NO TIME TO WASTE

Poverty and the Global Environment

Joan Davidson and Dorothy Myers
with Manab Chakraborty

Cover photo: Carrying water back to Tekkangel village in Senegal.
(JEREMY HARTLEY/OXFAM)

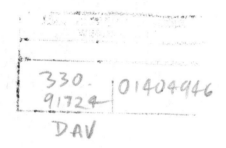

ISBN 0 85598 182 2
ISBN 0 85598 183 0 pbk

Published by Oxfam UK and Ireland
274 Banbury Road, Oxford OX2 7DZ
Typeset in 10 pt Palatino by Oxfam Design
Printed by Dotesios Ltd, Trowbridge, Wiltshire.

CONTENTS

ACKNOWLEDGEMENTS

This book is the product of many people working together – Oxfam partners, staff and volunteers. A number of case studies were specially commissioned and for those we are indebted to: Gabriel Banda, Ro Cole, Deborah Eade, Eric Gamalinda, Raja Jarrah, Mireya Sofia Trejo Orozco and Matthew Sherrington.

Several people contributed substantially to some of the chapters, we want to thank: Tricia Feeney, Omar Sattaur and Kevin Watkins, and also: Aisling Byrne, Piers Cazelet and Lucy Charrington.

Many busy people found time to comment most helpfully on earlier drafts, we are especially grateful to: Robert Chambers and Melissa Leach of the Institute of Development Studies, Sussex, Marcus Colchester of the World Rainforest Movement, Ben Jackson, Richard Jolly of UNICEF and Alison Jolly; Patrick Mulvaney of the Intermediate Technology Development Group, Richard Sandbrook and Camilla Toulmin of the International Institute for Environment and Development, Nigel Twose of PANOS and James Winpenney of the Overseas Development Institute.

We are indebted to our friends and colleagues in Oxfam for their willingness to comment on, and contribute to, many chapters – often at short notice: Odhiambo Anacleti, Renato Athias, Alison Barrett, David Bryer, Mary Cherry, John Clark, Belinda Coote, Pete Davis, Peter Drury, Claudia Garcia Moreno, Liz Gascoigne, Olivia Graham, Brendan Gormley, Vincent Homolka, Joe Human, Ian Leggett, Caroline Lequesne, Neil MacDonald, Ann Mackintosh, Roger Naumann, Robin Palmer, John Rowley, Richard Sexton, Susannah Smith, James Tumwine, Pramod Unia, Paul Valentin, Bridget Walker and Christine Whitehead. Other colleagues have helped – with great patience – on the research, editing, presentation and administration of various drafts of the text; we want to thank especially: Melanie Bradbury, Dave Hanson, Anna McCord, Geoff Sayer and Ann Simpson.

Lastly, thanks to Dianna Melrose for all her support throughout the writing – especially during the final stages. And our families for their encouragement.

Joan Davidson, Dorothy Myers
Policy Advisers in the Public Policy Department of Oxfam UKI

Manab Chakraborty
Formerly Overseas Programme Adviser
(Environment and Development) Oxfam UKI

April 1992

INTRODUCTION

The 'Earth Summit' in Rio de Janeiro in 1992 – 20 years on from the last United Nations Conference on the Human Environment – takes place in a very different world. Circumstances have changed dramatically – not least in the world's political shape. Environmental awareness is everywhere greater: in this respect there has been a transformation of attitudes.

But amid so much hope, action lags far behind the rhetoric. Conditions for the poorest people, in many countries, have not improved and the gap between rich and poor has widened – both within and between nations. People's lives and their land are still devastated by deepening poverty, environmental degradation and armed conflict.

The world faces two contrasting crises: one fifth of its people live in poverty and destitution while a quarter enjoy lifestyles of profligate consumption, using 80 per cent of the earth's resources.[1] A deteriorating environment links them both.

Environmental crises are no longer in the future: they are already here – and most of them hit hardest at the poorest people living in the Third World.* They are fundamentally dependent on the health and wealth of the natural resource base; they cannot draw upon a sophisticated, industrial way of life to buffer the effects of environmental stress which profoundly affect their lives.

What is happening is devastation on a grand scale. Added to the increasing number of environmental and human-caused disasters – cyclones in Asia, famines in Africa, deforestation in Amazonia – is the slow, insidious deterioration of local environments: trees cut down or damaged, soils lost or degraded, wells and watercourses dried up or polluted. Ozone depletion and the loss of biodiversity will bring

---

* There is no adequate term to describe collectively the poor countries in which Oxfam works. In this book 'Third World', 'the South', 'poor countries' and 'developing countries' have been used interchangeably in the text. They are taken to mean the poorer, less industrialised countries of the world, including the 43 Less Developed Countries which are so designated by the United Nations because of their low per capita incomes and little, if any, industrialisation.

disruptions to the global environment. Above all, climate change – the single most important influence on the earth – threatens a worldwide dislocation of weather, vegetation and cropping patterns.

Wasteful consumption of natural resources, especially energy resources by Northern countries, lies at the root of many of these problems and results in the pollution of land, air and water. Indeed, waste is an apt metaphor to describe what is happening to the earth and to the prospects for the poorest of its people. Both are being squandered.

It is increasingly clear that the environment, both globally and locally, in the North and the South, cannot be considered apart from the economic development which destroys or sustains it. Environmental degradation in many parts of the world is now seen as a major impediment to development of any kind.

This book is about Oxfam's perspective on these issues, drawing on its extensive field experience of working in relief and development with local organisations in 70 countries. In Chapter 1, which describes the links between poverty and the environment, and in subsequent chapters which deal with water, land, agriculture and forests (Chapters 3 to 6), the book looks at what is happening to the environments of poor people, and how they are responding to safeguard and improve the natural resources on which their survival depends. These chapters describe the work of Southern NGOs, including Oxfam's partners, who are increasingly active and effective at tackling poverty and environmental problems at the local level, while emphasising the need for national and international policy change to address the root causes of these problems.

Oxfam's experience of poverty and environmental degradation suggests that sustainable development is the only positive way forward:

> development that meets the needs of the present without compromising the ability of future generations to meet their own needs.[2]

Chapter 2 discusses the meaning and experience of development for the people with whom Oxfam works, and introduces the idea of Primary Environmental Care as a practical approach to sustainable development. Primary Environmental Care, with its three essential components of people's empowerment, securing basic needs, and caring for the environment, is illustrated through specific examples in this and later chapters.

Chapter 7 deals with the environments of urban poverty, and the importance of community organisations in improving living conditions for poor people.

But local action alone is not enough. Accelerating the transition to sustainable development means that the obstacles to it, at national and international levels, have also to be tackled – urgently. This requires action to end armed conflict and increase democracy, popular participation and good governance (Chapter 8). Chapter 9 looks at the factors involved in rapid population growth and emphasises the importance of tackling poverty, improving the education and status of women, and widening access to birth planning services. Alongside the need to reduce the inequalities within countries, is the urgent imperative of dealing with the structural inequities between North and South which stand in the way of sustainable development. Most important is the worsening economic situation of poor countries which are locked into a trade and debt crisis whilst investment and aid flows are falling. This is the subject of Chapter 10.

Because all the elements of the environment are interconnected, so too are the chapters of this book: their subdivision is, in many ways, arbitrary. The environment, especially for poor people, is impossible to categorise: it is the totality of the surroundings and circumstances which dominate every aspect of their lives – physical, social, economic and spiritual. As concern grows about acid rain, ozone depletion and global warming, people in the North are just beginning to see the interconnections. In an increasingly interdependent world, with the pressing need for much more global cooperation, there is growing recognition that sustainable development can only be achieved through far-reaching policy changes in international relations (especially on trade and debt) combined with a commitment to practical action locally.

Although this book will emphasises Southern perspectives on poverty and the environment, and the importance of action by governments, international agencies, NGOs and the business community, individuals in the rich world have a vital role to play in reducing the environmental problems of the poor world. It is their task not only to persuade Northern agencies to act with more responsibility and greater urgency, but also to adopt and promote personal styles of living which are more sustainable. Readers can participate in some of Oxfam's most successful 'environmental' ventures in the UK and Ireland – by recycling through the network of Oxfam shops, and through the Wastesaver Centre, and by buying goods through Oxfam's alternative trading scheme.

The 1992 United Nations Conference on Environment and Development (UNCED) was just a beginning: the action must not stop with the Earth Summit in Rio. The urgent need is for governments, intergovernmental agencies, NGOs, the corporate sector – and individuals – to continue to commit themselves to carrying out the policies and actions required for sustainable development. The real evidence of that commitment will come when nations address the causes of poverty and environmental degradation, not just the symptoms. The final chapter of this book focuses on Oxfam's priorities for a fairer, more secure and sustainable world beyond the Earth Summit.

Land degradation in Ethiopia. The hills were once well-wooded. Deforestation and over-cultivating the land has caused severe soil erosion.

1

WASTING PEOPLE, WASTING THE EARTH

When I visit this little valley of my childhood dreams, I feel the tragedy under my feet. Gullies stare at me, telling the story of soil erosion which was unknown before: the land appears exhausted. Firewood is scarce because every tree has been cut. Hunger is on people's faces.

Wangari Maathai, Coordinator of Kenya's Green Belt Movement [1]

THE POOR GET POORER

One fifth of the world's population – more than a billion people – live in poverty. They earn, on average, less than one US dollar a day. Even on this limited definition, and although poverty levels have fallen in some countries since the 1970s, worldwide, the number living in poverty looks set to rise to 1.5 billion by 2025.[2]

But being poor is about more than material deprivation. It is about powerlessness. Not only are poor people unable to meet their basic needs for food, shelter, health and education; they have few or no rights or freedoms to improve their position. They have little or no control over productive resources (especially land) and often little opportunity to use their own energies and capabilities to generate a better life for themselves and their families. They have limited access to the kind of public services which are taken for granted in the rich world, and their needs are frequently ignored by powerful, often corrupt, local elites.

Some 500 million of the world's poor live in Asia, whilst 360 million poor people live in sub-Saharan Africa and 340 million in Latin America. But Africa's development crisis means that by 2000, half of all Africans could be living below the poverty line.[3]

The inequalities between North and South are huge and widening: the average GDP per capita in the North is 18 times that in the South. The poor live shorter, harsher lives. While developing countries overall have increased their food output per person, a fifth of their people still go hungry every day. Two-thirds have no access to safe drinking water.

Illiteracy and unemployment lock the poor into their impoverished position: a quarter of adult men and half the women of the South have never been taught to read or write.[4]

The health of children is the real indicator of poverty. One child in six is born underweight and, every year, one in ten of all children born will die from waterborne diseases or malnutrition – most of them in the South. In the 1991 Bangladesh cyclone, more than 130,000 people lost their lives, but the same number of Bangladeshi children die every three months from diarrhoea or pneumonia.[5]

All these figures mask gross inequalities within the Third World – between rich and poor, between urban and rural areas, and between women and men. Poor Mexicans die some 20 years before their rich compatriots. Babies born to poor families in Colombia are twice as likely to die in the first few years as the children of richer families.[6]

Most of the Third World's poor live in rural areas: their incomes are, on average, 25 per cent – sometimes 50 per cent – less than those who live in cities. Even allowing for the importance of subsistence food production for rural families, this is still a major difference between urban and rural areas. Public and social services – water, sanitation, health and education – are generally inadequate or non-existent for those who live in rural areas.

Women make up 70 per cent of the world's poor and, over much of the South, they work harder but earn less than men. Poor Third World women not only work in the home, but contribute substantially to the family budget and grow most of the family's food: in parts of Africa, they are responsible for up to 90 per cent of subsistence food production. Yet, as a result of gender discrimination in the allocation of food, women are far more likely than men to be undernourished.

Women have limited access to income, credit, land, education or training, even where they are the head of the household. Most women do not own the land they work, the crops they produce or even the tools they use. In many Third World communities, women face restrictions on their freedom of movement and association outside the home. They may be forbidden to join women's groups or take up training and development opportunities. They are, even more than poor men, often excluded from development decisions which profoundly affect their lives.

Globally, one woman in three is illiterate, compared with one man in five – in South Asia, female literacy rates are only half those of males.[7] Because of their daily tasks – growing food and gathering water, fuel and fodder – poor women are especially dependent upon the natural resources of the environment and the first to suffer when the environment becomes degraded.[8] Girls are more likely than boys to be taken out of school to help their mothers with these tasks.

All these factors, which conspire to keep women poor and powerless, are rooted in the unequal distributions of power and status between the genders. This situation arises largely from cultural patterns but is reinforced by the legacy of colonial attitudes and practices.[9] Women, especially poor women, have become 'invisible', regardless of their contributions to the local economy and family welfare – and this has influenced the way development planners and policies have perceived them, as the next chapter shows.

The poverty trap

After walking for three days with her daughter Tombi, Christina Nguluba arrived at Malembo, the nearest food centre to her village in Chama District of north-eastern Zambia. They managed the trip by doing 'ganju' – or food for work – in the villages on the way. Christina's five sons are at home, also looking for 'ganju', and her husband is away in the Zambian Copperbelt, trying to find a job. But he has been gone for several years and has only once sent her any money.

Christina looks tired and her eyes are sunken behind high cheekbones. 'We sometimes go without a meal for days', she says. 'We have to live on mangoes, pumpkin leaves and wild okra. The wild pigs destroy the crops on our vegetable plot. We grow millet which will survive the drought but this is not our traditional crop. We grow it for brewing to raise money for food. And the maize has been failing because of the poor rains. Each year the land produces less and less. But I cannot leave my home: my parents and their ancestors were all buried there. How could I leave? Where would I go?'

It has not always been like this in Chama. A few years ago, the area offered a variety of food, especially wild game – elephant, buffalo and gazelle were all plentiful.

But the land around Chama has now become so degraded and eroded by drought and floods that it is no longer productive. What used to be the annual lean period has developed into a year-round shortage of food and chronic hunger. Government support is non-existent now: agricultural marketing and extension services have broken down and the emergency food supply system is totally inadequate. The government tries to sell maize rations to 50,000 people using three trucks. There is just one untarred route connecting Chama with other parts of Zambia and access to the villages is only possible between May and October – and then only by four-wheel drive vehicles. The price of fuel has increased dramatically and the food centre is often empty. People keep overnight vigil at the depot gate, huddled round a fire, and there is a dusty stampede for rations the day a truck arrives.

Meanwhile the lives of villagers like Christina hang in the balance.

Most families are in the same situation, especially women-headed households.[10] Many poor people are caught in this kind of poverty trap. They have little or no access to fertile land or to any other resource from which to earn a living. Industrial and service jobs are scarce, especially in the countryside. Corrupt local elites can ensure that people are powerless to exercise their rights to land even when these exist. Without productive land, they have no access to credit to buy other assets. Even with land, poor people's earnings are at the mercy of local markets, controlled by more powerful groups.

Along with falling prices for the goods they produce, poor people often face debts and high interest rates, so they can no longer afford food, shelter, health care or education. Added to these are other deprivations, including physical weakness and isolation, which lock the poor into their poverty trap.[11]

Of course, the causes of poverty are not just to be found at the local level. People remain poor because of the unjust distribution of wealth and power within their own societies, and economic development policies which bypass their needs. Moreover, they are at the receiving end of international pressures which damage their interests: massive indebtedness, high interest rates and falling commodity prices all restrict the incomes of poor producers. Inappropriate aid projects ignore or may even harm them.

Environmental degradation compounds all of these factors to force those who are already poor and vulnerable into a downward spiral of increasing poverty.

POVERTY AND THE ENVIRONMENT

Oxfam's experience is that livelihoods – indeed survival – for the world's poorest people depend fundamentally on the wealth of the natural environment and on resources such as soils, trees and water. Trees, for example, provide not only food crops, but also timber for building, fuel for cooking, fodder for animals and fibres for weaving. Trees perform a valuable role as savings and security for many in the South; they not only provide a future income, but are an insurance against contingencies – the need to spend on social occasions such as weddings and funerals, or to pay for medical care. Well-managed, accessible forests can be as valuable as productive cropland and pastures for rural living standards, especially for women.

Many poor people in the South have the knowledge – and the incentive – to manage renewable resources in sustainable ways. They apply traditional methods of soil and water conservation, they know which varieties of crops are resistant to drought and to pests, which trees provide wood to burn efficiently with little smoke, and which plants have medicinal properties. For centuries, Third World farmers have built and maintained terraces and other structures to retain soil and water. They practise complex systems of intercropping and crop rotation to increase productivity and reduce the risks of pest damage. Even where environmental degradation has already taken hold, local people are working to reverse the decline.

Looking after the trees

In the Puri District of the Indian state of Orissa, a remarkable environmental movement has emerged, showing how the timely actions of a group of villagers can eventually influence a whole region. Friends of the Trees and Living Beings is an Oxfam partner organisation which started formally in 1982. But it had its origins in the mid-1970s when a number of people from Kesharpur village decided that immediate action was needed to protect the nearby hill of Binjgiri.

With moderate, but highly seasonal, rainfall and poor soils, the natural cover of Binjgiri is dry, mixed deciduous forest. Its legal status is Protected Forest, which allows local people to collect wood and fodder only for domestic and farming needs. Despite this limitation, by the late 1960s, Binjgiri's 360 hectares were completely stripped of trees – with devastating consequences. Water was short because the springs had dried up. Gully erosion was so severe that fields at the foot of the hill could not be cultivated because they were covered with stones washed from the hillside. There was an acute shortage of fuelwood. Poor farming communities slid rapidly into greater poverty.

Starting in their own village (but in time working with seven others that shared rights to the hill) a group of campaigners began to persuade villagers to act. Using songs, slogans and rallies, they created – perhaps revived – an environmental movement which now covers 1,800 villages in Puri District.

Ten years later, the effects are highly visible. Binjgiri, and other hills in the district, have been re-greened and are now densely wooded. Wildlife has returned in abundance – monkeys, bears, rabbits, snakes and many birds. Recharged springs irrigate fields and gardens. Farmland is once more productive now the gullies have been plugged and the rocks cleared from the fields. Bhikan Hajary, a Buddhagran villager, writes:

Everyone planted trees here: civil servants, college students, passers-by, school children – and 100 people from the village. Seeing the trees grow we were all happy. For the last five years, the spring has come back; before that, for 10-15 years it had completely dried up. Clouds came but went away and rained on other hills. But we woke up in time.'

Less than two years separates these photographs. Above, most of the trees have been cut down and the soil is being washed away. Since the Friends of the Trees and Living Beings started a forest protection programme, the hillside is becoming green again as bushes and trees are re-established (below).

'We don't have more cash', says another villager, 'but we have much more security.'

Many factors lie behind the success of this movement. With perceptive and innovative leadership, Friends of the Trees and Living Beings is trusted by the village communities and has built upon the work of democratic village councils who already manage other village assets such as grain banks and common land. All the villagers face similar problems, as small marginal farmers and landless labourers, with few differences of caste or class and a strong sense of local equity. They recognise equal rights and responsibilities towards the forest and its products. Villagers have been directly involved in creating and implementing the rules to protect the forest, patrolling the regenerating woodland to keep out animals and illicit woodcutters.

Environmental education has played an important part, with children actively involved in creating tree nurseries and planting up hillsides. The movement has revived the traditional 'green culture' of the villages, including songs, poems and greetings, with frequent celebrations and tree-planting ceremonies. Although the movement has now reached 1,800 villages, there is still only one small office and two part-time workers; volunteers and associated local organisations do most of the work. This approach to 'thinking globally but acting locally', and the movement's Gandhian principles of non-violent persuasion and organisation, have gained support at all levels, from the village, the district and the state to international recognition among the 'Global 500 Awards' of the United Nations Environment Programme (UNEP).[12]

THE DOWNWARD SPIRAL

This is one example of how threatened communities can regain their livelihoods. But for most of the world's poor people, environmental devastation has already taken over. The rapid deterioration of their surroundings is undermining the daily struggle to maintain (let alone improve) living standards. In two decades of drought and deforestation, many villages in the Sahel – the arid land along the southern fringe of the Sahara desert – have lost as much as half their cultivable land. The fine balance between the earth and its farmers, sustained for centuries, has broken down because of the development model pursued by powerful elites. The people of Amazonia – the Yanomami and Kayapo Indians, for example – have survived for generations by managing the rainforest in a sustainable way. Now, millions of hectares of forest are burned and bulldozed each year to make way for land speculation, cattle ranching, mining operations, and oil drilling. Deforestation is also the outcome of poor families migrating from other parts of Brazil in search of land.

The Third World's poor are not a homogeneous mass: vulnerability to environmental stress varies in different places and among different groups, and between individuals, households and village communities. Children living in slums, and those without land – especially women – are particularly vulnerable. Estimates suggest that some 13 per cent of rural households in the South are landless and almost 60 per cent of all households, including those who live in city slums and depend on vegetable gardens, have too little land for subsistence.

Like the landless of Brazil who migrate to Amazonia, poor people are often pushed from marginal environments to ones that are even less productive and more ecologically fragile – arid lands, tropical forest at the edge of farmland, savannas, steep mountain slopes, mangrove swamps and the land around sprawling cities. Some 60 per cent of the world's poorest people live in ecologically vulnerable areas.[13]

The pressures of settlement and cultivation in these areas lead to further, often rapid, environmental deterioration. Poor migrants, who may have managed natural resources well in the past, are forced to degrade them. The gradual decline of the environment becomes both an extra cause as well as a consequence of their poverty: poor people then appear to be, at the same time, both the victims and the unwilling agents of environmental degradation – they are caught in a downward spiral.[14]

GEOFF SAYER/OXFAM

In Mwabuzo village, Daodi Paulo and his brother (*pictured above*) prepare the land for another year's cotton – the only cash crop that will grow successfully in the Meatu District of Tanzania's Shinyanga Region. Daodi and his brother will continue to grow cotton even though, with devaluation and falling producer prices, the profit margins are small. But this is not the only cause of their increasing poverty.

Land clearance to grow cotton for export is encouraged by the Government. When cotton is sold, extra cash is used to buy cattle and grow more cotton. This expansion, and the largely unmanaged cattle grazing, have left bare soils exposed to wind and water erosion. Gentle slopes are gullied and guttered, and tiny acacia saplings perch on earth mounds as the soil beyond the hold of their roots is washed away. The land has been stripped of trees: accessible supplies of fuelwood have already been consumed and wood is now too far away to collect except by oxcart. Crop residues and dung are burnt instead. These were previously returned to the soil as fertiliser; now soil fertility is not replenished and the soil is light and easily blown away. The downward spiral of environmental degradation leading to greater poverty continues.

Oxfam has recently become involved in helping the cotton-growers of Meatu to regenerate their land. Working cooperatively with the local agricultural extension officer, the farmers are now growing cotton more intensively but on smaller areas, clearing less land, planting trees around houses and among crops, and allowing surrounding woodland to regenerate naturally.[15]

A DECADE OF DISASTERS

In spite of their knowledge, and their 'coping strategies' developed over generations of adaptation to marginal conditions, poor people are ill-equipped to resist sudden environmental stress when this follows upon years of insidious damage.

For many of the world's poorest people, the 1980s were a decade of disasters. Oxfam has been called upon to respond to emergencies in many parts of the world – often several at a time: a cyclone in Bangladesh; conflict and famine in Ethiopia, Somalia, Liberia, Sudan, Angola and Mozambique; cholera in Peru; and typhoons and floods in the Philippines. Indeed, in Bangladesh, Oxfam has appointed a permanent Emergencies Officer, so frequent is the need for assistance. In some parts of the Third World, poverty, environmental degradation and armed conflict are creating an almost permanent state of emergency.

Disasters – natural and man-made – often strike at the most fragile environments: degraded arid lands, deltas and other low-lying coastal areas. It is here that the slow advance of poverty and environmental degradation can be suddenly tipped into a full-scale emergency by drought, cyclones or conflict.

Crisis in Africa

In 1991, famine was once again threatening 30 million people in Africa – many more than in the devastating drought of 1984-5. In ten years, some African countries had moved from food surplus to food deficit. Over much of Africa, the ravages of war have added to those of famine.[16] But a deteriorating environment has played a crucial part in the crises – as both a cause and a result of conflict, as Chapter 8 explains. For more than a decade, there has been massive deforestation, subsequent soil erosion and degradation, all of which has left the land difficult to farm and more vulnerable to drought. Combined with the loss of grain and seed stocks, these conditions bring a high risk of famine. Vulnerability and injustice ensure that the poorest suffer first and most severely. Even when they manage to survive, they are destined to become environmental refugees, uprooted from land and village. Worldwide, some 14 million people have had to abandon their homes because of environmental degradation.[17]

Ameth Kiros Germay is 54 and lives in Tseharte village in Tigray in the Horn of Africa. Erratic rainfall, periodic drought and serious deforestation of the marginal, overgrazed land has brought poor harvests and recurrent famine. In 1984-5 she and her husband did not migrate to Sudan with the younger farmers, but stayed behind in the village, getting small sums of money from REST, the Relief Society of Tigray, part-funded by Oxfam. With this she would walk to Makelle to buy food from other aid agencies. Her sick husband died, and she lost all five children in the 1984-5 and later famines. Her two oxen died and, after her husband's death, in line with local policies to redistribute land to accommodate population increase, her half-hectare of land was allocated to other farmers. She retained a small plot but this has produced little over the years of continuing drought – and nothing in 1990, when again she had to rely on REST. Now her sight is failing and she can no longer farm; she has lost everything.[18]

Floods in Asia

Cyclones are a fact of life in Bangladesh. But the one that hit the country on 29 April 1991 – with its accompanying tidal wave – was the worst for a decade. Within hours, more than 130,000 people were dead and four million were homeless. The cyclone killed thousands of animals, destroyed millions of pounds worth of assets, including all the crops. In a few hours, the livelihoods of millions of people were shattered. One week after the cyclone, an Oxfam fieldworker reported 'we are stunned at the scale of the devastation. Compared to those who are still alive, many people think that the dead are the fortunate ones.'

Hatiya Island, not much more than a large sand bar, is home to 300,000 people, three-quarters of them landless. It was just one of the areas devastated by the cyclone: 90 per cent of the island's inhabitants lost their homes and their crops, and fields were submerged under several feet of salt water. Overnight, years of hard work by local people were wasted. Dwip Unnayan Sangstha (DUS), a small local NGO supported by Oxfam, was one of the few organisations still able to help the stricken people, by distributing food and other essential supplies: 3,000 families were each given 5kg of rice, 1kg of lentils, some salt and matches. Since the cyclone, DUS has continued its longer-term development work, which is described in the next chapter.[19]

In the future, the effects of climate change and sea-level rise may exacerbate the scale and frequency of coastal flooding associated with cyclones. Some researchers consider that global warming may already be

SHAHIDUL ALAM/OXFAM

Damage after the cyclone that hit Hatiya Island, Bangladesh, in 1991. Poor people are often forced to live in vulnerable areas, and when disaster strikes, they have few resources for recovery. The outline of fields can be seen under the water.

a factor in extreme weather patterns of the kind which brought the 1991 cyclone.[20] Low-lying Bangladesh, with almost every inch of land already under cultivation, is one of the most vulnerable places on earth to sea-level rise: an increase of a metre could flood 16 per cent of the country and displace at least 11 million people.[21]

THE SCALE OF ENVIRONMENTAL DESTRUCTION

The daily fortunes of poor families – whether they eat or starve – are bound up with the state of the local environment, and that environment is changing rapidly. For those who must face drought or cyclones, their survival depends on adaptability and preparedness, but the pace of environmental change is now so fast that the capacity of poor people to respond is strained to breaking point.

Later chapters of this book will show how the environment is changing and how the poorest people are the hardest hit. Every year, more than 6 million hectares of land (an area approaching the size of Ireland) are degraded into desert-like conditions – more than double the rate over the last three centuries. If present levels of destruction continue, it is predicted that almost a fifth of the earth's cropland will have disappeared by the end of this decade. Throughout the world, health is seriously threatened by water polluted with human and industrial wastes. More than 20 million hectares of tropical forest (an area similar to that of England and Scotland) are cleared annually, mainly for subsistence farming, commercial agriculture and destructive logging. Up to 30 per cent of all known existing species may become extinct over the next 40 years; this rapid loss of biological diversity severely reduces the earth's potential to supply species of medicinal and economic value, and genetic material that could, for example, help countries adapt to global warming.[22]

Latest reports of ozone depletion in the northern hemisphere confirm scientists' warnings; the resulting exposure to increased ultra-violet radiation may lead to a widespread increase in skin cancers, damage human immune systems and have potentially devastating consequences for agriculture and fisheries.[23]

Global warming

Overall looms the threat of climate change. There is now substantial international scientific agreement that human activities are warming the surface of the earth. The clearing and burning of forests and – much more important – the burning of fossil fuels, accelerate the build-up of greenhouse gases which cause global warming. The industrialised nations, with a fifth of the world's population, contribute (from their past and present activities) two-thirds of the production of these gases.[24]

On present emission rates of the main greenhouse gases (principally carbon dioxide), global temperatures are widely predicted to rise by at least 1°C by 2025 – a rate greater than at any other time in the last 10,000 years.[25] Past changes of this kind took many thousands of years – species had time to adapt. Global warming could take place over just a few decades and there will be no time for adaptations, or places to migrate to. The effects will be felt first in the more ecologically fragile and unstable areas of the world – often where the poorest live. It is thought that global warming will raise ocean temperatures causing sea levels to rise, perhaps by a metre over the next century. This could devastate much of low-lying Bangladesh and northern Egypt, turning at least 50 million people in these countries into refugees.[26] Many more will suffer unless they can be helped to prepare and adapt quickly.

> The gravest effects of climate change may be those on human migration as millions are uprooted by shoreline erosion, coastal flooding and agricultural disruption.
>
> Intergovernmental Panel on Climate Change, 1990[27]

WAYS FORWARD

It is clear that the environments of the poor South are being damaged, indirectly and often irreversibly, by activities in other countries. The severity of cyclones and African droughts are thought by some to be, in part, linked to global climate change engendered mainly from the North.

The roots of local environmental degradation are often at the global level, in the economic pressures caused by an unjust trading system, indebtedness, and inappropriate aid policies. Misguided development policies at national level which ignore longer-term needs, favour the better-off and deprive people of any power over their own development are also to blame. Damage is also caused by poor people responding to their poverty: often they have no choice but to forgo tomorrow to survive today.

> The environmental balance is one that has been increasingly disturbed. But the environment should not be considered in isolation. Ultimately, it is people, not trees, whose future options have to be protected. Indeed, if people are not protected, the trees will stand very little chance... Environmental destruction... reinforces poverty. So, any plans for environmental action must be plans to reduce poverty. This approach is not merely better – it is the only approach that stands a chance of working.
>
> UNDP: Human Development Report, 1991[28]

There are many ways forward to break into the cycle and reverse the downward spiral of increasing poverty and environmental degradation, including a poverty-focused approach to national development, local action which blends environmental management with securing human rights and meeting needs, and international measures which not only tackle environmental damage directly, but also deal with questions of structural inequities between the North and the South. The following chapters look at all of these, concentrating on the ways in which local people are applying their own solutions to the problems of the downward spiral.

Iron ore from Carajás, waiting for shipment at the port of São Luis, Brazil.

2

WHAT KIND OF DEVELOPMENT?

Development is about individual people and their communities; it
is about these people taking control of their own lives and building
their own futures. Our task is to respond to their hopes, aspirations
and priorities.[1]

Serra dos Carajás, in north-east Brazil, is an opencast mine on a grand
scale. From here, iron and other ores go by rail to the coast to be
shipped to the United States, Europe and Asia. But this is no ordinary
development – the Projecto Grande Carajás will occupy some 10 per cent
of Brazil's land area. A new railway slices through 900km of the Amazon
rainforest and, along its length, the first of the iron and steelworks are
growing up. A series of dams is under construction to provide energy
for aluminium smelters and the national grid.

The scheme has already produced massive deforestation, with iron
smelters projected to consume charcoal at a million tonnes – or 50,000
hectares of forest – a year. Soil eroded from the cleared land has choked
waterways, bringing floods in the wet season. Huge dams are causing
the inundation of great tracts of land, including settlements and
territories of indigenous people. Because the land is not cleared before it
is flooded, rotting vegetation pollutes the reservoirs, which become
breeding grounds for disease-carrying insects. Air pollution from the
sawmills, the smelters and the charcoal burning causes respiratory
problems for people in the area.

Towns have sprung up, consisting of squalid, makeshift shanties,
spread out along the railway line to house the workers' families, and
those evicted from the countryside in violent disputes over land. But the
towns have neither the services nor the jobs to sustain such a rapid
influx of people. Some try to make a living extracting gold from local
minerals with mercury – further polluting the rivers of Amazonia.

This Brazilian experiment in industrial development is not only
unsustainable – it devastates the environment on which lives and

livelihoods ultimately depend. 'It is' says one commentator, 'an island of seeming modernity amid a sea of misery'.[2]

MODELS OF DEVELOPMENT

'Development' means different things to different people. Carajás illustrates the kind of large-scale, export-led economic development favoured by rich Southern elites, foreign investors, and intergovernmental agencies such as the World Bank. It damages poor people – threatening their rights, their livelihoods and their environments, offering few short-term benefits and no long-term employment.

In contrast, Oxfam supports 'people-centred development'. This necessitates social, economic and environmental policies that give priority to reducing poverty and to popular empowerment, so that people can participate fully in decisions which affect their lives and livelihoods.

Development models that rely on the idea of wealth 'trickling down' to the poor have been widely discredited, yet they are still pervasive. In many countries, economic development policies that have favoured powerful interests as engines of wealth creation have not yielded benefits for the poor majority. Instead, they have resulted in rapid short-run economic gain for a few, at the expense of wider social justice and long-term environmental security. Over much of Africa, development strategies have concentrated upon export-led growth to the exclusion of food security and incomes for the poorest people. Disparities in wealth have increased as the poor have become poorer. In Sudan, the average per capita income in 1991 was 25 per cent lower than in 1984. Economic development policies have not fostered local self-reliance, nor strengthened the coping mechanisms on which poor people rely during times of drought and famine.

Southern governments as well as Northern bilateral and multilateral aid agencies must share the responsibility for the failure to tackle poverty. Expensive infrastructure projects have proved unnecessary or damaging. Increased production of primary commodities for overloaded world markets has carried high social and environmental costs without increasing incomes. A neglect of the long-term health of the economy has been matched by a disregard for people's needs and for the natural resource base – depleted for short-term gains in a dangerous form of 'environmental borrowing'.[3]

SUSTAINABLE DEVELOPMENT: THE THEORY

The 1980s concern for the environment produced a new concept in development thinking – 'sustainable development'. *Our Common Future*, the report of the World Commission on Environment and Development (the Brundtland Report) defined it as development that meets the needs of the present without compromising the ability of future generations to meet their own needs.[4]

Sustainable development is an alliance of three essential elements – people, their environment and the future. Implicit is the idea of people-centred development which brings social and economic advances but also safeguards the environment and its resources so that options are not closed for the future.

The idea of sustainable development has bridged the traditional gulf between environment and development thinking. The old perception that environmental protection was a luxury impeding economic development was particularly damaging for the South, where so much social and economic progress is directly dependent upon the natural resource base – at national and at local levels. Sustainable development at last acknowledged the interdependence of environment and development. Moreover, worldwide sustainable development implied that Northern countries would have to commit themselves to reducing wasteful and polluting consumption, as well as transferring resources for poverty reduction in the South.

Economic growth

The World Commission on Environment and Development demolished the notion that economic and environmental gains were inevitably opposed. Economic growth, said Brundtland, is essential for sustainable development – what matters is the quality of that growth. Decades of change in the South have shown that economic growth does not necessarily bring equitable development – a rise in GNP is, in itself, no indicator of the welfare of the poorest nor of the health of the natural environment. Opting for growth at any price serves neither. But low growth or stagnation is not the answer.

> The approach of many environmentalists to this dilemma is to advocate a world of slower economic growth. While this may be superficially appealing to those already materially comfortable, it is both selfish and unwise. Given the extent and growth of mass poverty and the link between poverty and environmental stress, rapid economic growth in developing countries is essential...But growth must be qualitatively different from that experienced in the past: growth that contributes to sustainable development.

> Sir Shridath Ramphal[5]

Without growth, living standards for the poorest cannot rise. The resources needed by governments for public investment and the regular provision of services such as health and education will not be available except through an expanding national income. Creating jobs for a rapidly growing labour force cannot be achieved in a stagnant economy. What is needed are new patterns of economic development which serve the poorest and do not destroy the natural resources on which they depend. So the growth must be based, for example, on technologies that conserve rather than exploit resources, and the benefits of development must be spread much more equitably.[6] Some economists are already questioning the traditional concepts of economic growth which rely on increasing throughput of energy and raw materials, and underlining the importance of pursuing economic objectives which are less resource-intensive and which take account of the value of natural resource capital.

An international team convened by the Commonwealth Secretariat concluded that sustainable development, in practice, depends on a number of principles, including:

- the precautionary principle, which means that, in the absence of conclusive scientific evidence, policies which have environmental implications are formulated and implemented with care and restraint;

- environmental accounting, which means that where environmental assets are not used sustainably, then the full costs of depletion, regeneration and maintenance should be included in any costings; true 'economic values' will take account of environmental and social costs and benefits when projects or programmes are assessed; these do not appear in conventional financial balance sheets (this is further explored in Chapter 10);

- greater equity; sustainable development requires more equitable distribution of resources and decision-making powers between North and South and within developing countries, for – as Chapter 1 showed – environmental degradation is caused by both affluence and poverty.[7]

To these must be added:

- the polluter pays principle, whereby industrialised countries accept full responsibility for their part in causing environmental problems.

There will be conflicts of interest; growth, even when it is carefully managed, will increase demand for some natural resources, and for energy. But the evidence of Northern economies is that growth can be 'unhooked' from increasing energy demand, by improving energy efficiency and producing more from renewable sources. Much faster progress can be made on this if existing energy-saving technologies are applied more widely, and consumers can be persuaded to waste less energy and pay more for it, to reflect the true environmental costs of production. The optimistic growth rates envisaged by Brundtland – up to 4 per cent in industrialised countries and 5 or 6 per cent in developing countries – could only be sustained with a significant and rapid reduction in the energy and raw material content of every unit of production. 'Achieving significant changes in consumption patterns is one of the most challenging issues for environment and development', says a report from the UNCED Secretariat.[8]

New economic indicators are urgently needed; GNP figures may show impressive progress but this can be utterly illusory, for as it is presently defined, GNP takes no account of, for example, the distribution of resources, disparities in real incomes, the global and local depletion of forests, croplands and other environmental assets, or the effects of climate change.

Putting the poor first

From Oxfam's perspective, dealing with poverty is the overriding objective; the major goal of sustainable development must be to enable the poorest people to meet their basic rights and needs and sustain their livelihoods, while essential environmental resources are fairly distributed and well-managed.

Securing livelihoods is a key issue because so many other development benefits depend on this security. In resource-poor environments, vulnerable people need new forms of development that enable them to gain a secure and decent living for themselves and their children, where they are, and with the resources they can command.

> It is by starting with the poorer, and enabling them to gain the livelihoods they want and need, that both they and sustainable development can best be served... For the protection of the environment, poor people are not the problem, they are the solution.[9]

There is mounting evidence to show that where people have the rights and assets that ensure secure livelihoods, then they take the long-term view, safeguarding land and protecting natural resources to provide for their children. Putting the poorest first also means prioritising the rights and needs of women and giving them an effective say in development.

Women make up some of the poorest and most disadvantaged groups in many societies and they are the first to feel the effects of environmental degradation. In relation to sustainable development in the South, their needs and opportunities are especially important.

Women often play the major role in natural resource management, using their traditional knowledge and skills. It is normally the women of a community who gather water and fuelwood, and grow basic foods. Yet their work – most often unpaid – is largely invisible. As Chapter 1 described, women's unequal position in Third World societies, in communities and households, maintains their situation of powerlessness. This, combined with their excessive work burdens, ill-health, repeated and often unwanted pregnancies, limits their capacity to play a full part in the decisions and activities which affect their lives.[10]

Committee meeting of Samata, an organisation of landless people in Bangladesh whose work is described in Chapter 4. Samata has fought for women's rights to land, and women members participate fully in running the organisation.

Popular participation

In Oxfam's experience, popular participation is a fundamental requirement for sustainable development. Rights to participate in, and influence, decisions on the management of resources are necessary not only for reasons of social justice. Only when there is full participation – indeed, only when people have the power to improve their own lives and to challenge and influence decisions about resource allocation – will development activities have any chance of long-term success.

The latest policy documents of a number of official donors feature a new emphasis on addressing poverty and increasing participation as essential elements of sustainable development. At least on paper, if not yet in practice, some donors are acknowledging the crucial importance of poor people's empowerment. This has long been the approach adopted by development NGOs, which promote small-scale initiatives, designed to tackle poverty and powerlessness in partnership with the poorest people.

Many government and other donor agencies have now issued policy statements and adopted project guidelines on women in development. Some donors are more active than others in their consideration of women's needs and opportunities, but most are still better on paper than in practice. Few donors make a direct link between women and environment in the practical implementation of their policies. Where development assistance is directed at women, it often presupposes their role as victims and passive recipients of aid, rather than regarding them as active agents – and beneficiaries – of change.

It is certainly possible to see women as the principal victims of environmental devastation, and indeed – as Vandana Shiva argues – as victims of the man-made style of development that has become so destructive.[11] Women are still ignored in most large-scale development projects. They can even be ignored in smaller-scale projects, designed especially to restore degraded landscapes: some social forestry schemes, for example, have excluded the more beneficial fuel, fodder and fruit-producing trees which local women would have chosen.

Among some development agencies, women are beginning to be perceived as skilful environmental managers, with the knowledge and way of working cooperatively that can be valuable assets at the project level. But this view of women can, in practice, reinforce the perception that only men's work is economically valuable and increase still further women's unpaid work burdens, consigning to them a continuing role of invisible environmental carers. Instead, development should be empowering women in all their diversity to improve their incomes, skills, independence and status, and their ability to secure basic needs and livelihoods through greater access to land, credit, technology and training. At the local level, women need to be enabled to apply and communicate more of their own hard-won solutions to environmental problems and capitalise on their environmental roles – being recognised and remunerated for their part in sustaining the resource base for development.

A number of agencies, including Oxfam, are arguing for women to be seen as central figures in good environmental management, setting the agenda for action. Their experience is needed, at the earliest stage of development assistance, to shape effective policies and projects, and women deserve to benefit directly from this involvement. But this will require positive action by many institutions to recognise and enhance women's role in sustainable development – not just a commitment to reduce the damaging effects of conventional development on them.

SUSTAINABLE DEVELOPMENT: THE REALITY

In spite of the good intentions of governments and aid agencies, poverty-focused, participative and sustainable development is not happening in most areas of the world – North or South.

In the North, development continues (whatever the nature of national economic policies) along paths that are inherently unsustainable in terms of the global, if not the local, environment. Unchecked, the rate of fossil fuel consumption, with its accompanying emission of greenhouse gases, ensures accelerated global warming, threatening most of the world's croplands and forests. Some countries, the Netherlands for example, are trying to devise sustainable national strategies, but these remain paper plans so far.

In the South, as the example from Brazil illustrates, millions of people are either damaged or bypassed by existing forms of development. The land and water which poor communities rely on are taken away, eroded or polluted by powerful interest groups. Poor people are often forced out of their homes or away from the source of their livelihoods to make way for large-scale projects such as dams or commercial farms. They are denied access to (or must pay for) what had been 'free goods' from the environment – fuelwood, fodder and water. Or, as Chapters 4 and 5 show, they are forced to experiment with inappropriate forms of land holding and agriculture that stifle farmer initiative and traditional concerns for resource conservation.

Many factors conspire to prevent the transition to more sustainable forms of development, not least the lack of political will among those with vested interests (in the South and the North), and the severe economic pressures on poor countries, especially unjust terms of trade and massive indebtedness. Five years on from the Brundtland Commission Report, accepted by the UN and endorsed by many governments, not a single country has made any major change towards sustainability, though some are claiming limited progress.[12]

There is a reluctance to look beneath the symptoms of environmental damage to the root causes of unsustainability, particularly in the North. Indeed the preparatory work for the 1992 UN Conference on Environment and Development (UNCED) revealed, disturbingly, that the North had set the agenda along similar lines to the last UN Conference on the Human Environment in 1972. The concerns have been those perceived as important for the North – the protection of biodiversity, forests and the atmosphere – rather than the economic and political structures which underpin poverty and environmental degradation, and limit sustainable development.

This is one part of a growing difference of perception between North and South over what the real problems are and how they can be tackled. Whereas governments in the North are considering the details of technology transfer and additional resources for sustainable development, Southern governments and NGOs are much more concerned about finding solutions to the debt crisis and trade-related problems, including low commodity prices and Northern protectionism – issues which are further explored in Chapter 10. Without major changes in North-South economic relations, and in wealth creation and distribution at national level, positive action for sustainable development at the local level will always be undermined.

PRIMARY ENVIRONMENTAL CARE

For development to be sustainable, it has to be about change: change shaped by people to meet their perceived needs. This change must be firmly rooted at local level, but must be carried through to regional, national and international levels. From an Oxfam perspective, the most effective approach to sustainable development, especially at the local level, is to support individuals, groups and communities in the process of self-empowerment, to enable everyone, including the poorest, to secure their basic rights and needs while caring for the environment. This approach has come to be known as Primary Environmental Care.[13] It has three essential elements:

- popular empowerment

- securing basic rights and needs

- caring for the environment.

For effective Primary Environmental Care, all three elements must be tackled together. While environmental care is a key component, it is never the only one, but is integrated with other community-based activities to improve access to health care, shelter, education or income generation – a whole array of social and economic improvements.

For Oxfam, PEC is not entirely new – a number of Southern partners already approach local problems in this way. What PEC tries to do is to find integrated solutions to local problems and avoid a single-issue approach. Primary Environmental Care is appropriate in the North as well as the South – and there are examples of PEC in action in some of the poorer city districts of Europe and North America.

PEC is more than an approach to local action: it is a strategy which should guide policies at regional, national and international levels. Indeed, unless people can influence power structures at national level and have a say in decisions about the allocation of resources, PEC at local level lacks its vital enabling context.

Popular empowerment

Oxfam's experience suggests that sustainable development is about the process of change as well as the product. It is a process which enables people to become empowered so that their rights are recognised and their needs met. Empowerment is about supporting people in securing and defending their basic rights – the right to associate, to organise, to express their views and to participate in decisions. This means full and active participation of all parts of a community – individual women and men, children, households, and local organisations in all their different forms – so that their voices are heard and their knowledge and experience shared.

Securing basic rights and needs

The evidence from Oxfam's work is that meeting basic needs is about much more than improving the prospects for survival: it usually includes support for greater self-empowerment. It means ensuring that people are enabled to get access to the resources (especially financial, managerial and educational) they need to improve their incomes, food security, shelter, health care, education and training, sanitation and water supplies.

Caring for the environment

This takes many forms at the local level, including the rehabilitation of degraded environments, the protection of natural resources, for example by soil and water conservation, and the creation of 'new' ones – perhaps through the planting of trees or digging of wells. Oxfam supports various projects of this kind which combine, for example, tree-planting with water conservation, terracing and agricultural development. Building on local environmental experience is essential, for many poor people – especially women – have the knowledge to manage renewable resources in sustainable ways.

In both the North and the South, Primary Environmental Care is essentially empowering, enabling people to devise and implement their own strategies for self-reliant and sustainable improvements. This is especially valid at the local level, where the experience and skills locked up in a community are vital ingredients for success. Evidence shows that well-organised communities in resource-poor areas have been successful in meeting their needs while improving the environment – often with only limited outside support. Moreover, community-based projects of all kinds show high levels of effectiveness and efficiency in the use of human and material resources.

Some women's groups have become particularly effective in defending local natural resources and creating sustainable environments which provide food, fuel, fodder and building materials, as well as opportunities for income-earning enterprise. The Chipko movement in India, and the Kenyan Green Belt Movement are internationally known examples, but there are many other smaller groups of women who are successful at Primary Environmental Care. It is crucial that women – so often seen as unpaid agents for improving project success at the local level – become real beneficiaries of PEC programmes and projects.

PEC IN PRACTICE

PEC in Bangladesh – Dwip Unnayan Sangstha

The last chapter described how Hatiya Island, in Bangladesh, was devastated by the cyclone in April 1991. Dwip Unnayan Sangstha (DUS), a small, local NGO supported by Oxfam, not only provided emergency relief for the victims, but continues to help the islanders to campaign for their land rights. While land is constantly being eroded from the north of Hatiya Island, 'new' fertile land is added in the south as the sea deposits silt from the Bangladesh rivers draining into the Bay of Bengal. Like other islands in the Bay, Hatiya is being reshaped all the time. By law, the new land is set aside for the landless but it is often appropriated by rich and powerful landlords. With help from DUS, people displaced from the north of the island have successfully claimed land that is rightfully theirs, and they have been encouraged to protect it with embankments and tree-planting. DUS has helped some 700 landless families to get almost a hectare each, and has provided them with paddy and winter crop rice seeds. Some communities have excavated ponds for fish farming. DUS also works with women's groups to raise awareness about their rights and tackle some of the traditional forms of oppression – early marriage, polygamy and rape.

> Mokajjal Khatoun is a grandmother who has lived on Hatiya Island all her life – although river erosion has forced her to move house seven times. But now, for the first time, she is confident that she will not have to move again, because she has been able to buy land of her own, some way from the river. Through a women's savings group, set up with the support of DUS, she and some other women have been able to save enough money to add to a DUS loan to buy the land between them – and that land is in their own names, not their husbands'. They are raising the land before their homes are

built to make it less vulnerable to flooding and, with a loan from DUS, they are sinking a pond for fish farming.

But for some, the crisis remains. Momena Khatoun did not join the women's group, and she was not able to save any money. Her house still perches precariously next to the river and she will soon need to move. A widow, who lost both her sons in the 1970 cyclone, Momena lives with her widowed daughter: she does not know how they will move the house or where they can move it to.

After disasters like the 1991 cyclone, poor people are easy prey for unscrupulous moneylenders. Alone, they are very vulnerable. Now, with help from DUS, they have organised themselves in groups to pool labour and resources. DUS advises on land claims, creates jobs through reforestation programmes, and acts as a credit facility for small traders.[14]

PEC in India – the work of Seva Mandir

Starting out in 1969 with a literacy project in the villages of the Aravali Hills around Udaipur, Seva Mandir has grown from an NGO concerned with a single issue to one which promotes integrated local development. Its work shows how the concept of Primary Environmental Care can permeate an agency's philosophy, grassroots action and regional strategies.

Seva Mandir works mainly with the tribal people who live in 400 forest villages in the south-east of Rajasthan. Forests are the source of their livelihood, but the soils are impoverished and productivity is meagre. Systematic deforestation has been the cause and the consequence of increasing poverty. Yet the guiding philosophy of Seva Mandir is that only local people can protect and regenerate the forest in a sustainable way. Since 1985, the Wasteland Development Programme has not only promoted soil conservation, tree-planting and fodder production, but it has become a 'people's movement' to restore self-esteem and confidence in the long-term value of the natural resource base. Under the programme, Seva Mandir has been working with villagers to plant and manage a network of decentralised nurseries, which have survived in spite of three years of punishing drought. Local success has brought increasing recognition from government and forest administrators that a partnership with people and NGOs is the only effective way of restoring degraded forest.

The Wasteland Development Programme is just one element in a whole portfolio of social, economic and environmental activities which Seva Mandir generates or supports. These include adult literacy, informal education for children, health education, women's development, agricultural extension work, technical training and the formation of credit unions. In addition, there are physical developments – community centres, small-scale irrigation schemes and water projects, such as check dams and wells, for which Oxfam provided funding until 1985. Since then, Seva Mandir has been well supported from other state, national and international sources.

All the programmes enable poor tribal people, especially women, to participate fully in the process of rural development, while learning and applying leadership skills. 'Citizens' groups' are encouraged to analyse their problems in detail, determine priorities, negotiate with government and other agencies, then take action. Seva Mandir's goal is to help them to build their own organising and managerial capacity for sustainable development.[15]

PEC in Mauritania – Affolé

Many lessons can be learnt from Oxfam's experience in the Affolé district of Mauritania. Here, at the edge of the Sahara desert, agriculture is precarious. This region of scattered villages is hot and dry and droughts are frequent. Dams, built by the French in colonial times to trap the rains, have all been swept away by floods. People have had to rely on small dykes (or diguettes) but these are an uncertain source of soil moisture in drought years.

In 1983, Oxfam began to work with poor people in Affolé to manage the watersheds around some of their villages. First the diguettes were improved and then small dams were planned for the neighbouring watercourses. But the farmers were not enthusiastic about these improvements – they had other priorities.

Since 1988, the project has become more flexible, with wider local participation. Now, a larger range of activities has developed, responding more closely to the farmers' needs – for more wells, health care, the building of grain stores and the opening up of local markets. The village cereal banks and local trading are crucially important in helping farmers to tackle indebtedness – their overriding concern. Women's groups are especially active; they are in charge of the trading and, in some villages, they have taken to rearing small livestock which increases village food security.

The role of the project team has changed – from implementer to enabler, encouraging, advising and supporting the villagers. Now the villages are beginning to cooperate to build the larger dams necessary to catch flood waters and improve their sorghum production. But technical solutions like this, at first perceived by Oxfam to be the answer to Affolé's problems, are only a part of what is needed. The project has undergone a major change of emphasis over almost a decade, adapting to local needs as it has progressed. The priorities of its beneficiaries now

PEC in Brazil – extractive reserves

Since the 1960s the Government of Brazil has pursued a policy of 'opening up' the Amazon rainforest, encouraging ranchers and other developers to clear the forest. This threatened the livelihoods of Indians and rubber tappers who traditionally managed the forest in sustainable ways, collecting latex and brazil nuts.

Following years of bitter dispute – which included the assassination of their leader, Chico Mendes – the rubber tappers have pioneered the concept of 'extractive reserves' whereby their livelihoods could be protected in certain areas of the forest. In these reserves, they would continue to collect rubber and brazil nuts, as well as hunt and fish, without fear of harassment.

After persistent and effective lobbying of the Brazilian government by the rubber tappers' unions (supported by international agencies including Oxfam), the first extractive reserve was designated by the State Government of Acre, in 1988. Since then, more than a million hectares of extractive reserve have been mapped out (or are in progress) in the states of Acre, Amapá, Amazonas, Pará and Rondônia. The reserves are used to harvest natural resources – latex, brazil nuts and other forest products – in a sustainable way.[17]

The rubber tappers have built up an impressive alliance of support both within Brazil and around the world. The National Council of Rubber Tappers coordinates the views and activities of the local unions and, together with Indian groups, they created the Alliance of Forest Peoples in 1989. But the future for the extractive reserves is uncertain. The world price of rubber has fallen and competition from rubber and brazil nut plantations in Malaysia threatens to undercut the rubber tappers' production. Rubber tappers in Rondônia are earning 30 per cent less than the standard minimum wage in Brazil. Hunger will drive them off the reserves unless they can be helped to improve the transport of rubber and brazil nuts to market and to diversify their collection of forest products.

PEC in Chile – FEDEPA

Chile's Eighth Region, the third most important in the country's economy, contributes half of its timber supplies (the main export after copper) and a third of its fish production. The rate of clearance of the native forest has increased fourfold between 1970 and 1990. It has been replaced with pine and eucalyptus monocultures which acidify soils and destroy wildlife habitats. Likewise, fish catches have also quadrupled since 1970 to 2.5 million tonnes a year – twice the maximum catch to allow replacement of the fish stocks. The fish is used for fishmeal in animal feed; meanwhile fish stocks upon which people rely for food are come first. Affolé shows that self-help can lead to sustainability: when people help themselves they begin to innovate and adapt, finding the right solutions.

But arguably the most important part of the programme lies in the setting up of project committees, which will discuss community needs and organisation. The project will 'support a traditionally disempowered social group to take more control over the factors which have made them poor and insecure'.[16]

Rubber tapper at work, Brazil. The rubber tappers manage the forest sustainably, and the rubber trees will yield for many years.

Fishmeal factory, Chile. Over-fishing by commercial fleets has drastically reduced fish stocks in recent years, threatening the livelihoods of fishing communities. Waste from the factories pollutes the waters of the bay.

being depleted. Most of the fisherfolk are now working in the industrial fishing fleets and the fishmeal factories of Concepción and Talcahuano which pollute the Bay of Concepción.

The Caleta El Moro community has been fishing for shellfish, mackerel, sardines and salmon for more than a century. Now the shellfish have gone and the viability of the community is threatened by pollution and dwindling catches. Like other fishing communities in this part of Chile, people are sinking further into poverty: already, half of the Region's population is classified as poor, earning less than US$200 a month.

FEDEPA (the Federation Regional de Pescadores Artesanales) represents the local fisherfolk and helped to draft a new fishing law in 1991. This recognises the needs of small-scale fishers, and sets aside specific areas of sea for their exclusive use. It remains to be seen whether or not the industrial fleets respect these zones, and if pollution can be controlled. Meanwhile, FEDEPA and other local groups are exploring low-tech ways of smoking fish to add value and provide jobs without the need to increase catches. Related leadership training programmes are increasing the self-confidence of local fisherfolk as they fight for further protection of their livelihoods.[18]

PEC in the North

In the UK, Primary Environmental Care may be used to describe the approach of several NGOs working alongside local people in inner city districts. For example, the network of 29 Groundwork Trusts, begun in the early 1980s, emphasises empowerment and support for communities who want to repair their local environment and bring about associated social and economic improvements.

Sholver is a run-down housing estate outside Oldham – 1,000 feet up in the Lancashire Pennines. On this patch of the 'inner city' in the countryside, drug abuse, violence and truancy were common. In a place which offered little else to do, vandalism was costing the local council 10,000 a month in 1985. Led by an unemployed ambulance driver, some of the residents seized the opportunity to act together when their homes were threatened by demolition. With advice and support from Groundwork, they began by tackling dereliction and vandalism – decorating homes and communal areas and clearing rubbish. This demonstration of positive environmental action persuaded the local council to reverse their plans for demolition, and repair the houses. But the younger residents wanted more to do. A countryside ranger from the Oldham and Rochdale Groundwork Trust took them on trips to the countryside to respond to their interest in wildlife, and their

Children building the Skolga Serpent (from a Viking legend) in the wildlife sanctuary they have created on the Sholver Housing Estate, Oldham, UK.

enthusiasm for learning – and action. With support from various agencies, the young people set up the Sholver Rangers, building their own playspace and wildlife sanctuary on derelict land, and regularly patrolling the estate to check the safety of old people, protect homes from vandals and marauding dogs, and clear litter.

Attitudes have since changed on the estate: residents meet more often, get on better, and vandalism is much reduced. A number of Groundwork Trusts now work with other communities to transform run-down housing estates, enabling tenants to take more control. With support from the Trusts, they are working in partnership with housing authorities, not just on roof repairs and rent arrears, but to create neighbourhoods where people have some sense of belonging.[19]

Elsewhere in the UK, Europe and North America, there are other examples of local people taking action to meet their needs and build more resourceful communities. They are greening derelict land, recycling wastes and conserving energy, often creating new jobs and businesses at the same time.[20]

CREATING THE CONDITIONS FOR PEC

In all these ventures, it is clear that there are a number of preconditions for PEC to work. Communities must have some capacity to organise and to take decisions, with the assurance that they can influence development decisions. People have to be willing to work together – and foster a sense of community. PEC needs a supportive local context, with access to land and security of tenure for those who participate. In the South, the evidence from a variety of projects shows that when poor farmers are secure in their ownership of land and their rights to use the environment as they wish, then they will manage it well, conserving soil and water, planting and caring for trees.

Most importantly, PEC programmes and projects also need a national and an international framework which will allow such an approach to start and to flourish. Indeed, as with the rubber-tappers in Amazonia, the impetus for practical action may come from the regional level, rather than from local pressure alone. Likewise, it has to be possible for local innovations to influence national and international development practice. In a few countries, grassroots activities are already recognised and valued influences on higher-level policymaking but this is not common. In fact, governments often restrict any popular participation to the local level, so that the poor have no impact on the key economic decisions taken at national level.

Before Primary Environmental Care has any long-term chance of success, the obstacles to sustainable development at all levels – both within the South and between North and South – have to be tackled.

Lessons from Primary Health Care

The idea of PEC has grown out of various approaches to local resource management, including Primary Health Care. In part, PHC was a reaction against the domination of 'high tech' hospital medicine in favour of local – and locally managed – accessible health care, based on prevention as well as cure. Likewise, PEC is a response to locally expressed needs for environmental and social improvements – preventative as well as curative – which go beyond technical solutions alone. So PEC puts the emphasis on community forestry rather than reforestation, community-based conservation rather than nature reserves. As well as rehabilitating environments, real PEC programmes try to address the causes of degradation and enable local people to prevent further damage.

As PHC has done, PEC should recognise the key role of women, their experience, skills and needs. Best practice in PHC has enabled women to build on their existing roles and benefit directly from local improvements, taking up new responsibilities, realising opportunities and acquiring enhanced status. PEC should do the same.

Many lessons have still to be learnt from more than a decade of PHC. Political will and adequate resources are vital. Supportive structures are required for PEC which can provide personnel and technical training, help for local institutions, and access to resources such as land, credit, appropriate technologies, transport and marketing. Building on local knowledge and ensuring full participation will mean that PEC programmes must be – as in Affolé – flexible in their timescales and in their funding, with a style of management which enables people to take control. Durable PEC approaches typically begin small and do not seek to innovate continually, but to learn from experience, consolidate successes and explore the opportunities for replication. Most PEC schemes will be multi-sectoral including, for example, forestry, agroforestry, soil and water conservation, livestock and crop husbandry, and the creation of new enterprises. External inputs are usually modest and act in a catalytic way. PEC is based on planning from below, not centrally imposed 'blueprint' solutions.

WAYS FORWARD

Primary Environmental Care offers one route towards sustainable development, providing new opportunities for governments, aid agencies, NGOs and the private sector to support local communities in meeting both environmental and developmental objectives. Here is a practical way towards greater community self-reliance, which is already working. What is needed is massive replication of the approach (which acknowledges the likelihood that local solutions will be unique), with more support for new PEC projects and programmes to start up. These must be seen not just as a series of isolated, temporary, local schemes, but as a widening practical strategy for sustainable development.

The concept of Primary Environmental Care is gaining ground among NGOs, multilateral agencies and governments, including the British Government:

> The UK is keen to promote the Primary Environmental Care approach through cooperation programmes with developing countries and support to the NGO community. It is an approach which is affordable, replicable and applicable to multilateral agencies, national and local governments and NGOs, and it should be a key component of Agenda 21.
>
> UK Delegation Statement on Environment and Poverty: Third Preparatory Committee for UNCED, 29 August 1991

There are other advantages. PEC is a way of contributing to the solution of global environmental problems at the local level. The success of international measures to reduce land degradation, stem forest clearance and protect biodiversity depends in large part on what happens locally.

Primary Environmental Care is appropriate in the North as well as the South – and this provides new opportunities for North-South collaboration and the exchange of information and personnel, within and between countries.

Even so, Primary Environmental Care is only one essential element in a whole array of actions that are necessary to move towards sustainable development. PEC needs to be set in a context of large-scale programmes of conservation and environmental rehabilitation, environmental impact assessment and monitoring, and – of key importance – policy change on the issues which stand in the way of sustainable development, both within the South and between North and South. However successful the local action is, it will be undermined by a continuing deterioration in the economic and political structures which keep people and countries in poverty. These are the subjects of later chapters in this book.

3

WATER FOR LIFE

The number of water taps per 1000 persons is a better indication of health than the number of hospital beds.

Dr. Halfdan Mahler, ex-Director of the World Health Organisation

Gulabi's village, Khaspatti, nestles in the Garwal Hills of north-west India. In the distance are the snow-capped peaks of the western Himalayas, and the perennial tributaries of the Ganges criss-cross the land. But in summer the small springs on the hillsides dry up. The rivers run in deep gorges and are not easily reached by people who live in the hill settlements like Khaspatti. The more accessible rivers, such as the Bhagirathi, are a half-day's trek from the village, so Gulabi must make do with very little to drink. Her nearest source of water is a small stone tank in the next village, four kilometres uphill, beside an oak forest. The 'high-caste' women have first use of the tank in the early morning, then other families may use it according to their social standing. 'Low caste' outsiders, like Gulabi, come last. The pot of muddy water that she scoops from the bottom of the tank has to quench the thirst of her mother-in-law, brother-in-law and her children.

Life in Khaspatti is hard: wise parents avoid marrying their daughters to Khaspatti husbands. But Gulabi is from a local family so there was no question of her marrying outside the village. The daily drudgery of life in the hill settlements pushes many women to attempt suicide. They tie their limbs together and plunge into the whirlpool of the Bhagirathi River. Some escape to their watery graves. Others, like Gulabi, fail.

A failed suicide reflects badly on the family. Gulabi had to leave hers. She sought refuge in Swami Manmathan's centre for destitute women, an Oxfam-funded project. In 1986, Swami Manmathan encouraged the women of Khaspatti to stage a demonstration on the Tehri-Deoprayag road. They brought traffic to a standstill and their plight to the attention of the government. Today 250 villages around Khaspatti receive fresh water, piped from the Bhagirathi River.

NOT ENOUGH TO DRINK

Water makes up 60 per cent of the human body weight, is essential for all plant and animal life and sustains the world's industries. Yet water of high quality is scarce. While oceans cover most of the earth's surface, only about 3 per cent of the world's water is fresh and three-quarters of that is frozen at the poles. This means that less than one per cent is available in groundwater rivers and lakes, and those are unevenly distributed.[1] Whereas America uses the equivalent of 2,300 cubic metres of fresh water per person each year, in Ghana this figure is just over 30 cubic metres. Worldwide, over two billion people suffer from chronic water shortages.[2]

Consumption patterns vary widely. While in the South most water is used for agriculture, in the North the largest proportion is used for industry. The demands of both are growing rapidly – trebling since 1950. Industry and power generation now account for almost 50 per cent of all the water consumed in the United States.

More than half the people in poor countries have no access to safe drinking water and must rely on inadequate or polluted sources such as urban stand-pipes (shared by hundreds of families), or rivers, lakes and wells, which are becoming increasingly polluted, or drying up.[3] Water-borne diseases kill at least 25,000 people every day. More than 4 million children die from diarrhoea every year. Overall, UNICEF estimates that dirty water and insanitary living conditions account for 12.4 million deaths each year.[4]

As the industries and cities of Asia grow, its rivers become conduits for human and industrial wastes: they are now amongst the most polluted in the world. Even where laws to keep waterways clean exist, they are often not enforced. Industrial and agricultural wastes are believed to have polluted more than 40 of Malaysia's major rivers; and 54 of the 78 rivers monitored in the People's Republic of China are clogged with untreated sewage and industrial wastes. About 70 per cent of India's surface waters are polluted and barely 7 per cent of its towns and cities have any facilities to treat sewage.[5] The story is much the same over the rest of the developing world and is the main reason why Oxfam is so often involved in supplying safe drinking water.

A person needs a minimum of 15-20 litres of water a day (this is the amount which UNHCR reckons is necessary for people in emergency situations); but in the South few households have a water supply in the home and all the water needed by the family for drinking, cooking, and keeping clean must be collected and carried back home.[6] Collecting water is a gruelling daily task mostly done by women. They are forced to neglect their own health, their families, and their fields to spend hours each day carrying containers of water that can weigh as much as 20 kg.

Collecting water is traditionally women's responsibility. This can be a very demanding part of their workloads in terms of both time and physical effort. Women from Dhobghat village, Bihar.

As water shortages increase, women have to spend greater parts of the day collecting water. In rural areas this is likely to mean walking a greater distance and in urban areas it can mean queueing for longer at the source of supply. Women are usually the managers of water resources for their community, making decisions about collection, amounts and uses of water. A study has shown that when the role of women has been ignored in designing and implementing water projects, these have tended to fail.[7] In a water project in Wollo Region of Ethiopia, the male community leaders were consulted about the design of the project, but they had no knowledge or understanding of water sources. Initially, the project was not successful. For one thing, the water jar used by the women of the Afar community to carry water is round-bottomed and cannot stand upright on a concrete surface, and since the pump which was installed needed two hands to operate, the women could not hold the jar steady at the same time. One person could not collect water unaided. These problems were solved after consultation with the people involved in managing the resource – the women of the community.[8]

Coping with drought
Using water to irrigate crops in drylands may seem a good strategy. But most methods of irrigation are grossly inefficient: only a small amount of the water that reaches the fields benefits the crops, the rest runs away.

The larger schemes often waste more water than smaller ones. Big dams, with extensive networks of canals, often distribute water unevenly between the beneficiaries, are uneconomical and environmentally unsound.

Over centuries, farmers have developed many systems of harvesting water, including small dams, contour ditches and reservoirs. Traditional systems have much to offer. And the more farmers are involved in the design, construction and maintenance of irrigation schemes, the more efficient and productive such schemes become. Both large and small-scale schemes have a role to play in tackling drought, depending on the local situation.

> Rajasthan's Thar desert, in north-west India, receives less than 250 mm of rainfall annually and, in summer, strong winds blow away the dried-out top soil. Several years of drought prompted one Indian group called Gramin Vikas Vigyan Samiti (GVVS) to return to traditional methods of conserving water.
>
> In 1985, GVVS began to build embankments, locally called *khadins*, on hillsides to conserve rainwater, increase moisture in the soil, and check soil erosion. The *khadins* are almost 2m high, and 4m wide at the base and are built on three sides of the lower slope of a field. Rainwater is trapped behind the embankments and infiltrates into the soil. The work brings immediate results: improved soil conditions now give better crops of millet, pulses, sesame oil seed and mustard. Farmers have planted acacia and *ber* trees on the embankments to provide fuel and fodder. 'The families who made embankments have saved themselves from the severity of famine', says GVVS's leader.[9]

When is a drought not a drought?

Drought does not have to lead to famine. Indeed, occasional droughts are a fact of life for the Turkana and Samburu pastoralists of the semi-arid lands of eastern and northern Kenya. Centuries of living in this harsh environment have made them experts at surviving drought. As the dry season approaches they pack up and move on in search of fresh grazing, making the wisest use of available land.[10]

In 1984, the drought came after an epidemic of livestock diseases that had already weakened the animals. In some areas, 80 per cent of the goats and many cattle died. The price of meat, skins and hides fell until they were almost worthless. People were unable to buy cereals or other food even when they were available. Oxfam provided emergency food supplies linked to a destocking programme which gave pastoralists who wanted to sell their stock a fair deal. After the drought, consultation with local groups led to a restocking programme. Families were lent 'starter' herds of sheep and goats, and a pack animal. It was enough to liberate them from food distribution camps and get them back on the rangelands. The programme also helped to improve the marketing of hides, and trained herders to administer veterinary drugs.[11]

Water for the village
The droughts of the early 1980s dried up streams, the traditional sources of water in many parts of Ethiopia. In the south of the country, Wolaiyta was particularly hard hit, for it had few water resources and a high density of population, with people trying to scrape a living from small plots, competing for land, wood, pasture and water. The water table was so low, wells had to be up to 40 metres deep.

The people of Wolaiyta grow a combination of roots and cereals: *enset*, sweet potatoes, *taro*, yam, barley, maize, wheat and *teff*. Farmers cultivate the land intensively, all the year round, replenishing the fertility of the soil with animal manure. But a household has, at most, two animals, so manure is in short supply.

The women of Agoza Affar village have to walk for more than an hour to fetch water from a stream. In 1984, Oxfam started a programme to dig wells and cap springs in Wolaiyta. Oxfam funds pay for materials, technical support and, most importantly, the wages of people who dig the wells. Now Agoza Affar's 1000 villagers have two wells in the village. Each is lined with concrete rings and the well-head is fenced off to protect it from animals. Wolaiyta suffered again in the drought of 1991 but was better able to deal with the problems.[12]

Water for the capital
Cambodia's infrastructure had been destroyed by 1979, when Vietnamese troops drove Pol Pot and the Khmer Rouge from power. When people began to return to the capital, Phnom Penh, they found a ghost town, wrecked through years of conflict and neglect. Oxfam helped with machinery, spare parts and chlorination to provide safe water, a major priority.

In 1987, an assessment of the capital's drinking water supply concluded that the water pumping station could be made to work again. But the damage was so extensive, the water supply to Phnom Penh demanded total renovation. The problem was made worse by the lack of spare parts and equipment caused by the economic isolation of Cambodia, and by the scarcity of skilled technicians - most had fled the country or died in the Khmer Rouge purges. Oxfam drew up a three-year plan to renovate the water pumping station and train local technicians and engineers in repair and maintainance. Hydraulic

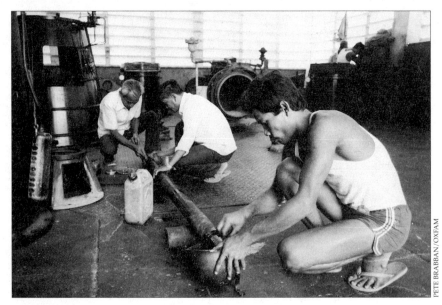

Inside Phnom Penh waterworks. Oxfam has helped to fund repair and renovation to the pumping station and water supply system in the city.

engineers eventually managed to repair and replace water filters and overhaul the electrical systems. Three new pumps now extract water from the river Tonle Sap and the plant that treats this 'raw' water has been repaired and improved.

The scale of devastation following the Pol Pot years and the Western aid embargo (imposed when the Vietnamese invaded) put Oxfam's work in Cambodia in a special category. Since 1979, Oxfam has spent more than £25 million in the country on relief and development work. Although the sum is large for an NGO, it is small in relation to Cambodia's needs. Oxfam allocated more than £1.1 million to rehabilitate the Phnom Penh waterworks, but could not fund such a scheme indefinitely. Now that the embargo on aid has been lifted, the hope is that bilateral and multilateral aid agencies will provide the capital investment needed to complete the restoration programme. UNDP has already identified the Phnom Penh water supply as a priority for action.[13]

COPING WITH FLOODS

Flood plains and the areas surrounding river deltas are fertile agricultural land. The plains of the Nile, the Yellow River, the Ganges, and the Mekong delta, are all densely populated. But the floods that bring the fertile silt and fish, can also cause destruction.

Heavy rains and melting ice can bring flooding when the run-off exceeds the local drainage capacity of streams and other shallow waterways. Deforestation in the catchment areas of major rivers can increase the likelihood of flash floods and overbank flooding. As vegetation is lost and topsoil erodes, the absorption capacity of the catchment area decreases and so the water reaches the river all at once.

Storm surges generated by tropical cyclones in coastal areas can also cause serious damage. Global warming – with sea-level rise and disrupted weather patterns – is likely to increase the risks of cyclone flooding. The destruction of coral reefs and mangrove swamps, which had formed a protective barrier along low-lying coasts, adds to the problems. On an increasing scale, mangroves are cut for timber and fuel, while coral reefs are lost when fishermen dynamite them to increase catches, and the coral is made into jewellery for sale to tourists, or used in cement or expensive floor tiles.

Bangladesh, Guyana, the Maldives, Vietnam, and the Netherlands, for example, have large parts of their land below mean sea level and are especially vulnerable to a rise in sea level. Whereas the Netherlands can afford to build expensive protective structures, poorer countries must rely on labour-intensive and low-cost solutions.

Vietnam, for example, is continually battered by the high winds and torrential rains that cyclones bring. Oxfam helped the people of Ky Anh to build a network of earth dykes to protect their homes and land from typhoons that blow in from the Pacific Ocean. These dykes, made entirely from earth and rocks moved by hand and compacted by machinery, stretch along 17 kilometres of river estuary, shielding 4,500 families. When an unusually severe typhoon in August 1990 destroyed much of the work, people immediately began a reconstruction programme. To fortify the dykes against future onslaughts from the sea, a team of 3,000 local people and nine bulldozers worked every day for six months.[14]

Floods in Bangladesh

Much of Bangladesh is made up of the deltas of two of the world's mightiest rivers – the Ganges, Brahmaputra – and a third, the Meghna. Flooding is a familiar part of life, and vital for Bangladeshi agriculture. The annual monsoon flood brings water needed to irrigate jute and rice crops, and silt that renews soil fertility. Floods also bring fish – an important source of protein and income for poor people who can fish in the flood waters. During floods, small boats ferry people about. Although floods are inconvenient, people expect them, need them and know how to cope with them.

But the floods of 1988 were on a different scale. They were the worst in living memory, submerging two-thirds of the country and affecting 45 million people. Many people died and millions lost their homes. Two million tonnes of food were lost, nearly an eighth of the country's annual production.[15]

It is tempting to conclude from two consecutive bad years, 1987 and 1988, that Bangladesh has become more prone to flooding, perhaps because of environmental degradation in Nepal and India. But the records that are available do not entirely bear this out. The delta has always been a dangerous place and, as the rivers change course, there have been major floods throughout history.[16] Although there is no conclusive evidence to suggest that the incidence of serious floods is increasing, it seems clear that their impact is now more severe, mainly because of deepening poverty.

The poorest people often live in exposed positions and their houses are made from fragile materials. They have few resources for recovery when disaster strikes. Many are landless and in debt to landowners and moneylenders. Poor people do not have reserves of food or money to call on in times of need. They sell their livestock – cows, goats, chickens – but get a low price and have lost their source of food and income. When the floods are over, livestock prices rise out of reach for poor families. An alternative to selling possessions may be to borrow money

BADAL/OXFAM

Floods are a familiar part of life in Bangladesh, which people are prepared for and can cope with. But the floods in August 1988 were much worse than usual. This photograph was taken near Dhaka.

during the crisis, from moneylenders who demand even higher rates of interest during times of great need. Once again, the borrower may be forced to sell possessions to repay the loan; or will have to work on the moneylender's land next season at a low rate of pay, and so the family will be even poorer when disaster strikes again.

The last resort is migration. After the 1988 flood thousands of people moved to the capital. Many could be found sleeping on the streets of Dhaka, forced to beg for a living. Moved off land that they once worked, poor people may also migrate to marginal land that is more likely to flood. On the coast, landless people perch on *chars* – mudflats newly formed from silt washed into the Bay of Bengal – in danger of being hit by cyclones and tidal waves.

The Flood Action Plan

The Bangladesh floods of 1988 prompted the international community to look for long-term 'solutions'. France, Japan, the US and the UNDP all sent experts to investigate and make recommendations.

The World Bank pooled elements from four reports to produce a five-year Flood Action Plan, which the Bangladeshi Government accepted. The Plan could cost US$5 billion to implement. It calls for immediate strengthening of the existing embankment on the right bank of the Brahmaputra, with flood protection for greater Dhaka and some other vulnerable towns. It recommends further feasibility studies for more embankments, drainage canals to divert water, and 'compartments' to store the floodwaters. These are enclosed by embankments, and can be flooded or drained as required, with gates in the embankments to allow water in and out of surrounding fields.

The Plan is founded on detailed studies of the problems of flooding, but from a technical point of view. It seems that less attention has been paid to the hundreds of thousands of people living in the affected areas and the potential impact that major embankments and flood compartments might have on them. To contain floods like those of 1988, the embankments will have to be set well back from the rivers. Up to five million people could then find themselves living in an area which would become more, not less, liable to flood. In crowded Bangladesh, there is nowhere else to live.

Moreover, landowning elites are likely to control the gates, perhaps charging for their use. Embankments would also reduce the amount of fish that arrive with floods. The record of maintaining public works in Bangladesh is poor; if people living in threatened areas fear that the embankments might be breached, they are likely to breach them deliberately at a place where they can predict the consequences and control the flood waters.

Living with floods

Whatever the outcome of the Flood Action Plan, the poorest people will need help. The approach favoured by Oxfam relies less on elaborate engineering and more upon enabling local people to live with floods. This 'soft engineering' approach has the advantages of being comparatively cheap and more easily designed and implemented by local people according to their own priorities.

The elements of this approach are simple. Refuges are created on higher ground and villages are supplied with boats for use in emergencies; stocks of food and medicines are maintained at strategic locations. Seed banks, run by local groups, will help farmers after the floodwaters fall, and revolving loan funds and credit facilities will support income-generation projects. Communities, at hamlet level, are linked with local authorities who issue flood forecasts and warnings.

After the 1988 floods, many people built another floor in their houses, just under the roof, where they could store their possessions above flood level and even shelter themselves. Banana tree trunks make excellent rafts when lashed together. Water hyacinth plants, normally seen as a pest, stifling crops and blocking drainage channels, can be made into platforms for use during floods.

Most of these solutions come from the villagers. Working at the local level, Oxfam has helped partners in Bangladesh, and also in Vietnam, to implement village-based flood preparedness programmes which encourage people to think through how they can be better equipped. Some groups plan to save money and food, or build up land to serve as flood refuges. Floating coops can protect chickens, and certain varieties of trees are more resistant to floods. People are exploring alternative sources of income so they are not so dependent on agriculture. Groups can buy boats to rescue people when needed, which double as ferries during the rest of the year.

Self-help in Lalmonirhat

In 1989, the river made Zamrun homeless when it eroded the embankment on which her tiny house was perched. The surrounding land was flooded, which meant no work for her husband, Zekander Ali. Zamrun had no idea how she might feed her six children. The family once had nearly two hectares of land. But the River Teesta changed its course and washed their land away. They fled to the precarious spot on the embankment with such meagre possessions as they could salvage.

When the 1989 floods came after floods in the two preceding years, Oxfam began to wonder whether giving emergency support to people was the best way of helping. Was there a way in which the community could become less vulnerable to the effects of a disaster? Oxfam discussed the problem with a small local organisation, Own Village Advancement. OVA and Oxfam agreed that they had to give immediate relief but also that the community should explore ways of becoming more independent.

Zamrun worked for two weeks on a project to raise the earthen foundations of a school above flood level. The income she earned enabled her to feed her family until the crisis was over and until her husband could again find a job. It was the first time she had earned an income of her own.

Zamrun and her husband Zekander Ali, with the help of friends and neighbours, are moving house - literally. The embankment they lived on was unsafe after the severe floods of 1990. Houses in Bangladesh are made of light materials, so it is possible to move them to a different site.

With the encouragement of an OVA worker, Ahadullah, they and the other families on the embankment formed small groups to try to work out longer-term solutions. The group that Zamrun joined elected her President. First, they set up a savings fund. Zamrun has little spare cash, but saves 2 Taka (about 4p) a week by holding back a little rice from the cooking each day. She saves it until she has enough to sell. The fund is to see them through crisis periods and to invest in small money-making ventures such as bamboo weaving, fruit-tree cultivation and goat-rearing.

The groups resolved never to ask for emergency relief again. Zamrun and Zekander Ali set up their own small business, weaving bamboo for housing: they do not earn much, but it gives them more security than searching daily for agricultural work. From Ahadullah they learnt about a programme to distribute government-owned land to landless people: they applied for a plot nearby, safer than the embankment.

The groups formed a federation and chose representatives for a committee to coordinate all their activities. This federation has two Presidents, a man and a woman, a brave step towards equality in a society in which women traditionally take no part in public life. The federation aims to represent landless people, helping them to gain access to public resources such as government-owned land, a water supply, and health care.

August 1990 brought more floods. The people of Lalmonirhat took loans from their savings funds to buy food. The embankment was breaking up so people resolved to take immediate possession of the government land. Oxfam only contributed wages for an earthworks project during the floods of 1990, plus the salaries of the OVA staff who had encouraged the groups to plan for the future with confidence.[17]

THE PROBLEMS OF LARGE DAMS

It seems to make sense to store water, particularly in drought-prone areas that have large rivers with reliable flows. Dams create reservoirs of fresh water to be released when needed. Networks of canals can take water to homes, fields and factories. Controlling the flow of water can reduce the risk of floods, supply water for irrigation, and also generate hydroelectricity.

But large dams are expensive to build and they often cause massive displacement of people and wildlife. Deforestation, or neglect of the river catchment area, can increase the rate at which silt builds up in the reservoir, reducing its useful lifespan. Aims may conflict: full reservoirs drive turbines efficiently whereas empty reservoirs give the flexibility needed for flood control; but full reservoirs can cause flooding when unexpectedly late rains are released through the spillways to prevent dambursts or overtopping. Large areas of stagnant water can provide breeding grounds for malaria-carrying mosquitoes and canal networks can spread the snails that carry the bilharzia parasite. Local power structures usually ensure that those adversely affected by large dams – poor people, displaced from their homes – do not get their fair share of the benefits.

The needs of poor people are often ignored in the rush to recover investments in large dam projects. Generating power may take precedence over irrigation; and irrigation is more likely to go to large-scale cash crops than subsistence food production. Power, irrigation and water for industry are usually seen as more important than the provision of drinking water, because all three can contribute to making the dam, power houses and canal networks pay for themselves.

For all these reasons, and many more besides, the success of large dams has been mixed. The earliest dams were built on well-chosen sites, usually in temperate countries with ample rainfall. Many provided cheap electricity and were seen as attractive options by developing countries. But the list of suitable sites is finite and dams are now being built in places that some engineers view as wholly inappropriate. A host of interrelated factors – deforestation, intensive land use, centralised planning, inequitable land distribution – can undermine the effective working of these large schemes.

The high Aswan dam on Egypt's Blue Nile may have effectively controlled flooding but it has starved the downstream areas of the flood water that used to cover the land with fertile silt. Irrigated areas, meanwhile, have been degraded by a build-up of salts.

Part of the huge Narmada dam project under construction in India, which has displaced many thousands of people from their homes and land.

Narmada

India's Narmada Valley Development Programme (NVDP) is one of the most ambitious schemes ever contemplated. Over the next half century, 31 large dams, 135 medium dams and 3,000 minor structures will be built to exploit the waters of the Narmada river and its 41 tributaries. Work on one of the large dams, the Sardar Sarovar Project (SSP) in Gujarat, is now well under way.

Indian law demands that compensatory reforestation be carried out by projects that cause deforestation. The Government of Gujarat has begun tree-planting in the catchment area, to decrease siltation of the reservoir and increase groundwater flows – important for those farmers whose land will not be irrigated. There are plans for much more of this catchment area protection in neighbouring Madhya Pradesh, but doubts about whether the plans will be carried out.

The Sardar Sarovar dam and its canal projects have been much criticised. Rural people who will be displaced by the reservoir are concerned about being moved with no compensation. Environmental groups stress the ecological impact of the scheme on forests, wildlife, soils · and hydrology. Indian development groups, and some international NGOs, fear that the interests of industrialists and large landowners who want to grow cash crops (such as sugar cane and bananas) will take precedence over subsistence food producers, and rich farmers will benefit at the expense of the poor.

Moving out need not mean losing ground
The people of the tribal village, Mankhakhada, were unaware of the Narmada project until a farmer, Lalubhai, saw a group of workmen driving white marker stones into the ground. Lalubhai wondered whether they were signposts for a road connecting his village with the rest of Gujarat. In fact, the workmen were marking the level to which the water would rise once the reservoir of the Sardar Sarovar dam had filled. The thatched houses of Mankhakhada lay below the white markers. That is how Lalubhai and his village learnt about the Narmada project.[18]

Dam officials later told villagers that the dam would bring prosperity to all by providing Gujarat with the electricity and irrigation water that was so badly needed. The drought-prone areas of Kutch would get drinking water. But 70,000 people in Gujarat, Madhya Pradesh and Maharashtra would have to move because they lived within the area destined to be flooded by the reservoir. Among them would be thousands of Bhil tribals like Lalubhai.

The officials said that those who owned farms would get replacement land. But because Lalubhai and the people of Mankhakhada were living on forest land without legal title, they would get no land. The forest officially belongs to the Government, and farming within it is illegal. This ruling dates back to colonial times, when land ownership laws were introduced into India, and vast tracts of communal land were declared to be government property. The fact that people had cultivated land there for generations was not taken into account.

The efforts of local people, national and international NGOs, and the World Bank, in pressing for a fairer resettlement policy eventually succeeded. Today, Gujarat has an excellent resettlement policy, not least because of the unremitting work of an organisation called Action and Research in Community Health (ARCH), one of Oxfam's partners.

ARCH was started in 1978 by Anil and Daksha Patel. They decided to use the medical knowledge they gained in India and the epidemiology and health care they had studied in Britain, in setting up a community health programme in Mangrol – a small village in rural Gujarat. People came to realise that low-cost health care was sound and effective. Village health workers were soon treating more than 3,000 patients as confidence in ARCH grew.

In 1980, ARCH found out that several of the tribal villages in the project area were being acquired for the construction of the Sardar Sarovar dam. There was no programme for resettlement; the people of Gujarat were to be excluded from the awards for compensation set years earlier by the Narmada Water Disputes Tribunal. Working with the tribal people, ARCH enabled them to challenge state government policies in the Supreme Court. ARCH argued that the Gujarati 'oustees' should get the same treatment as promised to those of Maharashtra and Madhya Pradesh. The Gujarat Government improved its rehabilitation policy in 1987, in line with the Tribunal's award. ARCH pushed for yet better terms. The outcome is that Gujarat has significantly improved its policy.[19]

Under the new policy, those displaced by the dam will have access to essential amenities such as drinking water, schools, health services, housing and road networks. It guarantees all heads of households, including women, at least the same areas of land as they lose and a minimum of two hectares for people who had no land before. Moreover, the land will be irrigated once the system is in operation. People from Madhya Pradesh and Maharashtra whose land is to be submerged by the Sardar Sarovar reservoir and who wish to move to Gujarat will get the same benefits. So far, 3,000 people from 19 villages in Gujarat have received their land. Compensation for people in Gujarat affected by the building of Sardar Sarovar Project's irrigation canals has not been adequately addressed by the State Government. Little progress has been made in Maharashtra and almost none in Madhya Pradesh, the two states most affected by the dam but which will derive far fewer benefits than Gujarat. ARCH, with Oxfam, is monitoring conditions at the village level to ensure the agreed rehabilitation policies are carried out fully.

The Sardar Sarovar dam has polarised Indian NGOs. Some, like ARCH, believe that completion of the dam is inevitable and so try pushing for more progressive resettlement terms for all those displaced.

But many NGOs reject the Narmada project unconditionally as a symbol of inappropriate development and view any agreements on resettlement as a sell-out to the developers. Anti-dam organisations argue that it will be impossible to rehabilitate all the estimated 90,000 people affected by the dam. Critics allege that the project is completely uneconomic; costs have escalated and financing is inadequate. They question whether the dam waters will reach drought-prone areas of Gujarat and are sceptical about the project's ability to produce many of the benefits claimed for it, such as increased crop yields.

THE RIGHT TO WATER

Elsewhere, water can be a source of international conflict. Because water is so precious, secure rights to it are vital for sustainable development, and access gives power. Landowners with wells on their land can dominate the local economy. Nations which control the headwaters of major international rivers can use the water as they wish, affecting water supplies and agricultural productivity in neighbouring countries.[20]

In the Middle East, water has been a source of conflict for centuries. The River Jordan, with Syria, Jordan, Lebanon and Israel within its watershed, is already insufficient to meet the needs of the countries it serves. In the 1960s, Syria, Jordan and Lebanon tried to divert the flow after Israeli attempts to do the same in the demilitarised zone of the Israeli-Syrian border. The threat of diversion, which would have reduced supplies to Israel, was serious enough to bring the countries close to military conflict.[21]

Israel's 1967 occupation of the West Bank and Golan Heights (where the Jordan rises) helped to safeguard its access to the river on which it relies for 50 per cent of its water, and to give it control over the aquifers of the West Bank. The Jordan water is used to irrigate wheat and citrus fruits from Galilee to Jaffa and in the Negev Desert. The old River Jordan is now nothing more than a trickle. Some observers believe that the groundwater reserves of the West Bank are the reason for Israel's determination to retain control over the territory. The Israeli Ministry of Agriculture has stressed the importance of controlling water resources:

> It is hard to conceive of any political solution consistent with Israel's survival that does not include complete and continued Israeli control of the water systems. Water is, in many ways, the limiting factor on the country's future development.[22]

Israel controls most of the estimated usable water resources of the West Bank and Gaza. Both Israel and the West Bank are described by experts as facing 'serious water stress',[23] with populations expected to double within the next 20-30 years.

*Palestinian farmer,
cultivating his land.
On the nearby
hillside is a new
Israeli settlement.*

Palestinians in the Occupied Territories argue that 80 per cent of the water in their aquifers is being diverted to irrigate Israeli fields.[24] Since 1967 there have been prohibitions on Palestinians drilling new wells for irrigation and only three wells have been drilled; at the same time, Palestinians have had no say in determining water policy.[25]

To increase the flow of information and expertise to the people of the West Bank, Oxfam supports the Palestinian Hydrology Group (PHG) which carries out research and practical development projects. Before the PHG, there were no easily accessible sources of information for planning purposes in the Occupied Territories. The Group's first project was a survey of more than 300 natural springs in the highlands of the West Bank; now it is building a comprehensive data base on local hydrology. The Group is also involved in water development projects, promoting more effective use of existing resources by giving advice on irrigation, water management and efficient technologies. Oxfam has subsidised the cost of cement and iron needed to build rainfed cisterns, which are a cheap way of providing water for both domestic and agricultural use. Abdul Rahman Tamimi, a hydrologist and Director of the Palestine Hydrology Group, is critical of the current distribution of water supplies in the region:

> You won't find any Israeli settlement without water – they have lush lawns, even swimming pools – while there are scores of Arab villages with wholly inadequate supplies.[26]

For poor people, like these Palestinian farmers, rights to water which are secure, publicly recognised and protected are essential for their livelihoods and yet customary rights to water are generally even less secure than customary rights to land – the subject of the next chapter.

The high plains where pastoralists graze their flocks in Erigavo, Northern Somalia (Somaliland). When communal lands were taken into private ownership, grazing pressure intensified, leading to land degradation. Run-off increased after heavy rain, causing erosion in the valleys. Below, an eroded valley where the force of the flood water has created deep gullies and uprooted trees.

4

THE STRUGGLE FOR LAND

Land means self respect and security. It enables poor people to start planning for the future. When disasters come, they can lose almost everything but still have their land.[1]

The total number of very poor people is growing. The rural poor are having to provide for themselves on dwindling amounts of land which is becoming less and less productive; the problems of access to land and land degradation are closely related. Whoever owns land also holds power; yet most of the earth's poorest people have no control over the land where they live.[2]

Somalia – land tenure and environmental degradation

The Erigavo district is in the far northern region of Sanaag in Northern Somalia (Somaliland). There is a high escarpment in the north near the coast, and vast high-lying plains to the south on which sheep, goats, camels and cattle graze. The plains are crossed by a series of steep-sided, fertile valleys which produce a rich variety of fruit, vegetables and maize. Few people live in this part of Somalia: more than three-quarters of them are pastoralists and the rest are farmers. Rainfall is low and comes in short, intense storms. Frequent droughts dry out the soil and, if it is not bound by vegetation, the wind blows it away.

In recent years, changes in land tenure have brought increasing environmental degradation. Communal grazing land has gradually passed into private hands and been enclosed. Encouraged by high livestock prices, pastoralists have enlarged their herds at the same time as communal pastures have been shrinking. Meanwhile, steep hillside areas which were not formerly grazed have become overused and eroded. Denuded of its vegetation cover, the land no longer retains water: rainfall rushes off the hard surface, causing sheet erosion on the plains and gullying in the valleys. The loss of vegetation and soils hits farmers and pastoralists alike, but women and children suffer most, for they are often left alone to fend for themselves while the men search for new pastures. Women carry the responsibility for feeding their families, which can mean going hungry themselves. Community tensions increase and marriages break up.[3]

Efforts to deal with the problems of soil erosion by high-tech, capital-intensive methods made things even worse. An extensive and costly gully-control programme was started in the late 1970s, using outside experts and funds. Large dams were built across valleys to check the seasonal rush of rainwater. But the dams either collapsed, or diverted the flow of water so that new gullies formed: flooding became uncontrollable and valley farmers had to abandon their land. The combined effects of the transfer of common land into private ownership and increasing land degradation was a disaster for the community.

When Issa's farm in the Medishi valley of Erigavo was flooded because of these unsuccessful attempts to reduce erosion, he and his family left their fertile land and their permanent home. They took their sheep, goats and camels into the hills nearby to live as herders. As Issa explained:

> We tried to cultivate the land for a few years, but in the rainy seasons, our crops were destroyed by floods. So we moved into the hills with our stock and stayed there. In the dry season, I came back to see what had happened to the land, never to cultivate – that was impossible.

In 1984, Oxfam began to work with the people of Erigavo, listening to their perception of the problems; involving them fully from the start was essential. After much discussion, it was agreed that the people of the community, working with hand tools, would lower the big dams, and construct spillways, check dams and irrigation canals. When this work had been done, the valley farmlands became usable once more: one year later, Issa was able to return to his land to farm again.

It was clear that people saw gully erosion as the main issue; they were reluctant to accept that grazing pressures could be a part cause of their problems. Oxfam started working with the pastoralists on the plains, demonstrating better methods of stock control and ways of encouraging revegetation. Tree-planting was popular: one village elder, Mohammed Farah Yusuf said:

> We wanted trees because we were looking to the future for our children. We hope that others in our community, and even other communities, will see what we have done and will do it also.

Groups of volunteers took part in workshops on conservation, and began to use their new skills and knowledge in their own communities. People from other villages began to get involved in training. But small-scale action of this kind is limited if it cannot address the root causes of the problems. The issue of land ownership was never far from the surface. As one workshop participant put it:

> Our animals have not enough places to graze since most of the grazing areas have been given to individuals, to make permanent farms.

For the pastoralists of the Erigavo plains, the crucial issue was land enclosure and the disruption of traditional patterns of livestock grazing. They decided they must form grazing associations and press for the return of the 'commons' to communal ownership.

LOSING THE LAND

Land degradation is a term which covers a wide range of processes related to soils, vegetation and climate – including the deterioration of drylands, soil erosion, salinisation (of irrigated lands)[4] and the damaging effects of pesticide and fertiliser use. Every year, land which could have produced 12 million tons of grain output[5] is lost because of land degradation of all kinds. The amount of land lost through soil erosion alone amounts to 20 million hectares each year and this could bring a decline in the output of rainfed crops of more than 20 per cent over the next two decades.[6]

The problem is most serious in dry zones with uncertain rainfall. The term 'desertification' has been much used to conjure up a dramatic

Deforestation and drought lead to loss of fragile soils in sub-Saharan Africa. This is a dried-out lake bed in Chad.

JEREMY HARTLEY/OXFAM

image of the desert encroaching upon villages, destroying farmland and pastures forever. But grand schemes to combat the threat of an advancing desert have usually failed. Oxfam field workers in the Sahelian region of Africa have observed that desertification is a rather complicated process. Land, particularly if it is overused, is eroded by wind and rain, and the soils that remain are so lacking in humus they can support very little plant growth. The lack of vegetation leaves the soil vulnerable to further erosion and this produces conditions that resemble a desert. The removal of tree-cover for fuelwood and the deforestation of upland watersheds also play their part in the process. Experience has shown that, even in these conditions, it is possible to restore soil fertility; 'desertification' is not so permanent as popular imagination would have it.[7]

The underlying causes of 'desertification' are complex. Often, the lack of secure land rights can discourage people from taking a long-term view and conserving resources for the future. When people are displaced into marginal areas of poor land, they are often forced to adopt farming practices which lead to soil degradation.

Although the restoration of degraded or 'desertified' areas is difficult, some progress has been made in parts of the Sahel. Here, Oxfam's programme has included large-scale emergency relief when the situation called for it, and longer-term development work with pastoralists and agro-pastoralists. Education, training and network building to encourage the sharing of ideas and experience between different communities across the region are essential; conservation works best when people are fully involved in designing and implementing the measures which will protect the natural resource base on which they depend.

Burkina Faso: regaining ground

From Burkina Faso, one of the many countries of Sahelian Africa affected by severe land degradation, comes an example of how degraded land can be restored. Yatenga Province is part of the Central Plateau and has, by Sahelian standards, a high population density. Rainfall has decreased significantly within the last 20 years, and much of the land is badly degraded.

Efforts in the 1960s to provide irrigation through the construction of large-scale earth dams were not successful because water was not directed to the fields where small farmers wanted it. They were not consulted about the dams nor did they participate in the irrigation projects. Because the dams did not fit people's needs, they had no interest in maintaining them. As conditions worsened during the 1980s, the people of Yatenga were faced with the choice of either improving their land, which was becoming less and less productive, or migrating.

MARK EDWARDS/OXFAM

Farmers in Burkina Faso at a training session, watching a demonstration of the technique of building stone lines along the contours. The dykes hold back water, allowing it to penetrate the soil, resulting in much higher crop yields. This is one of the most successful environmental regeneration schemes supported by Oxfam.

A solution was urgently needed – which gave the impetus for Projet Agro-Forestier, an Oxfam-supported initiative.[8]

The original idea was for tree-planting on common land, but this approach was not successful, because people were not interested in planting trees for the future when they could not grow enough food in the present. After much discussion, it was decided to revive and improve the traditional practice of building simple stone-lines to conserve soil and water. By adapting the technique and building stone-lines along contours (using water-tubes to measure contour levels), rainfall run-off could be spread behind the stone-lines and allowed to seep into the soil. In this way the amount of moisture available for the crops was increased and conservation of top soil improved.

As well as water-harvesting, other techniques have been developed such as composting, fencing in stock, and village fodder plots, in an integrated approach to village land-use management. But the key to it all is popular participation. Local people are involved in all stages of planning and implementation through village committees. An effective training and extension system, in collaboration with the national extension service, helps to spread the techniques. The popularity of these methods of renewing the land is clear: in 1981, stone-lines had been built on only seven hectares. Now the area covered exceeds 8,000 hectares, in over 400 villages. The combination of the stone-lines and deep planting holes ('zai') has led to harvests increasing by about 50 per cent, sometimes by as much as 100 per cent.[9]

ACCESS TO LAND: COMPETING INTERESTS

People, poor or otherwise, must have some kind of secure tenure of their land if they are to invest in it and manage it in a sustainable way. Some would argue that private ownership is necessary for this to happen; others think that security of tenure is more important than the form of tenure. What does matter is that the tenure system must fit with the customary systems of resource management and decision-making. Moves towards privatisation of common land or inadequately enforced state ownership can create conditions of insecurity which lead people to 'mine' natural resources.

Access to land can be a matter of gender. In their work as farmers growing food crops, women often find it very difficult to get the resources they need. In conditions of land scarcity, women often have difficulty in protecting their land rights on the basis of either local or state procedures and customary usage, and they lose out in the competition for land to the men. Cash cropping often means that good land goes to the cash crops and women are left to provide for their families on inferior land.

The 'tragedy of the commons'

Poor people often depend on 'common property resources' to supply their needs for food, fuel and grazing for their animals. The theory of the 'tragedy of the commons', which was put forward in the 1960s,[10] contended that where communities have access to communal resources they will tend to over-exploit them, because the benefit of, for example, extra animals on the common will go to an individual or family, whereas the cost will be shared out amongst the community. Only if resources were privately owned would people use them sustainably in their own long-term interests. More recent research has disproved this theory and shown that local communities with secure communal rights often take good care of shared resources. Individuals will act in the interests of the community to preserve common rangelands, forests or water resources for the future.[11] This sense of community welfare extends to pooling land where plots are small, so as to cultivate more efficiently.

Common property resources play a vital part in the household economy of many poor people, especially in times of hardship. But common lands, forests and water are more and more under pressure from private or state interests, and the poor who depend on them, particularly women, are increasingly deprived of their rights to use them. The result is that poor people must pay for the fuelwood, fodder and water, which was once freely available. For them, this dispossession from the commons is the real tragedy.[12]

Today, too, the 'tragedy of the commons' is being enacted at the global level. Benefits of using the atmosphere as a 'free' dump for waste products resulting from energy consumption, for example, accrue to the large energy consumers – the industrialised countries – whereas the costs in terms of global warming are spread throughout the global community.

THE RIGHT TO LAND

Unequal land distribution is a feature of many countries both North and South. But the consequences are more far-reaching for people in the South, most of whom still depend on land for their survival. FAO estimates that 30 million rural households worldwide have no land and 138 million are almost landless.[13] Poor people are often forced out of their homes or off their land by powerful groups to make way for large-scale projects such as dams, mines or commercial farms and plantations. Tax and incentive systems often encourage the rich to appropriate and speculate in land. Land-hungry people are pushed into forest areas which often cannot sustain intensive agricultural use. In a recent Oxfam report on the Philippines, Rosalinda Pineda-Ofreneo comments:

> ...the landless poor try to eke out a living by encroaching further and further into forest lands. If trends continue, Philippine forests will completely disappear within this decade, which means floods, droughts and landslides.[14]

The tribal people who lived in the forest areas and who used to practise more sustainable methods of farming have become marginalised. (Deforestation is discussed in Chapter 6.)

Brazil: land, power and conflict

In Brazil, the land distribution issue can be, quite literally, a matter of life and death. It is also crucial for the sustainable development of the country and especially for the Amazonian forests. Brazil is a country with gross inequalities in the distribution of land which have their origin in its colonial history. When the Portuguese first colonised the northeast, for example, land grants were made to prominent people who set up large estates which were used to produce single export crops. This land tenure system still prevails today. In 1984, Oxfam reported that:

> The trend in recent years has been towards increased concentration of land ownership in the hands of large landowners. International loans have helped to consolidate the growth of the industrial

farming sector. The World Bank has recently pledged US$202 million to provide agricultural credit; but little of this money will find its way to the domestic food producers, given the emphasis on agricultural export promotion.[15]

In 1984, according to a rural workers' group – the Movement of Landless People – 1 per cent of farmers owned 44 per cent of the cultivable land, while the poorest 71 per cent of people were squeezed on to one-tenth of the land. There are 23 million rural workers living in poverty in Brazil;[16] almost 11 million farmers are classified as having either insufficient land to support their families or no land at all.

Government tax policy coupled with rapid inflation have made land much more valuable as an economic commodity – not only for its productive potential but as a speculative investment. Because of this, vast tracts of land are under-used. The Brazilian NGO, IBASE, estimates that 280 million hectares of farmland are lying idle. According to Anthony Hall, a former Oxfam country representative:

> Most large estates are held principally as a real estate investment and as a hedge against inflation.

The situation seems to be getting worse for the dispossessed peasant farmers who are forced to turn to wage-labour, squatting on vacant land, and other short-term strategies.

Violent conflict over land is widespread. The Pastoral Land Commission of the Catholic Church (CPT) reports a dramatic increase in violent incidents since 1985. In this period, CPT registered 600,000 peasant families in land conflicts with big landowners – and the deaths of 560 people (including Chico Mendes, the trade unionist who organised the rubber tappers' campaign to protect forest resources).[17] The number of rural workers demanding land rose from over half a million in 1985 to 1.5 million in 1990. The disputed area more than doubled, to 20 million hectares, over the same period.[18]

In Rio Maria, an isolated town of some 15,000 people in the south-west of the state of Para, peasant leaders have been targets of contract killings by gunmen allegedly hired by local landowners. According to the Pastoral Land Commission (CPT), the city is one of the main fronts in the war between big landowners and landless peasants. But the killing of Ribeiro de Souza caused an international outcry and forced the authorities to take action. Expedito Ribeiro de Souza was President of the Rural Workers' Union of Rio Maria. The Union was active in defending the interests of rural workers in the region and Ribeiro de Souza had received many death threats; he had repeatedly asked for official protection. He was returning home one evening in February 1991 after a meeting when a man crossed the street and shot him dead at point-blank range. The killer ran off and vanished into the night. Three other people had been killed the week before, and only a month later, there was an attempt on the life of the new President of the Union, Carlos Cabral.[19]

Father Ricardo Rizende, a member of CPT based in Rio Maria, whose own life has been threatened, commented:

> In Rio Maria we live within a context of the most terrible criminality. There are seemingly random crimes against anonymous rural workers whose unidentified bodies are secretly buried. But there are also more selective crimes, carefully planned to eliminate peasant leaders and to crush the rural trade union movement.

Despite the increasing conflict and violence, successive Brazilian governments have shown extreme reluctance in tackling the land question. Since the 1950s, every President has promised land redistribution and land reform but little has happened. President Sarney promised land totalling about 42 million hectares to 1.4 million landless families but, during his five-year presidency ending in 1990, only 1.36 million hectares was distributed, to only 46,000 families. The next government announced a five-year plan to resettle 380,000 families, but according to CPT there has been very little progress.[20]

Amazonia: migration and speculation

The issue of land tenure and access to land are factors in the deforestation of Amazonia.[21] A recent study on the future of Amazonia noted:

> The policy bias in favour of large landed interests, as well as four-digit annual inflation rates, have encouraged land concentration in every successive Amazon frontier zone. Large landowners are the biggest culprits in the process [of environmental destruction]... though the growing population of migrant farmers is under increasing pressure to engage in more destructive cultivation and occupation techniques.[22]

There is no single, simple answer to the question of why Amazonia is being destroyed. Most of the explanations on offer are at best partial; other popular views are wrong. Brazil is not dependent on Amazonia's resources for its development; the forest is not being chopped down to provide pasture for cattle for hamburger beef; it is not being exploited to service the foreign debt. The pace of deforestation has much more to do with small farmers, pushed off their land in other parts of Brazil, who

This road slicing through the Bolivian Amazon rainforest will speed up deforestation of the surrounding area. Once a road is constructed, the area is opened up, land values increase enormously, and land speculators take their profit.

then migrate to Amazonia; and land speculation by rich Brazilians.

Throughout Brazil the increasing number of landless families existing side-by-side with large, under-used holdings owned by absentee landlords is one of the country's social time bombs. For a while, the opening up of Amazonia seemed to offer an escape valve. Ironically, the development of Amazonia is reproducing the same pattern of landholdings concentrated in a few hands that exists in the longer-settled areas of the south and north-east of the country. Smallholdings that fail are being bought up by large landowners and speculators, and settlers are being forcibly evicted where their presence clashes with the landowning interests.

Most people arrive in Amazonia with the intention of becoming small farmers. But only 20 per cent of agricultural land has ended up in their hands. For a small farming family that migrates to Amazonia, there is often no turning back – they have spent all their resources getting there, and have no cash to pay their return fare – even if they have anywhere to go back to. The land they try to farm quickly loses its fertility once the rainforest is cleared. The new farmers are susceptible to diseases such as malaria; or subject to intense pressure from local landowners and face eviction. Their options are to move on to a new frontier – or into one of the growing urban slums. The towns of Amazonia are growing fast and fully 50 per cent of the population is now classed as 'urban'. This urban growth is totally unplanned, and as Chapter 7 describes, living conditions are terrible.

Whilst the primary motivation for opening up Amazonia was political rather than economic, financial gain for the rich has been a major driving force. The business community wasted no time in taking advantage of government incentives to buy and clear land and develop cattle ranches, plantations and mining concerns. Investors acquiring a tract of rainforest quickly set about clearing and burning to establish possession – until recently, with the aid of a hefty government grant. Many such land 'owners' have not legally purchased the land, but occupied it by a mixture of force and deceit. In order to legitimise their dubious claims, they clear as much forest as possible to show that they have put it to 'productive' use; rough grazing qualifies in the eyes of the authorities. In time, the same authorities will open up an access road and the land value will then increase perhaps one hundred-fold.

South Africa: new approaches to conservation[23]

> The ultimate lesson of apartheid's ecological toll is that inequitable social institutions ... are not compatible with environmental sustainability.[24]

South Africa offers the clearest example of a country, like many of those in which Oxfam works, where First World affluence rubs shoulders with Third World poverty. The difference is that in South Africa the 'rich-poor' divide was deliberately created and reinforced along racial lines by the policies of apartheid. Widespread environmental devastation is one of the legacies of apartheid. The government's push for rapid industrialisation and economic growth in the face of sanctions paid little regard to the environmental consequences. Black townships sprawl in the shadow of mines and factories, their atmosphere and water supplies heavily polluted. The land tenure system of apartheid is a major cause of environmental degradation, tension and conflict, as large numbers of people have been forcibly removed from their land and crowded into ecologically fragile areas which rapidly become degraded.

Until recently, environmental initiatives in South Africa were confined to the demarcation of substantial tracts of land as national parks from which whites were excluded except as visitors, and where blacks were not allowed at all. South Africa's wildlife parks have received much international acclaim. But there is a stark and paradoxical contrast between the parks and the surrounding environment.

The Richtersveld, in the north-west of Cape Province and with a climate similar to the Sahara, is prized by environmentalists for its remarkable diversity of plants (including over 300 varieties of succulents). Although this was already designated as a 'coloured reserve', this did not stop white farmers and mining companies encroaching on the land. Without any consultation, a decision was taken to zone part of the area as a national park, threatening local people with removal. The community acted together and, with help from the Surplus People's Project (SPP), funded by Oxfam,[25] they got legal advice and drew attention to their case, winning a court injunction in 1989 to stop the park.

After two years of negotiations, an agreement was reached which satisfied the needs of local people as well as conservationists, and the Richtersveld National Park was established. To stop further overgrazing, the number of animals in the park will be restricted and farmers will have access to other grazing grounds. Most importantly, the community will get a sizeable income and have a role in managing the park. There is no doubt that the success of the Richtersveld community reflects the changed political environment in South Africa: it would have been almost impossible only a few years ago, and it illustrates a new awareness of the importance of meeting the needs of the local community whilst conserving the environment.

In KwaSunduza village, in the 'independent' homeland of Transkei, erosion gullies scar the fields and hillsides. The hills are bare through over-grazing and the collection of firewood, because so many people have been forced to live in this small area. Chitibhunga Magibili, now retired, tends the trees which have been planted around the village to retain the soil and help the environment to regenerate.

Conservation has not usually helped the black communities of South Africa. In a country where three-quarters of the people have been allocated only 13 per cent of the land (often of the worst quality), 6 per cent of the country has been set aside for protected national parks and game reserves. The 'homelands' that make up that 13 per cent are now home to 15 million people, more than half the black population (estimated at 27.5 million in 1989).

Since 1960, 3.5 million people have been forcibly moved from their homes, 2 million of them to the homelands. The aim was to preserve as much of the best land as possible for the white population, while maintaining a reliable pool of cheap, black labour for the cities, farms and mines. Lying between the fertile corridors of white farmland, the ten homelands occupy some of the poorest land in South Africa – nearly half is classified as semi-arid.[26] The average population density is ten times that of rural white South Africa. Population pressure in the homelands (which blacks were not allowed to leave) has led to overgrazing and deforestation. This, in turn, has brought severe erosion, lowered soil fertility, and declining agricultural yields; in some areas, food production per person has halved over the last 50 years and health standards have fallen dramatically, with two out of every five children severely malnourished.

Access to sufficient land for those who were dispossessed and crowded into the homelands remains an issue that will have to be addressed, in the interests of South Africa's political and environmental future.

Bangladesh: moves towards land reform

Many countries in Asia have land reform programmes but few have implemented them. Bangladesh is no exception yet the need for land reform has never been more pressing. It is estimated that over 65 per cent of the population is landless in a country where people are almost totally dependent on agriculture.[27] There have been numerous attempts at land reform over the years. In 1950, the Government of Pakistan (Bangladesh was then East Pakistan) tried to curb the influence of wealthy landlords. After the War of Liberation in 1971, the ruling Awami League proposed radical land reforms and a better deal for sharecroppers, but again the landed classes blocked it. After President Sheikh Mujibur Rahman's assassination in 1975, President Ziaur Rahman proclaimed a commitment to land reform but, with his party dominated by powerful landowners, the promises came to nothing.

The proposals put forward by the next President, H M Ershad were comprehensive. Following the recommendations of a Land Reform Commission on the Causes of Rural Poverty in 1983, all government-owned common lands were to be distributed to the landless, sharecroppers would have legal protection and a just share of their crops, and agricultural labourers would receive a daily minimum wage. Although these proposals became law, they were never adequately implemented. In 1987, an NGO committee was formed to coordinate a programme of conferences and publicity on land reform. The most significant result of these efforts so far has been to establish women's rights to land. Married women are recognised legally as equal owners of redistributed land, and in the event of divorce or separation that title will not be affected. It remains to be seen whether or not the new government, headed by the widow of the previously assassinated President Ziaur Rahman, will implement the Ershad legislation. However, thanks to the involvement of NGOs, landless people, including women, are being awarded land. But it never happens without a great struggle and the land is not always free of encroachment.

Samata is an organisation of landless people in Pabna District on the north bank of the Ganges.[28] For several years, its members have been pressing claims to hundreds of acres of government-owned land in the areas around their villages. This has been farmed by rich individuals who have no right to it but are supported by the local authorities. As Samata grew, the members were able to gain titles to redistributed land but were still harassed by officials. Samata now has over 1,000 women members, who will not give up the struggle until they have land. More than 400 groups are affiliated to Samata, believing that it is only this kind of collaborative strength and pressure that will ensure that land reform happens.[29]

This government-owned land at Ghu Ghu Daha, Pabna district, Bangladesh, has been secured by Samata for some of its landless members. Hasim and Idrish are gathering hay after the paddy harvest.

It is hard to be optimistic about the future. With the degradation of pastures and croplands increasing, there are few signs that land rights and access for the poor are genuinely improving. Even governments which have committed themselves to land reform – from Brazil to Bangladesh – have generally been unwilling or unable to act on their stated intentions.

Secure land rights that are publicly recognised and protected provide incentives for sustainable development by making it possible for people to invest in the future. The World Bank recognises the need for large-scale land redistribution as a means of reducing poverty.[30] There are significant political obstacles to change, and so the needs of poor people and their environment demand more determined efforts at agrarian reform. Organisations such as the rural trade unions in Brazil, Samata in Bangladesh and the Surplus People's Project in South Africa, all point the way forward.

But problems remain even when the struggle for land is successful. At local level, solutions are called for which enable poor people to sustain their livelihoods, even in fragile areas, or to intensify production in areas of high potential.

5

FOOD SECURITY AND SUSTAINABLE AGRICULTURE

The disappearance of soil fertility and water supplies – the two basic life-support systems that keep rural areas going – are the areas which do not concern global decision makers.

Vandana Shiva, interviewed on a TV documentary shown in October 1991, *Greener on the Other Side.*

Poverty and food security

A simple definition of food security is for all people at all times to have enough food for an active healthy life.[1] Food security is a human necessity and should be regarded as a basic human right. But tonight and every night, 700 million people will go to bed hungry despite the fact that the world produces enough food for everybody to have a more than adequate diet.[2] This paradox of people going hungry when some parts of the world produce massive food surpluses, much of which is fed to livestock, is at the centre of the food security debate.

Two-thirds of the people who go hungry are in south Asia and a fifth in sub-Saharan Africa, and the majority live in countries with very low average incomes.[3] The situation is especially serious in Africa where Oxfam has been called upon more and more in recent years to provide emergency food aid, especially in the countries afflicted by conflict such as Sudan, Ethiopia and Mozambique, where longer-term development efforts aimed at food self-sufficiency have been seriously hampered (see Chapter 8).

But having enough to eat is not only a question of overall production or the average amount of food per head of population, although total production is obviously important. It is also about distribution at household, community, national and international level.

At the household level, it is a matter of being able to grow food, having money to buy it, or the capacity to be lent or given it by relatives or friends. For the poorest people surviving on the margins, often without land or sources of income, environmental or economic shocks can suddenly undermine their capacity to feed themselves. Poor people face starvation when they are totally deprived of food; but many poor people are regularly hungry because they do not have access to enough food each day.[4] Food security at the household level can be a matter of gender. In India, for example, nearly half of the country's households cannot provide for their nutritional requirements so many children are deprived. But malnutrition is far more prevalent among girls than boys, a situation which continues into adulthood. Women and children do not receive a fair share of the food available.[5]

Women farmers are at a particular disadvantage. Women grow at least half the food crops around the world, and in Africa they are responsible for between 60 and 90 per cent of food production, processing and marketing. National surveys significantly underestimate women's agricultural work because it is unpaid and therefore 'invisible' in economic statistics. There has been a gradual polarisation of agricultural production along gender lines in recent years. When agricultural projects and innovations are analysed, almost all the beneficiaries are found to be men. Women's groups are not targeted for extension training, and new technologies and development aid go to cash-cropping rather than subsistence food-growing. Effective and innovative women farmers may be ignored in development programmes in favour of less effective male farmers.

Women are responsible for most of the food grown in Africa. These farmers in the Mahoney Valley in Tigray are harvesting teff, a cereal which grows well in that region.

At the national level, food security means self-sufficiency in production, having goods to trade to acquire foreign exchange to pay for food, or the capacity to be given it by aid agencies.[6] Poor countries face food insecurity if their agricultural systems fail or if their exports cannot pay for the food imports they need. In seeking to provide for their food requirements, the poorer developing countries face formidable obstacles. If they are not food self-sufficient and rely on imports, they are exposed to the vagaries of the international trading system. It is one thing to depend on the export of competitively priced manufactured goods, especially where food self-sufficiency is clearly impossible (as in the case of countries such as Taiwan, Singapore or Hong Kong); quite another to be dependent on agricultural commodities whose prices are fluctuating on a downward trend (as are Rwanda, Ethiopia or El Salvador). FAO has identified 65 low-income food-deficit countries which are potentially vulnerable in the current international climate, many of which have not been able to increase domestic food production. The list includes 17 African countries, and 4 in Latin America.[7] Oxfam works in most of them and has been called upon to provide emergency relief or support for local communities' efforts to enhance food self-sufficiency. These countries include Ethiopia, Tanzania, Burkina Faso, Angola, Kenya, Malawi, Mauritania, Mozambique, Rwanda, Somalia, Zambia, Sudan, Bolivia, El Salvador and Haiti.

But even where Southern countries have the purchasing power to import food to meet their domestic requirements, there are uncertainties in relying on global surpluses. The present pattern of surpluses may not continue. Production decisions in the main surplus-producing areas, over which the South has no control, can affect the volume of cereals coming on to the world market. If climate changes take place as predicted, there could be serious negative effects on the main cereal-growing areas of North America, and areas such as the Sahel and south-east Asia, which are at present vulnerable to drought or floods, could suffer further.[8] Demands from Eastern Europe are likely to increase, and this could also affect the amount of food available to food-deficit countries in the developing world since those demands will probably be backed by hard currency.

It appears that for the most vulnerable countries, a considerable degree of self-sufficiency in food production is desirable, plus some additional capacity for export of agricultural commodities. But the efforts of vulnerable countries towards achieving such objectives are often hampered by both the international system and difficulties at national level, notably the transition time needed to convert to greater self-sufficiency. A major problem is the dumping of cheap food produced in the North as a result of subsidies and income support for farmers. This can undermine Southern farmers' production of food staples by depressing local prices, while at the same time, urban people benefit from, and acquire a taste for, cheap imported food.

Sudan

Oxfam has been very involved in the provision of food aid in Sudan in recent years, and in efforts towards longer-term development work to improve food security. Millions of people in Sudan have become vulnerable to famine largely due to factors beyond their control. Poor people in Sudan starved in 1984 and 1985; in 1986 the harvest failed again but was followed by good years in 1987 and 1988. Two poor years followed in 1989 and 1990 and people who had not fully recovered from the famine of the mid-1980s were still vulnerable. By the end of 1990, Oxfam was once more planning food aid: in 1991, almost 8 million people were in need of over 1 million tonnes of emergency supplies.[9] Once poised to become the bread-basket of the Arab world, now the country cannot even feed itself.

The Sudanese economy is heavily dependent on the export of cotton. The north of the country is more economically developed than the south, which aggravated cultural, religious and economic differences, eventually leading to a long-running civil war. Emphasis on export-led development made the country vulnerable to fluctuations in the international market. When the world price of cotton fell, the government promoted large-scale production of sorghum as a cash crop for sale overseas as animal feed. Landlessness increased as large-scale farming enterprises took over vast tracts of land forcing out pastoralists and small farmers.

This large-scale production for export brought with it environmental problems related to inappropriate cultivation methods and misuse and overuse of dangerous pesticides. Large-scale agriculture often gives rise to large-scale pest infestations. The cotton-growing areas, for example, have been affected by pest resistance due to overuse of toxic pesticides, which has given rise to serious health and environmental problems.[10]

Sudan, having invested heavily in capital-intensive agriculture, became severely indebted when commodity prices fell and oil prices rose. When it was again hit by a serious food crisis in 1991, the government made an increased effort towards food self-sufficiency by converting some of the large-scale irrigated farms to growing wheat instead of cotton. But this strategy will meet only the needs of the urban people rich enough to buy bread; it fails to meet the needs of the rural poor. Support for the poor who rely on rainfed agriculture or pastoralism, and who have been disadvantaged by the emphasis on export crops, is missing from the strategy. The result is that poor people

SARAH ERRINGTON/OXFAM

The animal feed programme in Sudan encourages pastoralists to feed molasses block to their herds when fodder is in short supply. On the left is the Oxfam veterinary adviser.

ιn Sudan are increasingly undermining their longer-term survival in order to survive in the short term.

Oxfam has been heavily involved in the provision of emergency food aid in famine-affected areas of Sudan in recent years, particularly in Darfur and the Red Sea Hills, home of 600,000 Beja people. The Beja practise both pastoralism and agriculture in order to spread the risk in times of hardship. When Oxfam first arrived at Port Sudan in 1984 in response to the famine, conditions in the province were bleak. Rainfall had been poor throughout the 1980s, people were very malnourished and a large number of their cattle had died. The Beja economy was in a state of collapse and people had started to move to the towns and road-sides in search of food and water. In their struggle to survive, people had begun to exploit their environment, and their activities had become increasingly destructive. For example, they were cutting wood and making charcoal to sell as fuel in the towns. One study[11] has shown that tree density in the province has declined significantly between 1960 and 1990 largely as a result of human activities. Oxfam found that the crisis for most of the people was not simply one of food availability; people were unable to buy food because their herds had been lost and they had few other sources of income. The problem for the Beja was poverty.

At first Oxfam only provided food relief but after a year or so this was followed by a combination of relief and development work aimed at helping the Beja to sustain themselves in the longer term. The food relief programme helped to stave off continuing famine, and livestock losses were reduced which helped herds to recover. Movement of people to the towns was stemmed. By 1986, the worst of the famine was over and Oxfam became much more involved in rehabilitation, using food as a way of boosting economic recovery. The aim was to support people in their efforts to become more self-reliant but food aid had to be resumed in early 1991, as a result of harvest failure, and there are further food aid requests for 1992. Once again, rehabilitation and development work has been subsumed within relief provision. An Oxfam report concludes that the impact of people on the environment in the province continues to cause problems which may undermine the long-term viability of the Beja economy and make them vulnerable to food insecurity in the future.

For the longer term, the emphasis is on appropriate local development and securing policy changes at national and international level. Oxfam has been working with 16 village centres at Kebkabiya in North Darfur province since 1986 providing support for efforts to achieve local food security through sustainable agricultural practices.

Families in this area had previously supported themselves by growing millet, getting meat and milk from their animals, gathering wild fruits and berries and buying other things with money from the sale of their livestock, craft work or labour. The region of Darfur was one

*Collecting berries from a desert shrub, mukheit (*boscia senegalensis*) in Darfur. The berries and their kernels are poisonous but, if soaked in water overnight, become safe to eat. This is an example of a 'famine food', which people can resort to as part of their coping strategy in times of hardship.*

of the worst hit in the 1984-5 famine: villagers produced less than half their normal grain and seed requirements – some only managed to produce 5 per cent of their needs. Grain prices soared as people tried to survive. After the famine, the villagers wanted to find ways of preventing another disaster. They began to plant wheat and vegetables to supplement the millet harvest: even poor villagers, with no land of their own, managed to get access to land on credit to plant food. People provided seeds for their neighbours until they grew their own and farmers, eager to learn about the new methods and crops, began to experiment.

Sixteen seed bank committees, each serving a cluster of villages, were formed in Kebkabiya during the relief period. Each committee provides a representative to the Project Management Committee. Farmers here are now experimenting with a range of new and improved techniques. They have built seed banks and organised revolving seed credit programmes. More than 30,000 people have benefited directly from the first phase of the project, which has greatly improved food security. The second three-year phase involved handing over management and financing to the local committees: they are now responsible for making sure loans are repaid and the seedbanks are restocked. Phase Two has not been without its problems: the rains failed in 1990, leaving farmers with no seeds to sow, or to restock the seedbank. Tribal conflicts erupted and grain stores were burnt. Loans could not be repaid, but villagers eventually managed to buy seeds and to re-establish credit.

During Phase Three, the food security project will gradually become wholly managed by the Kebkabiya Smallholders' Charity Committee – a local autonomous organisation responsible for its own budgeting and accounting, capable of seeking funding from a variety of sources. What started out as a relief project has developed into an integrated programme which includes a seed bank, veterinary services, pest control and increased use of animals for ploughing. Already the project has improved food security in the area, and empowered communities by providing them with the resources and skills to continue working in the longer term. Moreover, the Kebkabiya project looks set to become a model that could be followed in other parts of northern Darfur affected by drought and famine.

SUSTAINABLE AGRICULTURE: A WAY FORWARD?

Ecological systems, or ecosystems, consist of an association of living things, soils, water, climate, slope, and aspect. They are highly complex and diverse, self-regulating and sustainable and if undisturbed, have a built-in equilibrium. Agriculture transforms ecological systems to meet human needs for food, fuel, fodder and fibre by promoting the production of certain species of plants and animals.

Sustainable agricultural systems are those which are able to maintain their productivity, stability and equilibrium in the face of stress or shock indefinitely into the future.[12] Ecological relationships can be used to make agricultural systems more sustainable, for example, agroforestry (mixed plant/tree associations), intercropping, rotations, green manuring, biological pest control and integrated pest management. Agricultural systems which mirror the diversity of natural systems are more resilient than monocultures. The risk is spread amongst the crops and harvests are spread throughout the year and over longer periods.[13]

By contrast, modern agriculture in the North and the 'Green Revolution' in the South, have relied on systems of monocropping which, in order to be productive, have called for high levels of fertilisers, pesticides and technology. With substantial economic resources, these systems have maximised productivity. Yet they have often been costly in terms of pollution and depletion of soil fertility and are now looking less and less sustainable. Environmental problems resulting from over-intensive production require costly solutions.

Sustainable agriculture is not just about survival now, but in the longer term; it is about systems which are productive, stable and equitable now – and in the future. The Northern agricultural systems have been productive and profitable in the short term but are looking increasingly unstable and inequitable. It is generally accepted that the European Common Agricultural Policy, which has produced massively but at great cost, must be dismantled and replaced with a system which is more financially and environmentally sustainable.

Increased self-sufficiency in the South through sustainable agricultural systems is a way of working toward better food security. A dual strategy could be adopted, aimed first at further increases from high potential land (which is fertile, irrigated and flat and can produce surpluses to meet national food needs), and secondly at marginal lands which may be rainfed, less fertile and hilly. Experience in Burkina Faso described in the last chapter shows that even marginal lands occupied by the poorest people can be highly productive. If the right techniques are used in the right social and economic context and, most important, if the local people are involved, then productivity can increase dramatically.

The Green Revolution:
a sustainable agricultural system for the South?
Throughout the 1960s and 1970s, concern about food was largely about the need to increase total production. Development thinking at that time concentrated on growth as a way of alleviating poverty, hoping that the wealth created would 'trickle down' to the poor. Increased food

production was seen as a way of overriding some of the problems of uneven distribution within countries. These were the years when there were famines in India and Africa was, in general, an exporter of food.

Increases in food production in developing countries since the 1960s have been achieved largely because of the implementation of 'Green Revolution' technologies. The Green Revolution is the popular name used to describe a set of technologies which included the introduction of semi-dwarf wheat and rice varieties, initially produced at the International Centre for Wheat and Maize Improvement (CIMMYT) in Mexico and the International Rice Research Institute (IRRI) in the Philippines. These varieties had exceptional potential for higher yields if provided with high inputs of fertiliser and water. Subsequently the term 'Green Revolution' has come to be popularly used to describe a broader range of agricultural methods based on new varieties of crops.

Green Revolution technology is especially suitable for the best agricultural land which is fertile, flat, and has plenty of water. The technology has little to offer farmers in low-potential areas such as the arid and semi-arid areas of Africa or those farming steep slopes with poor soils. India, Pakistan, Mexico and the Philippines are countries which have benefited substantially from these technologies and became self-sufficient in food at national level. But there have been trade-offs in economic, social and environmental terms.[14]

Green Revolution crops, do best on flat, fertile, well-watered land and need high inputs of fertiliser and pesticides. Here, rice is being transplanted in South Sumatera.

Even though food self-sufficiency was achieved, the benefits have been rather unevenly distributed, partly as a result of disregarding the social and economic context into which the technology was introduced. The poorest people, especially women, have often lost out because they were not able to afford the inputs needed for the new varieties to thrive. Recognising the social and economic problems, the Green Revolution scientists, charged with the emergency task of helping to avoid mass starvation in Asia, warned that theirs was a 'holding' operation to achieve food security nationally and that others must tackle the problems of social and economic inequalities.[15] The Green Revolution technology achieved high productivity but was not necessarily a stable, equitable, or sustainable system of agriculture, as shown by experience in India.[16]

India

During the 1950s and 1960s, India had come to rely on massive imports of food grains to feed its people. Continuous droughts from 1964 to 1967 and famine in Bihar left thousands starving. More recently, the drought of 1986-88 affected all the main agricultural states and led to a shortfall in food production comparable to that of the Sahelian droughts of the 1980s – but this resulted in neither mass starvation nor mass emigration. Buffer stocks were in hand to tide the country over until the next successful harvest. Indian agriculture has been transformed since the late 1960s by the Green Revolution. At Independence in 1947, India produced 50 million tonnes of food grains per year; by 1989 the harvest was 170 million tonnes per year – a 240 per cent increase. The population grew in the same period by 140 per cent.[17]

The impetus for Green Revolution research and technology derived partly from the difficulties in implementing land reform in post-Independence India. Increased production was seen as a way of defeating famine without recourse to land redistribution which was strongly opposed by the landed classes. The Green Revolution strategy aimed to 'build on the best' by promoting the new system to farmers who had flat, irrigated lands and fertile soils. Those who could afford the whole package of inputs did well. Those farmers who could not found that their yields were lower than they had been with traditional varieties.

The majority of India's farmers are poor subsistence farmers involved in rainfed agriculture, often in hilly areas. For the most part, the Green Revolution has not helped them. It has been argued that emphasis on wheat and rice has disguised failures in the production of pulses, oilseeds and other cereals which are important to the diet of poor people. Production of these crops has barely increased since the 1950s.

There have also been heavy costs in environmental terms. India has lost vast areas of prime agricultural land because of salinisation and water-logging in the irrigated areas. Intensive monocropping has made crops vulnerable to pest problems and the overuse and abuse of pesticides has given rise to widespread environmental and health problems.[18] Large quantities of fertiliser are needed for the high-yielding varieties of plants grown and can leave water supplies contaminated with nitrates. Use and knowledge of traditional plant varieties and techniques has been reduced or lost.

However, a recent study in North Arcot, in the state of Tamil Nadu, over a ten-year period, has shown that small farmers and landless people can gain as much as bigger farmers.[19] The area studied is not a particularly favoured rice-growing region of India and the impact of the Green Revolution technology was modest in comparison to that in other parts of India. But because the State Government was committed to equitable land distribution and spreading resources fairly, small farmers benefited from new technology, and the local economy was stimulated to the extent that even people who were not involved in farming became better-off. The authors of the report believe that these widespread improvements can continue if the Government's commitments remain the same, and that future growth will be driven by crop improvements based on genetic manipulation of plants.

In India, the Green Revolution is only half the story of agriculture. With limitations on the further gains that can be expected from capital intensive Green Revolution farming, the concern now is to improve traditional farming systems.[20] Most Indian farmers do not grow only one crop. They use intricate systems of farming which may involve planting up to five different crops in different patterns in the same field. This is to try and get the maximum amount of food from the land, while spreading the risk by making sure that if one crop fails there will still be something left. These intercropping systems often lead to healthier crops by reducing predators and provide special benefits for the soil as well by fixing nitrogen and conserving fertility. But farms are getting smaller and smaller as population pressure grows.

Zambia

Green Revolution technologies have been important in parts of Africa in recent years but have not been without problems for poorer people. Starting in the 1960s, great efforts were made to convert to Green Revolution technology through extension services and adult literacy programmes. By the 1980s, Zambia was self-sufficient in food and had begun exporting, with as much as three-quarters of the production being grown by small farmers. But in the 1980s, falling commodity prices and an increasing debt burden precipitated an economic crisis. The government came under pressure to adopt 'adjustment' policies. Subsidies were removed and prices shot up, which seriously affected farmers needing Green Revolution inputs.[21]

Recently, farmers of the Chiyanjano and Tiyeseko women's groups, two groups supported by Oxfam in Kazimule area of Chipata District in eastern Zambia, found themselves in great difficulty.[22] The women had become accustomed to planting several types of Green Revolution maize in addition to the local or traditional maize variety. The traditional planting methods of intercropping and field rotation had been abandoned for a monocropping system in straight lines, as promoted by the agricultural extension officers. The hybrid seeds must be bought each season, since they do not breed true to type, and they need a high level of soil nutrients which can only be supplied by artificial fertilisers. The women were faced with buying both seeds and fertiliser each season. The price of both increased dramatically when subsidies were removed as part of the government's adjustment measures. Some seeds were five times as expensive, others as much as ten times.

Fertilisers, besides being very expensive, were hard to obtain as a result of shortfalls in local production and lack of imports because of foreign exchange difficulties. When the farmers did produce a surplus and wanted to market it, they were faced with yet more difficulties. The state marketing system had been abandoned in the wake of market liberalisation. The only way to sell was on a barter basis to traders coming from the capital, Lusaka. Increasingly, people were having to leave their homes to go in search of food, often at times when planting should be done in preparation for the next season. The women found themselves in an impossible situation. Old farming methods had been abandoned and they could not afford the new ones. The result was increasing hardship for the women and their families to the point of sever food shortage in some cases.[23]

Faced with spiralling input costs and decreasing food security, the women of Chiyanjano, Tiyeseko and other groups met in August 1990 to try to work out ways of tackling the problem. Growing widespread poverty was put down to over-reliance on chemical fertilisers. They decided to diversify into crops such as beans and groundnuts which needed less expensive inputs, and to use intercropping methods once again and local maize varieties which require less fertiliser. The yields were slightly lower but they did not have to buy fertiliser so they had a higher net income. Composting and application of cattle manure (hitherto little used) is also part of the integrated system. In this way at least the household food needs can be met. One of the women of the Tiyeseko group, Tisauke, is delighted with the results:

The results have been outstanding. This year I have no hunger in my house. I recall my parents cultivating by these methods but somehow modernisation has overshadowed our traditional experience. I want to see on my own if I can revive it in my field.

Another important element was improvement of marketing in the area. The Chama District Disaster and Development Group (CDDD), funded by Oxfam, developed a marketing system to buy surpluses from the farmers.[24] The scheme is based on participation by community groups which have authority over the buying, storage and selling of products in their locality. In the process of working together to achieve a better marketing, supply and distribution system, group members have gained insights into the processes at work which caused hunger in the District – even at the level of national and international influences.[25]

THE BIO-REVOLUTION: NEW POSSIBILITIES FOR FEEDING THE WORLD?

The shortcomings of technical solutions for what are really socio-economic problems are highlighted by the mixed success of the Green Revolution technology. In many quarters, the 'Bio-revolution' is promoted as the next agricultural revolution, the solution to the shortcomings of the Green Revolution and to hunger in the developing countries. The basis of the new revolution is biotechnology, a range of biological techniques which are used to modify living organisms. It is based on the manipulation of genes which are the parts of the living cell which carry messages which control the development of particular characteristics in the whole organism. New varieties can be developed by introducing bits of genetic material which carry desirable characteristics. Genes, or genetic resources, are the underpinnings of the new biotechnologies developed in the past twenty or thirty years. Developments and inventions are moving extremely rapidly in the industrialised countries.[26]

The potential benefits of the bio-revolution appear to be endless and there have already been some amazing achievements – plants for poor soils, plants for arid conditions, plants which make their own fertilisers and pesticides. Applications in developing countries are so far limited but research is well advanced on a range of crops grown in those countries, for example, cassava, cacao and coffee. There are reports from Kenya of smallholder tea producers using improved varieties developed by a local tea research organisation.

But the bio-revolution may well be a double-edged sword. For example, research is going ahead on herbicide tolerant plants, which will permit big increases in the use of herbicides, when there are already problems, especially in developing countries, with misuse and overuse of toxic chemicals. There may be costs as well as benefits if the bio-revolution results in short-term gains at the expense of long-term sustainability and if the social and economic context is ignored.

Genetic resources

Retaining a diverse array of wild and locally bred living things is essential for our very survival. Each species has numerous different and genetically distinct varieties which have adapted to different local climatic conditions and ecosystems. Diversity is fundamental to efforts to sustain or improve crops and animals and a crucial requirement if natural systems are to respond to change. Throughout history, farmers have played their part in encouraging biological diversity (or biodiversity) by contributing to the selection, development and maintenance of thousands of different plant and animal varieties suitable for different situations and needs. Preserving a rich array of plant varieties and the genes they contain is the way in which the small farmer spreads his risks, and conservation at the local level is part of the survival strategy of the poor.

The majority of global biological diversity is located in the tropics in developing countries and is now seriously threatened (Chapter 6). The forces which deplete these vital resources are wide-ranging, including destruction of tropical forests, construction of large-scale dams, exten-sive monocropping such as that associated with the 'Green Revolution', and destruction of agricultural systems in areas of conflict. Faced with hunger, people eat the seed they have stored for the next season.

The genetic resources which are being depleted are not only the underpinnings of new varieties which may develop naturally in the future, they are also the building blocks of the new developments in biotechnology which are at the centre of the bio-revolution. But seeds which were once entirely the property of the farmer have now become a commodity to be traded. At present, big companies involved in biotechnological developments acquire genetic resources, free, from the developing countries, since they are regarded as a 'common heritage' of humankind. However, if the inventors of the new biotechnological products and processes succeed in patenting their inventions, genetically modified plants may well be sold back to the very countries which provided the genetic raw material free.

Kenya: Preservation of agricultural plant genetic resources

So far as preservation of plant species goes, the role of women has been especially important. The work of seed collection and storage has often fallen to women, who also play an important role in promoting and maintaining traditional crop varieties in their farming systems and making sure that knowledge about the use of varieties is not lost.

Olembo and Bolo are two women's groups which are part of Kenya Energy Non-Governmental Organisations (KENGO), a coalition of about one hundred small groups working on environmental and development issues in Kenya. For the last ten years, often with support from outside organisations like Oxfam, KENGO has been promoting the use of indigenous trees and crops in Kenya. This activity is seen as a way of maintaining the stock of both the plants themselves and the associated body of knowledge about how they are used for food, medicines and other purposes. It is a small-scale local initiative to protect the genetic resources of specific parts of the country. When the indigenous vegetables programme started four years ago, knowledge about indigenous crops and their uses was in decline. Research showed that plants which were often regarded as 'weeds' are more nutritious in protein and vitamins than 'imported' varieties such as spinach, cabbage and cauliflower. Building on the research, the approach has been to develop public awareness about the value of these 'people's crops' and to stress the importance of knowledge about them. As Monica Opole, in charge of the vegetable programme, says:

> We want to show that these plants can be as productive as the major crops, if given as much attention in research and extension.

Olembo women's group on the shores of Lake Victoria in Western Kenya is rediscovering the value of these traditional trees and plants. Nerea Ongango explained the value of the Ober tree (*Albizia coriaria*):

> We use the wood for timber and fuel, the leaves for covering ripening bananas and for the children to play with, and the bark is cooked up to make a medicine for treating children's ailments.

Across the bay from Olembo group, Bolo women's group is building up a nursery for indigenous trees. They sell the tree seedlings in the local market where they find an increasing demand. Like the Olembo group, the women have their own farms but they work together in the nursery.[27]

Activities of this kind are crucial in maintaining the stock of plant diversity which is the underpinning of sustainable agricultural systems. It seems that the form of agricultural development that will work best in the longer term is one which poor people at the local level initiate and manage themselves, with the right kind of support. Evidence from all parts of the world shows that when farmers have secure tenure to land and are paid fair prices for what they produce, then most poor farmers even on low-potential lands can produce surpluses using locally available resources.

6

THE VANISHING FORESTS

The dark clouds pour rain on the forest,
The forest gives it to the land.
Without the forest, friends,
Our land would be only rock and sand.

Song of the Friends of the Trees and Living Beings, Orissa, India.

Sr José lives in a small shack in one of the shanty quarters of Marabá –
a boom town since the discovery of iron ore in the nearby Carajás
hills. Sr José recalls:

> When I was a child, this place used to be brazil nut forest. I
> remember coming here to collect nuts for the landlord. The whole
> family came. It was a hard life – it always is for the poor, isn't it?
> For three or four months that is all we would do. Then we would
> go to the landlord's store and sell the nuts to buy food. The store
> manager had the power of life or death over the nut collectors and
> you always ended up in debt.[1]

Now the forests have gone. What remains is an expanse of beaten red
earth. The pig iron smelter and other industries burn charcoal and the
forests have been felled to provide it. Landless people from outside the
region have flocked to Marabá to find work, some of them as charcoal
burners.

Both the forest and the people are getting a bad deal. The forest is
disappearing fast: and lost with it are the fruits, the timber and the
wildlife that in the past provided a livelihood to people like Sr José.

TROPICAL MOIST FORESTS

Forests in the tropics, covering 14 per cent of the earth's land surface, are
of two kinds – moist and dry. Tropical moist forests are both evergreen
and deciduous, with a closed canopy where the tops of the trees touch.
Rainforests are one type of moist forest found mainly in Latin America,

West Africa and South East Asia. They thrive on poor soils and lie near the equator where rainfall is heavy (1500 – 2000mm) and the average temperature is high. Tropical dry forests are more open: trees shed their leaves during the driest season and are usually much smaller than those in the moist forest. Most of the world's dry forest is found in Africa, where much of it is degraded. (Particular environmental issues affecting tropical dry forests are considered later in the chapter.)

Charcoal burners, Brazil. Many of Brazil's industrial plants run on charcoal, and trees are being cut down at an ever-increasing rate to meet the demand.

The value of forests

Tropical forests, especially rainforests, are home to many indigenous groups and settlers whose livelihoods are dependent upon a wide range of forest products including fodder, fuelwood, fibres and timber, and on the wild animals living in the forests. Indigenous people know how to use forests productively and sustainably: their farming methods improve forest soils and they use thousands of plant species – as medicines and food, and for building and craftwork.

The tree canopy and leaf litter of forests protect soils from the impact of heavy rain; tree roots bind the soil, reducing run-off and erosion, and helping to prevent floods and landslides, providing vital protection for watersheds.

Forests play a major part in regulating the world's climate and – through the earth's carbon and oxygen cycles – they influence the rate of global warming. Although fossil fuel burning in industrialised countries is the major source of carbon dioxide (the main greenhouse gas), the burning of tropical forests makes a substantial contribution. Forests also act as 'carbon sinks' trapping carbon dioxide from the atmosphere and storing it in the form of carbohydrates in their tissues. When forests are burned on a large scale – as continues to happen in Amazonia – the carbon dioxide released accelerates global warming.[2] Forests also regulate rainfall: one study from the Amazon basin shows that 75 per cent of the rainfall is generated by water evaporating from forest land.[3]

Tropical forests are a rich storehouse of biological diversity.[4] Rainforests, for example, cover only 7 per cent of the earth's surface but they are home to at least 50 per cent of all species of plants and animals.

A whole range of economic benefits come from forests. Commercial wood products – lumber, saw logs, pulp – and medicines (25 per cent of all prescription drugs come from rainforests) are worth over US$150 billion a year.[5] Forests are the source of many products – fruits, honey, gums, latex, bush meat and dyes – as well as some 7,000 medicines used in Western practices,[6] yet virtually none of the profits from this multi-million dollar industry ever get back to forest people.

The loss of forests

Tropical forests – both moist and dry – are being destroyed at unprecedented rates. Most of the remaining forest is in the Amazon basin, an area approaching half the size of the United States. No one knows exactly how much tropical forest is destroyed every year. Differences in the definition of destruction and in the methods of analysis produce widely differing figures, but the clearance probably amounts to over 20 million hectares each year.[7] Many more millions of hectares of forest are being degraded.

Rainforests suffer the worst losses, and replanting is nowhere keeping pace with the devastation; forest areas are being cleared almost 30 times faster than they are being planted. In several countries where Oxfam works – El Salvador, Haiti, Bangladesh and the Philippines – the productive forests have largely been stripped. Given the present rates of clearance, most of the world's remaining primary forests will be lost by 2020.[8]

The causes of tropical deforestation vary from region to region. In Latin America, most of the clearance comes from felling and burning to create small farms and cattle ranches, or to open up areas for hydroelectric dams or major mining projects such as Carajás. In South East Asia, logging and agricultural expansion are the main agents of loss: much of peninsular Malaysia's forest, for example, has been cleared and replaced with plantations. Africa's tropical moist forests still cover large areas, especially in Zaire, but they are increasingly threatened. Dry forests are being degraded by fuelwood cutting and the needs of small-scale agriculture. But whilst these are the immediate causes, there are underlying pressures deriving from national and international economic structures which drive the destruction. The burden of massive debt servicing, the international trading system and inadequate aid programmes all have an effect, as do national policies which foster land speculation or fail to carry out land reform.

Conversion to agriculture

The conversion of rainforest to farmland accounts for more than half of all deforestation in tropical areas.[9] Movement of settlers into forest areas can reflect an official policy to expand agriculture or to resettle people. In Latin America and Southeast Asia, large areas of land are often owned by a small minority, and this inequitable distribution of land, along with rapid population growth, has brought new demands for the conversion of forest to agriculture. In Brazil, for example, migration of poor settlers into forest areas has been officially encouraged in the absence of more fundamental land reform. Forest land is also cleared for large-scale agriculture to produce crops for export, often because of an urgent need for foreign exchange. Forests have been cleared in Malaysia for rubber and palm oil, and in Thailand thousands of hectares of forest have been cleared by poor farmers to grow cassava which is turned into tapioca for export to Europe as animal feed.[10]

Deforestation for agriculture may be the result of economic policies but is seldom based on sound economics. For example, the net present value of a good Amazonian cattle pasture has been calculated as only one-third of the net present value of a tract of productive forest in Peru, from which products such as latex, fruits and medicines can be

Cattle grazing where the rainforest used to flourish, Rondônia, Brazil. This land will rapidly become degraded as the soil cover is thin and infertile.

extracted.[11] Cattle pastures are able to sustain only a low density of animals for a short period – they rarely last more than eight years before they must be abandoned. Conversion of forest to cattle ranching is only 'economically viable' because landowners are given tax incentives, and stand to make a profit if the land rises in value.

Logging

Vast tracts of forest are opened up by the roads which logging companies build. This initial clearance is then followed by people who settle the land and clear yet more of it. The logging itself is highly destructive: in a typical operation, for every tree cut, a further three are destroyed and the soil is sufficiently disturbed to prevent regeneration, leaving a badly degraded environment.[12] Cleared areas dry out quickly and easily catch fire. In the fires which swept through 3.5 million hectares of East Kalimantan in Indonesia in 1982-3, a total of 55 million cubic feet of timber was destroyed with an estimated export value of US$55 billion to Indonesia.[13] At the end of 1991, after a long drought, fires were again widespread in East Kalimantan.

Some governments encourage logging for foreign exchange which may be needed to service debts. The expansion of export production under structural adjustment programmes also leads to forest clearance. While there is no simple correlation between indebtedness and deforestation, the revenue from timber exports or processed woods is of great importance to tropical forest countries. One study in the Philippines concludes:

> There is a link with national debt: the scramble for foreign exchange encourages the export of forest resources, and the resulting denudation of land destroys watersheds.[14]

Ka Rudy Sambajon who works for Pamalakaya, a fishing federation in the Philippines supported by Oxfam, comments:

> The connection is quite simple. Aquino merely continued the Marcos policies on foreign borrowing, as a result, our natural resources became open to foreign companies who used Filipino loggers to cut down our forests and export the logs.[15]

Faced with a debt burden of US$28 billion in 1988 (equal to 65 per cent of its GNP)[16] the Philippines has to repay $10 million a day.[17] The prospects for Philippines forests are not good: 55 per cent of forest was lost between 1960 and 1985.[18] The effects of forest losses have been dramatic; livelihoods have been destroyed, watersheds eroded or flooded, and coastal fishing grounds silted up.

The major beneficiaries of the international timber trade are the developed market economies – especially Japan and the UK, which together consume three-quarters of the world's exports of tropical timber.[19] Yet only 1 per cent of this production comes from sustainable sources. The conclusion must be that present patterns of pricing and consumption in the North are contributing substantially to the elimination of the world's remaining tropical forests.[20]

Worldwide, the consequences of indiscriminate deforestation are almost always the same. The needs of poor people are not met, the productive capacity of forests is damaged irreversibly, and valuable environmental resources are lost. The potential for soil erosion and flooding is increased and global warming accelerated. Long-term benefits are sacrificed for short-term financial gain. For all these reasons, deforestation is not socially acceptable, ecologically sustainable nor economically prudent.

The rights of indigenous people

The basic human rights and needs of indigenous people have been largely ignored in the process of tropical deforestation. Indigenous people represent about 4 per cent of the world's population and number some 200 million. Many have been killed when their lands were seized; others have died when new diseases were introduced to their area by colonisers. Over 90 different groups of Amazonian Indians are thought

MIKE GOLDWATER/OXFAM

People have lived in the forest for many generations, and have evolved sustainable life-styles, and varied, individual cultures, using a variety of forest products. But their existence is under threat as forests are destroyed. These are Campa Indians who live on the borders of Brazil and Peru, in the Amazon rainforest.

to have died out this century.[21] Some people who live in the forests are hunter-gatherers. Other groups have practised systems of sustainable farming, usually involving shifting cultivation, for millenia; but these ecologically sound ways of life are now under pressure. The future for indigenous people is seriously threatened and, even if they manage to survive, they may lose their cultural identity in the process of assimilation into other types of society. Their accumulated knowledge will also be lost, together with their understanding of how to live in harmony with their environment. India's forests, which are being lost at a rate of more than 1 million hectares a year, were home to 400 tribal groups – some 54 million people (7.5 per cent of the population). Today, relatively few tribal people live in India's forests; without land, they have become some of the poorest and most vulnerable members of society.[22]

Vietnam

The Hmong people, with whom Oxfam has worked in Vietnam, are changing their way of life and taking up sedentary agriculture. Their traditional system of 'slash-and-burn' farming was sustainable when population densities were low. They occupied specific areas, recognised by other groups and held in common. Because the land 'belonged' to one family or group, there were incentives to use it in such a way that soil fertility was maintained. They farmed up to one hectare for three years, growing maize and sweet potatoes, then left it fallow until they returned a dozen or more years later. But this system of cultivation is no longer possible. Declining forest area and growing population pressures have reduced the periods of fallow and the land has no time to recover. The government of Vietnam is encouraging the Hmong to adopt settled agriculture systems which can support more people on smaller areas of land. But the transition is not easy, and farmers need a great deal of support. In Hoang Lien Son, Oxfam is helping them to make the transition by providing technical advice and agricultural equipment. Those who have access to a market and are well served by roads have moved into small-scale cash cropping, growing bamboo, spices, tea, or coffee.[23]

Brazil

In Brazil, Oxfam has worked for many years with the Yanomami Indians of Roraima. There are about 9,000 Yanomami living in the forest on the border with Venezuela. They are the largest of South America's tribal groups to have retained their traditional way of life, living in large family groups of up to 150 people usually sharing a communal long-house. They are hunter-gatherers but also grow some crops. The influx of outsiders – particularly the gold-panners – has brought disease, poisoned the waterways and degraded the forest. The Yanomami have been badly affected by malaria: in some communities more than 90 per cent of the people are infected.

In March 1989, eight Latin American countries agreed to set aside areas for national parks and demarcate lands for indigenous groups, with an emphasis on popular participation in their planning and development. The countries agreed not only to provide essential services such as health and education but also to help the groups become more economically self-reliant. In December 1990, President Collor promised to carry out the long-deferred demarcation of land for the Yanomami Indians. In the face of opposition from the army and mining companies, little action was taken. Despite official assurances, progress is still slow. The Commission for the Creation of the Yanomami Parks (CCPY), an organisation supported by Oxfam,[24] claims that outsiders are continuing to pan for gold and that health services are totally inadequate to deal with the malaria epidemic. It was not until November 1991, and against strong military opposition, that the President announced that 9.4 million hectares of rainforest would be demarcated for the Yanomami Indians. Despite continued pressure against demarcation, funds have been approved for the work to start in 1992.

Zaire

Covering some 360 million hectares, 80 per cent of Africa's tropical rainforest, the Zaire basin is home to 200 different tribes, numbering some 50 million people.[25] Zaire alone has 13 per cent of the world's total rainforest and is Africa's richest country in terms of animal and plant species. The forests are home to 200,000 Pygmies and 300,000 Pygmoids. Largely as a result of foreign investment, the forests are being destroyed at an increasing rate. The National Forest Plan of Zaire anticipates a ten-fold increase in logging to 6 million cubic metres by 2000, including the supply of 20 per cent of Kinshasa's charcoal needs. It is estimated that by 2050 Zaire's rainforests will have largely vanished. The Pygmies' nomadic hunting and gathering way of life is being supplemented by agriculture as they seek to survive in increasingly difficult circumstances. In a report prepared for Oxfam,[26] John Beauclerk explains that the survival of the Pygmies is inextricably linked to the fate of the forests:

> It is important to retain the picture of Pygmy social organisation as inextricably linked to the forest, non-hierarchical between sexes and ages to a degree unknown among African cultivators and without definition on inheritance or private property. They are too mobile and have no concept of land ownership. Theirs has been a successful formula for at least 5,000 years, though it will be tested as never before in the next 20 years.

During the 1970s the government tried to force the Pygmy groups to settle in villages. They became ill and found it hard to become cultivators. More recently, as the forests are being opened up by loggers, the Pygmies are being drawn into the world of the immigrants, serving initially as hunters before being reduced to dependent day-labourers and eventually dispossessed altogether.

Evidence suggests that there is a major effort under way to exploit Africa's forests in which the World Bank may play a significant part.

> The motives have to do with profits to meet debt repayments and to fuel further development. The environmental and social costs are foreseeable; as in Amazonia and Southeast Asia, the destruction of the forest will cause an increase in poverty rather than its resolution... The 'opening-up' of the Zaire basin will inevitably result in destroying the Pygmies economically and physically... None of this is inevitable; governments wishing to avoid forest loss and the dissipation of non-renewable national resources have a variety of options. In adopting these they also need to look carefully at the social inequalities that provoke forest destruction; this will concern them as a priority with land rights and new

legislation. The misinterpretation of Pygmy needs makes most development efforts on their behalf ineffective. Ultimately their only real hope lies in control and ownership of their forests.[27]

Embracing the trees: the Chipko movement

Third World women play a central role in providing food, fuel and fodder, production of which depends on and is derived from natural ecosystems, especially from forests. Women's responsibility for providing for their families is not reduced because the forests disappear; women must still provide, even if it means walking further and working longer hours. In India, deforestation of the Himalayas led to floods, landslides and soil erosion which in turn gave rise to the creation of a popular protest movement known as the Chipko movement. The movement has been largely organised and sustained by women. 'Chipko' means 'to embrace' which is what the women did when the trees were about to be cut down by logging companies. The differences between the interests of the men and the women in the communities were highlighted in some of the confrontations. The needs of the women for the food, fuel and fodder which the trees could supply were at odds with the needs of their menfolk for the cash income they would get from employment by the logging companies to cut the trees down. Women have been known to hold out against the forest department and their own husbands to protect a patch of trees, and have protected the forest by their physical presence against grazing and lopping and cutting. The results have been that in time the forest successfully regenerated. The movement has spread throughout India and is an inspiration to many 'green' activists all over the world.

WAYS FORWARD

Action at several levels is required if the destruction of forests is to be reversed and the livelihoods of forest people protected. The first need is for local level initiatives which support people in their efforts to meet their needs and care for their environment. It is the people who live in the forest – the indigenous people and the settlers – who have a vested interest in its survival. At international level, the need is for more commitment to sustainable development on the part of the large agencies such as the World Bank. Appropriate policies and actions at national level are also crucial.

Fiscal and agrarian reform

The principal direct causes of the deforestation of Brazilian Amazonia are cattle ranching, road building, smallholder agriculture, urban growth and large infrastructural projects. Cattle ranching has been the most important direct cause of deforestation but it would not have been possible without roads and has been closely linked to land speculation. But the underlying cause lies in the uneven distribution of land and the economic and social instability associated with high inflation rates.[28] Subsidies and incentives, and inflation throughout the 1970s and 1980s, encouraged land speculation and the conversion of Brazil's forests to cattle pasture. One researcher on Amazonia suggests several options for tackling the deforestation problem: taxes should be levied on the speculative use of land; pastures fraudulently established in order to claim land ownership rights should not be recognised; construction of highways should be controlled; and processes of environmental impact assessment for big development projects should be strengthened.[29] Another important step towards reducing deforestation would be agrarian reform, including secure, recognised and visible rights to land, together with access to credit and technical help if needed, for the poorest people. This would make it possible for smallholders to stay put instead of being evicted by more powerful interests and moved on to other parts of the forest.

Sustainable agriculture

Progress is being made towards sustainable farming and the development of extractive reserves – two initiatives which could prevent deforestation. The work of organisations like the Oxfam-supported Centro de Educacao, Pesquisa e Assessoria Sindical e Popular (CEPASP),[30] which provides agricultural training and advice, is a contribution towards helping people to stay on their land and farm it in a sustainable way.

New styles of forest management are emerging among some of the settlers. They are planting forest trees on farms and cultivating annual crops along with commercially valuable tree species. This mixed agroforestry system is labour intensive, diverse and resilient and yields high incomes.

In the Brazilian town of Castanhal Araras near Marabá (the town where Sr. José lives), 150 families, who have each been granted a 50 hectare plot, are taking a new initiative. Instead of felling their trees for charcoal, raising a few crops and then being forced to sell their exhausted land to land speculators, the people of Araras, with the advice of an agronomist provided by CEPASP, have prepared a land use plan for their 7,500 hectares and the neighbouring forest.

First, they plant seedlings in the forest to increase the density of large useful species such as brazil nuts and cupuacu fruit trees. Next, they plant tree or shrub crops such as coffee, cacao and fruits on the cleared land along with cassava and maize. The tree crops protect the soil from torrential rains and scorching sun as well as providing leaf litter to enhance fertility. Then other useful species are introduced into areas that have been left fallow to recover from cropping. In this way the secondary forest regrowth is rich in trees that can yield an income. The scheme also involves setting up marketing cooperatives to transport the produce and reduce costs. A start has been made on processing the crops to add value: the group began with a rice huller and plans to introduce a freezer for the cupuacu pulp. The Araras experiment is demonstrating that basic needs can be met from forest farms, and the settlers are persuaded to leave the remaining forest intact. Land distribution to smallholders in this way is far more socially and environmentally beneficial than concentrating forest land in the hands of a few cattle ranchers.

In Peru's Urubamba valley, the Centre for the Development of Amazonian Indians (CEDIA)[31], funded by Oxfam since 1982, helps the Machiguenga Indians obtain their land rights. Under Peruvian law, Indian territories are only partly protected. If some areas are not considered to be 'used' properly, the land can be confiscated and given to colonists. As a result of conflict between the Indians and the colonists, CEDIA encouraged the Indians to plant boundaries. These 'living' boundaries not only served to reduce conflict, but also protected the land and provided the Indians with a source of cash crops. CEDIA estimated that within two years of its introduction, 25 communities were tending plots of between 8 and 26 hectares. CEDIA is now encouraging families to diversify the crops they plant to improve their diet and gain an income. Agricultural production increased by one-third between 1984 and 1988. As a result, the communities are increasingly self-sufficient. They intend gradually to plant and reforest poor and exposed land. This could be a blue-print for the whole of the Urubamba valley, where there are large areas of useless, degraded land.

This 'Primary Environmental Care' approach to forest management is guided by the same principle as the rest of Oxfam's development work: it is only by supporting the capacity of local people to organise and empower themselves that poverty and environmental degradation can be tackled. But the quest for empowerment is fraught with difficulty and sometimes danger, as the assassination of the Brazilian rural workers' trade union leader, Chico Mendes, has demonstrated.

Extractive reserves

Chico Mendes played a crucial role in organising rubber tappers in the Amazon state of Acre. From 1985, under his leadership, the National Council of Rubber Tappers mounted a campaign for the creation of 'extractive reserves'– areas of forest set aside for the exclusive use of rubber tappers working in the traditional way, in areas they have long occupied, as described in Chapter 2. They developed a non-violent form of protest, *empate*, modelled on the Chipko movement, preventing loggers cutting down trees by occupying the threatened area. Three reserves were declared in 1988, including land on the Cachoeira Estate, owned by a local landowner, who was bitterly opposed to the creation of the reserves. Later that year he shot and killed Chico Mendes. It was only after Mendes' death that the Chico Mendes Reserve, on the old Cachoeira Estate near Xapuri, was officially designated by the President. Mendes also inspired the creation of the Forest Peoples' Alliance, which was founded in 1989. The Alliance unites rubber tappers and Indians in a joint movement to defend their livelihoods and habitat from encroachment by ranchers, timber merchants and land speculators.

Social forestry

Social forestry programmes are primarily designed to satisfy the needs of rural people for fuelwood, small timber and fodder and to provide an income for poor farmers. Despite such worthy objectives, the results of many social forestry programmes have been disappointing. In India, the social forestry programme is geared to afforesting public lands to produce trees for industrial use, and to tree-planting on private farms and community lands for fuelwood and fodder. Poor rural people depend on the resources of the communal forests and have little cash to buy fuelwood. Their needs would be better served if the trees planted enriched the environment in the longer term and provided useful products.[32] Eucalyptus was a popular species for farm-forestry in the north-west states of India in the first half of the 1980s. But since then, market saturation and production problems have reduced farmers' interest in trees as a crop.

Oxfam has been involved in monitoring social forestry programmes in south-west India where they have been seen as a way of tackling serious deforestation problems. A World Bank/ODA social forestry project in Karnataka was part of a scheme to plant 5 million hectares of forest each year.[33] It had three components: farm forestry (providing seedlings to farmers), nurseries (providing plastic bags and seeds to families), and tree planting on government-owned common land for fuel and animal fodder. An Oxfam report concluded that poor people were not being helped, and the benefits of the project appeared to go to the wealthier farmers. One study found that 12 per cent of the trees were being cut down each year, of which 78 per cent were going for fuelwood to Bangalore. Smaller farmers could not participate in the programme for they could not afford to wait up to ten years for returns on their investment. The eucalyptus trees were no good for fodder as animals refused to eat them. Because they were not directly involved, local people were unaware that the project was meant to benefit them, and so took little interest in the fate of the trees. In some areas, land formerly used for growing subsistence food crops had been given over to growing commercial trees, mostly eucalyptus. Tree-planting on farms has reduced the jobs available for labourers and women have lost out more than men. An Oxfam field worker comments:

> ... Here, exploitation takes the form of planting a eucalyptus forest on land previously available for villagers. Cattle and sheep could be grazed there; local craftsmen could gather the grass and vines needed to weave baskets and mats; women could gather branches and leaves for cooking fuel; seasonal fruits and herbs could be picked free. Since the area was planted with eucalyptus saplings, the poorest villagers have been the hardest hit. Nothing else grows where eucalyptus is planted; no grass, no undergrowth, no flowers; no animal will touch its bark or leaves. No birds sing, for no bird will nest there...[34]

Well-organised and well-publicised campaigning by local NGOs has resulted in changes. Eucalyptus is no longer the only tree planted: trees for fruit, fodder and fuel are appearing. Important lessons have been

On Sabu Island, school-children are being taught how to stall-feed goats, and fence them in. By preventing goats from grazing freely, young trees are protected and forest regeneration is encouraged.

learnt from the Karnataka Social Forestry Project. In future, collaborative management systems need to be established which bring foresters and communities together so that the needs of the poorest people can be met as the area is reforested.

A new project for the Western Ghats Forests, which cover a range of mountains parallel to the Karnataka coast, is to be funded by the ODA. The Western Ghats are important as the source of all the major rivers in south India and as the location of a unique variety of forest types concentrated in a small area. Over the years, the forest has suffered from excessive exploitation, and little regeneration is taking place. The project's aims are to assure the livelihoods of those who depend on these areas and at the same time rehabilitate the forest. Local people will be involved in project planning through village committees which will enter into management agreements with the Karnataka Forest Department.

Community forestry can work well, especially when it is initiated by local people. For a number of years, Oxfam has supported the activities of Friends of the Trees and Living Beings,[35] a local NGO in the Indian state of Orissa. The work of the organisation (described in detail in Chapter 1) covers a range of integrated activities which link meeting basic needs with forest regeneration.

Re-greening: Ie Rai

Sabu Island, off the coast of West Timor, is one of the poorest parts of Indonesia and has been almost totally deforested. Soil erosion is widespread. Perennial drought is broken by flash floods. The island has a population of 60,000, most of whom are very poor subsistence farmers. Ie Rai is a local NGO established in 1981 with Oxfam support.[36] It now runs several projects on the island. Forty villages have been involved in soil conservation and terracing, fencing, well-digging and establishing tree nurseries. The most popular tree for people to plant is one called *lamtoro*, which has the capacity to increase the nitrogen content of the soil and produces highly nutritious fodder. The aim of Ie Rai has been not only to 're-green' the island, but to strengthen associations of small farmers by encouraging participation in programme planning and decision making, so that people can take control of their own environment. Awareness of environmental issues has been built up, and people have become highly motivated as they have seen the benefits of the environmental management schemes. The work is expanding into agroforestry and the establishment of fodder plantations aimed at increasing agricultural yields. This is an example of community management, where people take control of natural resources and manage them sustainably and efficiently for the benefit of the whole community, both now and in the future.

International Forestry Agreements
The International Tropical Timber Organisation

This organisation was established in 1985 to follow up the International Tropical Timber Agreement of 1983, negotiated under the auspices of UNCTAD. Eighteen producer countries and 23 consumer countries are members of the ITTO, and together account for 90 per cent of the global trade in tropical timber. ITTO is charged with the twin tasks of coordinating tropical timber producing and consuming countries and encouraging national policies for the sustainable use and conservation of tropical forests and their genetic resources. Many NGOs have criticised ITTO's failure to fulfil its conservation function, influenced as it is by trade interests. It has also been accused of ignoring the needs of indigenous people who depend on the forest for their livelihoods.[37]

Tropical Forestry Action Plan

Established in 1986 under the auspices of the FAO, the TFAP is an international mechanism to coordinate assistance to the forestry sector, identify and plan priority actions and fund conservation projects. The TFAP's funds come from bilateral arrangements and are not directly under TFAP management. In some countries, notably Peru, Cameroon and Papua New Guinea, the funds pledged have merely served to intensify logging. Some national plans have been shrouded in official secrecy, and people who live in the forest have not been involved in the planning process.

In spite of its potential, the effectiveness of the TFAP remains to be proved. Oxfam, like many other NGOs, has called for reforms to ensure a participatory planning approach that involves the communities concerned and NGOs. A strong emphasis needs to be placed on securing the lands and livelihoods of rural communities, especially forest dwellers, on promoting plantations of native species and on developing the sustainable production of non-wood products such as nuts, fruit and herbs. As yet, there is no firm indication of any shift away from the large-scale projects normally funded under the TFAP nor any evidence that reforms have begun. Indeed, some observers believe that confrontations between North and South in the run-up to UNCED set back progress. Discussions of national sovereignty over resources have excluded the broader considerations of forest conservation and the welfare of forest people.[38]

Forestry and the World Bank

With aggregate lending of US$23 billion by early 1990, the World Bank is a major actor in forest development. Under continual pressure from NGOs, the Bank has moved from industrially-oriented operations towards forest schemes which address the interests of forest dwellers. There is now an emphasis upon social forestry and community participation in tree-planting and watershed management.

In 1990, the Bank developed a new Forestry Policy and Oxfam has been actively involved in the consultations on revision. It is Oxfam's view that unless the needs of traditional forest dwellers and the rural poor are urgently addressed by the Bank in its lending programme, then environmental objectives will not be met. Indigenous people, Oxfam argues, should never be displaced. This has to be a central element of the Bank's approach.[39] The new Forestry Policy will focus on financing international technical assistance, promoting national policy reform, supporting the sustainable production from forests and providing funds to help preserve primary forest areas. The Bank has set out conditions for loans, which will only be given to governments displaying a commitment to sustainable, conservation-oriented forestry and respecting the rights of forest dwellers. Perhaps most importantly, the World Bank has stated it will no longer finance any commercial logging in primary tropical moist forests. Some 20 countries, accounting for 85 per cent of the world's remaining tropical moist forest, will be given special attention. It remains to be seen whether or not the International Finance Corporation, an organisation of the World Bank group, which holds equity investments in timber extraction projects, will adhere to this directive.

Oxfam has drawn attention to the important relationship between debt servicing and tropical forest degradation in the South and to the need for a creative approach by the Bank to debt reduction. The new World Bank Forestry Policy is forest-focused rather than cross-sectoral, and fails to address projects which are not in the forestry sector which may lead to destruction of forest and forest people's livelihoods, such as road construction projects which can open up forest areas to exploitation.

The draft conventions

Efforts to develop legally binding international conventions on climate change and biodiversity have been under way for several years. Loss of tropical forests has far-reaching implications for both biological diversity and global warming and yet the gap between North and South is currently very great on this issue. The North is calling for a binding agreement to protect tropical forests, whilst the countries of the South are insisting on their sovereign right to use their forests in the ways they choose. Given the rate of forest destruction, some form of international agreement which also addresses issues of people's rights and access to resources is essential. Parties to the agreement should accept targets and instruments and commit themselves to undertake policy measures which promote conservation and sustainable use of forests.

TROPICAL DRY FORESTS

Around the world, there are nearly 800 million hectares of tropical dry forest. Most is found in Africa, but there are also extensive tracts in South and South East Asia, Latin America and Australia.[40] Because of their accessibility and ease of clearance, 3.8 million hectares are being lost each year.

Although they attract less attention than the rainforests, dry forests are significant for a number of reasons. They absorb large quantities of carbon dioxide, and conserve moisture in areas where rainfall is low and uncertain, helping to build up soil fertility. They contain many species which are resilient under abnormal weather conditions, both dry and wet. Semi-arid woodlands are capable of supporting higher densities of people and stock than rainforests and they play an important complementary role in the pattern of semi-arid agriculture as well as providing many minor forest products including gums, resins, fruits and berries and a supply of fuelwood and building materials for urban and rural areas.[41]

A burning issue

One of the major threats to tropical dry forests is the fuelwood requirement of urban people. Where they are close to urban areas, dry forests are under threat not only for wood but also for the land they occupy. As we saw in Chapter 5, charcoal burning is a major cause of degradation in Darfur province and Red Sea Hills Province, but is a source of income and part of the coping strategy of people threatened by food insecurity.

Two billion people are short of fuelwood to cook their food. FAO forecasts that some three billion people will be a part of this crisis by the end of the century. The problem is already acute in the arid and semi-arid areas of sub-Saharan Africa, throughout the arid and mountainous regions of Central America, and the populous areas of South Asia.[42] For poor households, there is no alternative to wood; any other fuel is too expensive. More and more forests in rural areas are cut – both for wood and for charcoal – to serve urban markets.

Because of the shortage of fuelwood, poor families often burn dung and crop residues which they would otherwise return to the soil. In Nepal, it is estimated that this practice reduces crop yields by 15 per cent.[43] And in areas where wood is scarce, the remaining trees are often damaged by the lopping of young and green branches, and continued cutting means that the trees cannot recover. The burdens upon those

Collecting wood, Burkina Faso; traditionally a woman's task. There is a growing shortage of fuelwood in many parts of the world.

who collect fuel – mainly women – are increased. They must walk long distances to find and carry home bundles of wood, allowing less time for other tasks in the fields and in the home.

In the Eastern District of Zambia, Oxfam field staff report that people are finding it harder and harder to gather wood. Elderly people in Mulolo village in Chipata District recall that, before the tobacco farms moved into the neighbourhood and started using wood for curing, there was no shortage of firewood. As recently as 1980, there were plenty of trees near the village, but now the women have to walk five kilometres to a place called Mutucha, and even there the supply is close to exhaustion because of over-cutting. A widow describes her daily struggle to gather fuel to cook her family's food:

> We leave home very early about 5 a.m. before the sun is up. We arrive at Mutucha at 7 a.m. I move through the area trying to break wood with my hands and collect dry branches and twigs. Sometimes I can find only very small pieces like match sticks and sometimes we are forced to get fresh wood which will burn only with a strong fire if you don't keep them. You have to have small and big pieces. You have to think about the distance to carry the wood and how strong you are. I can only manage a little wood. By the time I cook 'nsima' and relish in the evening the wood is finished. The next day I have to go back again.[44]

Women try to cut down on their use of wood; they may not boil water, and sometimes dangerously undercook food, both of which create health risks. As wood supplies are reduced, families must buy their fuel rather than collect it, straining already limited budgets. Even in Amazonia, where there is an abundance of wood, a week's supply of charcoal can cost a family some US$2 – 14 per cent of the average wage. In South Asia, buying fuelwood and charcoal can take 40 per cent of the family earnings.

WAYS FORWARD

There are various ways in which the problem can be tackled – planting more trees, burning wood more efficiently, or by using different sources of energy. The World Bank estimates that meeting the world's fuelwood needs requires a five-fold increase in the planting of fast-growing trees to reach a target of 2.7 million hectares each year.[45]

Experience of tree-planting schemes in Nepal, Senegal and South Korea shows that there are some critical ingredients for success. It is essential that farmers – especially women – are involved in management. They should own the land which is planted, or be entitled to the trees grown on common land. Supportive technical services are vital, supplying seeds and seedlings, testing soil, giving advice. Tree-planting works best where there are strong incentives for people to protect trees for their own use as well as for sale. Of crucial importance is the choice of species to plant, which should fit local conditions and be adaptable, resilient and capable of multiple uses. Users can show strong and varied preferences; often men would choose different tree species from women.

In the Shinyanga region of Tanzania, people have adopted a simple method of re-greening with advice from HASHI (Hifadhi Ardhi, Shinyanga), a land conservation training centre, supported by Oxfam.[46] They protect the degraded forest which, left to itself, will regenerate. An area of land is demarcated and protected from grazing animals and fuelwood-collectors. First the grasses grow, then bushes are followed by trees, and finally animals return to the forest. But this style of natural re-greening demands a good deal of community cooperation.

More efficient use of woodfuel

Improving the efficiency of cooking stoves is another way of responding to the woodfuel crisis – and reducing the heavy burden upon women. But all the experiments show just how important it is to match local needs. One Oxfam supported group – Lok Chetna Manch – in the Garwal hills of India has popularised more fuel efficient stoves in homes and on tea stalls.[47] These stoves cut wood consumption by up to 40 per cent. Translated into time, that means that women save about eight hours walking on their twice-weekly trips to gather wood. The simple technology not only reduces their drudgery but decreases the demand on the village woodlot. Young men from the village have been trained to install the stoves (which cost US$2) and maintain them.

Left to itself, dry tropical forest can regenerate rapidly. HASHI, in Tanzania, is supporting schemes of forest protection, to prevent grazing and wood collecting in designated areas. Here, Charles Mwandu, an elder of his village, and chosen as a warden for the growing forest, is patrolling the regenerating area.

INTERCONNECTIONS

The last four chapters have looked at separate aspects of the environment of rural people, but it is clear that water, land, agricultural systems and forests are closely related parts of the ecosystem. The loss of tropical forests, land degradation and water shortages threaten the survival of many millions of people who depend on these natural resources for their livelihoods. Forest losses in particular have far-reaching implications for biological diversity and global warming, and may disrupt climatic and ecological patterns such as the growing season, soil formation and water supplies, which in turn could have profound effects on the ability of poor people in rural areas to produce the food they need. The next chapter looks at the very different problems facing the city dwellers in the Third World.

La Esperanza, a shanty town on the outskirts of Guatemala City.

7

LIVING IN CITIES

I came to the city because things started to go wrong where we lived. In the country, if you don't own land you can't earn a living. There's only agricultural work and that is hard work for women. Here you can do laundry or ironing or work in a house. I work in a school and do washing at the weekends and sometimes I fry snacks for people. Services are very few, practically non-existent. We don't have refuse collection, people just throw it on the street. Water is very scarce, I have to go a long way to fetch it. There is no school, no hospital – the nearest one is a maternity hospital, but there is no doctor. I cannot use the private clinic – I have no money.

Basidia Rulesindo, a woman from the Dominican Republic.

Thirty years from now, for the first time in history, more people will live in cities than in rural areas; and it is in the Third World that the urban explosion is taking place. Over 5 billion people will be urban dwellers by 2025, almost 4 billion of them in the South. In the North, where most people already live in cities, urban growth rates have decreased to less than 1 per cent a year, whereas in the South towns and cities are growing by an average of 3.6 per cent – four times as fast. Of the 24 mega-cities with over 10 million people by the end of the century, 18 will be in the Third World.[1]

Many factors are at work in the growing cities of the South. The prospect of employment, better standards of living and the amenities of urban life all pull people to the city, while increasing poverty, landlessness and conflict push them from the countryside. High rates of natural increase within cities add to the numbers of migrants. Urban populations in the developing world are now growing more than three times as fast as the populations of rural areas. Even though a high proportion of the citizens of Mexico City are unemployed, people still stream into the city in search of work and a better life.

Mexico City: an urban nightmare

The capital of Mexico is home to more than 20 million people. In the past 50 years, the population has expanded nine-fold and is expected to reach over 25 million by the end of the century. Mexico City suffers from severe air pollution, a lack of water, high unemployment and a critical housing shortage. One-third of the city's people live without sufficient water and electricity. Half of the city's rubbish is left on the streets to rot.

Lying in the crater of an extinct volcano at 2,500 metres, Mexico City was built on the site of the old Aztec capital. Even without the effects of people, the environment is a problem: the valley is flooded in the rainy season and there are dust storms in the dry season. The city, which lies on the San Andreas fault, is prone to earthquakes; the ones in 1985 killed at least 10,000 people and damaged or destroyed 500,000 homes. Excessive use of subterranean water has caused Mexico City to sink – in some parts over 9 metres. Now, water is so scarce that the only option is to pump it to the city from more than a hundred miles away over the mountains, at costs that are unsustainable.

Respiratory problems, and skin and eye infections are commonplace in Mexico City because of the high levels of pollution. A total of 130,000 factories and more than 3 million vehicles pour 5 million tonnes of toxic smoke and fumes into the city every year. During the rainy season, layers of cold air trap these pollutants in the valley, turning it into a hot gas chamber. Almost every day of 1991 saw the air register as unsafe by WHO standards. Although the public transport system is good, it is simply not good enough to cope with an ever-expanding population: pollution from private vehicles continues to increase. But industrial sources, including oil refineries, contribute most of the pollution. In March 1991, the Mexican government ordered the closure of the country's largest refinery – in the heart of the city – which was responsible for much of the city's pollution (up to a third was quoted in Mexico). The land is to be turned into a park. Attempts are also being made to slow down migration to the city by locating new industries in other parts of Mexico.

A new government programme aims to reduce pollution by almost 40 per cent within the next five years through a combination of measures including conversions from fuel oil to natural gas, tree-planting, and traffic management schemes, which include restrictions on vehicles entering the city on one day each week. But although there are already many rules and regulations to govern atmospheric and water pollution by industry, these are often openly flouted. NGOs like Casa Y Ciudad (described later in this chapter) are working with community organisations to promote a new approach to urban planning which will improve living conditions in the poorer districts of Mexico City.[2]

THE URBAN ENVIRONMENT

Urban expansion is happening at such speed and on such a scale that the capacities of most Southern governments are severely strained. They cannot manage urban growth, nor provide for the basic needs of their citizens. The consequence is that there are unplanned, informal settlements in and around most of the major cities of the South where the basic infrastructure is inadequate and services are largely absent. The poorest people suffer the worst living conditions. They can only afford to live in makeshift settlements at the city margins on land unfit for housing, or in crowded city slums. Homes are constructed on unstable hillsides, on land subject to flooding or in contaminated areas close to industry. There are few or no basic services such as water supply, sewerage, garbage removal or electricity, except those organised by the slum-dwellers themselves. Roads and transport facilities are poor, medical care is inadequate and there are few schools. Air and water pollution levels are high, and there may be no opportunities for growing food, collecting fuel or safely disposing of waste. Sometimes a half of all the people in large Third World cities must live in these desperately overcrowded slums and squatter settlements. Employment is limited: few have jobs in the formal sector and in the world's poorest and most rapidly growing cities, up to 70 per cent of the population depends on income from activities in the informal economy.

Urban environments cannot be considered in isolation from the countryside: they are interdependent. Cities are major centres of production, consumption and communication but they depend on the hinterland for labour, resources and energy and draw in water, foodstuffs, and fuel from the surrounding areas. Cities also produce great quantities of waste: domestic and industrial as well as air and water pollution.

Supplying the materials that cities need is a major cause of environmental change: croplands, forests and water resources can all be degraded as urban areas grow. In Brazil, urban development has exacerbated deforestation and land erosion where, for example, trees have been cleared to make charcoal for industry and for urban markets. In India, the discharge of raw sewage and toxic chemicals into the Ganges from cities along the river has posed a major threat to the livelihoods of fishermen and to drinking water sources in the downstream villages. The Hooghly estuary, near Calcutta, is choked with untreated industrial wastes from more than 150 major factories around the city. Two thirds of Calcutta's population suffer from pneumonia, bronchitis or other respiratory diseases related to air pollution.[3]

Most Third World cities are without effective water and air pollution regulations, while standards for handling waste are poor or absent. In consequence, bad health is a major environmental hazard of living in the city. It pervades the daily lives of poor urban dwellers – especially women and children – and erupts periodically in major disasters.

Cholera is a disease closely associated with urban poverty. By the end of April 1991, cholera had reached epidemic proportions in Peru: more than 166,000 cases had been reported and 1,075 people were dead. The epidemic began in the shanty towns along the coastal plain, then spread to the rest of the country – and across the continent. Cholera has now been identified in Ecuador, Colombia, Chile and Brazil, although it had been absent from these countries for decades.[4]

Farmers to shanty dwellers

Cities can consume great quantities of arable land. By the end of the century, total urban area in the Third World will be more than twice the size it was in 1980.[5] As urban areas grow, villages become towns and the farmers who are shifted out of agriculture move into the shanties. Some move because they have no incentive to produce for urban markets where imported food is subsidised. Others are pushed off their land by large commercial developments.

Marabá, in the Amazonian State of, one of Brazil's fastest growing towns, today has 250,000 people, having grown twenty-fold in as many years, since the discovery of iron ore in the nearby Carajás mountains (Chapter 2). People have come from all over the country: some were small farmers, evicted from their land by violent conflicts; many were labourers who came to work on the construction of the Carajás railway or the Tucurui dam. And thousands came in search of gold. Others came to Amazonia to find a plot of land to farm, only to be disappointed. They all end up in Marabá.

The officials and technicians working on the new Carajás railway and in the industrial zone live on the highlands. Poor people live in the shanties built on land that no one else wants – it is too dry and too polluted. Their shacks are made of whatever they can find: wooden planks, poles, straw, cardboard and, if they are lucky, iron beams. The wastes of the industrial park end up in the Itacaiunas river, Marabá's water source. At night when the wind dies down, charcoal smoke and sulphur settle on the shanties.

Marabá has nowhere near the level of services, housing or employ- ment to cater for the new residents. There is no clean water, sewerage, refuse collection, public transport, schooling or health care. Some of the poor migrants work at casual jobs on building sites and seasonally with the cattle ranchers. The women work as maids or in other menial jobs, or are forced into prostitution, as well as carrying the domestic burden – for most men are itinerant workers.[6]

Living in the city

Poor people in Third World cities use a wide variety of ways to gain a living space. Most live in illegal settlements in houses or shacks constructed from simple materials, often on public land. A few are lucky enough to be able to buy land and build on it – often without legal permission. Some may participate in official settlement schemes which upgrade existing slum areas or offer serviced sites to those who can afford to build their own homes. The rest will have to rent rooms or bed spaces for the night in crowded tenements, where conditions encourage accidents and the spread of disease. Poverty and powerlessness restrict their access to environmentally safe housing. The worst-off live on pavements and railway stations and under bridges.

Squatting on public or private land in self-built makeshift hovels has become the way of life of most of those who flood into the cities of the South. They hope that official permission will eventually be secured but, in the meantime, they may have to pay bribes to political parties and city officials to secure protection against removal. The common official response has been to clear these homes or at least to exclude them from civic amenities like water, roads, fair price shops, health and education. But without other options, poor people are forced to continue to squat.

> On the night of 28 November 1988, Shanti lost her meagre possessions in the fire that consumed the makeshift houses in the Salimpur Netaji Colony, one of the many slums beside the railway track running through Calcutta. Shanti's shack was made of highly inflammable materials: plastic sheets, bamboo, jute bags and whatever else would give protection against scorching sun and torrential rain. For a colony of illegal squatters, occupying public land, no government services were available. Fortunately, the Calcutta Social Project, an Oxfam partner, provided emergency relief. Shanti is not alone; two-thirds of Calcutta's 11 million people build, buy or rent illegal dwellings, because they cannot afford even the cheapest legal house.[7]

The urban environment, both inside and outside the home, has a particular significance for women – a fact which is reinforced by cultural patterns. As home-makers and child-rearers, women are directly affected by the lack of water and sanitation. Their daily domestic tasks – cooking,

Doing the washing is difficult when there is only one tap to supply several hundred families. Shanty town, Lima, Peru.

washing and child care – confine them to the environs of the house. Women in seclusion, particularly in Islamic countries, must remain inside most of the time. Yet the internal environment is often dangerous: fumes from open wood and charcoal fires damage eyes and lungs. Household accidents are common where there is little protection from unguarded stoves and heaters, and where perhaps seven or more people live in one room.

Environmental disasters, too, can affect women more severely. In the aftermath of Bhopal, many suffered menstrual and other gynaecological problems; pregnant women gave birth to deformed babies; some infants were blind. In the demonstrations which followed the gas leak, women were especially active in protesting about the damage to themselves and their families.[8]

Community action

We, the poor, have to organise because we have no alternative. The poor must help the poor and hope that society will change.

Dionisia Acosta, coordinator of an Oxfam project in the Dominican Republic.

One positive development of the growth of cities has been the evolution of community organisations to articulate the needs of poor urban dwellers like Shanti and find new ways to promote their interests. With the extension of political democracy and fair voting, the slum dwellers have been able to exert political pressure to try to solve their problems. Environmental disasters can sometimes be the spur to community action which brings long-term benefits.

Preventing disaster in the Rimac Valley: PREDES
Every year, between December and April, floods and violent mudslides destroy lives and homes in Peru's Rimac Valley – a densely populated area of poor settlements close to Lima. From 1980 to 1983, villages and farmlands on the valley sides and floodplains were flooded or buried under more than 140 mudslides, caused by the collapse of waterlogged terraces. The two major routes connecting Lima to the rest of Peru – the central railway and the main highway – were severed. Damaged water supplies caused shortages in the capital throughout the long, hot summer months and when the Rimac River was blocked, hydro-electric power to the city was cut off.

Mudslides are not just natural disasters: human activity creates the conditions which precede them. Because the Rimac Valley has been stripped of its vegetation for fuel and building materials as the land has been settled, heavy rains do not infiltrate the soil, but cascade off the bare ground. Some of Peru's poorest people have settled here, close to Lima with its (largely illusory) attractions of better jobs and incomes. They try to farm the fragile slopes and floodplains.

There is evidence that, in the past, the Incas managed this vulnerable valley by careful terracing and water management. Where the terraces have survived, there is no erosion. Present farmers do not maintain the terraces and they farm in a different way. As market prices for their crops have fallen in the city, they have abandoned cultivation in favour of raising sheep. The result is overgrazing, more deforestation and eroded terraces.

Since the mudslides of 1983, a local NGO, Centro de Estudios y Prevencion de Desastres (PREDES), has been working with the poor communities of the Rimac Valley, first on disaster relief, lately on long-term measures for rehabilitation. The geologists, engineers and social scientists of PREDES have given advice to local groups on how to build defences against the floods and mudslides using local materials. They have helped people to choose safer sites for their homes, clear the rivers to cope with extra flows and build bank reinforcements. More important, PREDES has enabled local people to lobby the local and national government for assistance and better flood-planning services.

PREDES, an advisory organisation set up to help people living in vulnerable areas in the Rimac Valley, Peru, encourages communities to work together to build river defences in order to minimise the impact of floods and mudslides.

The underlying goal is to raise awareness of the environmental dangers and provide people with the technical skills to design and implement preventive measures and the political skills to negotiate with local government for the resources they need.

PREDES has been highly successful in persuading local community groups to organise and maintain disaster prevention programmes. When severe flooding and mudslides came again in 1987, the benefits were obvious. In one valley where there had been no preventive work, 40 people died and all the houses were reduced to rubble. Where PREDES had worked with a neighbouring community, the defences had withstood the floods: there were no deaths and only a few homes were destroyed.

Since 1984, PREDES has been funded by Oxfam and the ODA and it has moved on from disaster relief to concentrate on the day-to-day social and economic needs of the Rimac Valley residents. In one area of the Valley – Chosica – PREDES is widening its area of concern, to raise consciousness about human rights issues. And it is designing a comprehensive approach to the problems of the Chosica district – from disaster relief through recovery and planning to reconstruction – which can be used as a model for community groups in other parts of Peru.

PREDES shows that community organisation is the key to reducing the vulnerability of poor people to environmental disaster while at the same time tackling their poverty. PREDES operates not as a funding agency (though it helps groups to procure funding) but as an independent adviser. PREDES believes that the gradual, bottom-up approach of changing the social, economic and political relations between marginal groups and the state is the only way forward. It responds to the capabilities of local people, attracts government resources and is more successful than the large-scale plans and projects of large agencies.[9] The PREDES way of working is a good example of the Primary Environmental Care approach discussed in Chapter 2.

Throughout the poor districts of Third World cities, community organisations are springing up to find collective solutions to common problems. These organisations rally communities either in the defence of basic rights (such as shelter or public services) or in opposition to projects and programmes which threaten freedoms, livelihoods or their environment. Community organisations may begin with a single issue, but they soon find themselves dealing with many other problems.

Changing attitudes

Poor citizens show a great capacity to plan and build their own homes, and organise and defend their neighbourhoods. They often understand far more about local needs, incomes, climatic conditions and resources than do government officials. Many governments and NGOs are beginning to see the advantages of channelling this energy and cooperating with poor communities to create better settlements.[10]

In the past, official attitudes towards squatters have varied from neglect to outright hostility. The authorities would try periodically to bulldoze informal settlements and push squatters beyond the city limits. Wherever the land they occupied attracted commercial interest, the pressure on squatters increased.

In recent years, there has been a shift of attitude among policymakers and planners towards recognising slum and squatter citizens as part of the solution. Informal settlements are increasingly seen as living environments better suited to the priorities and resources of poor people. Changes in official thinking and the growth in strength of community organisations have brought a number of experiments in low-cost settlement which involve people directly in the design and construction of homes and neighbourhoods.

Two approaches have achieved some success: settlement upgrading and site-and-service schemes. The first includes legalisation of an existing settlement and allocation of land titles as well as the provision of services. Security of tenure is believed to be the key to encourage squatters to invest in home building and improvement through their own savings or bank loans. In site-and-service schemes, families are allocated land and provided with basic infrastructure (roads, communal water taps, drainage) and services (post office, schools, clinics). Families are free to make their own design and complete their dwelling in a reasonable period of time. Often, building materials are supplied at subsidised rates. Families can use their own labour or engage contractors of their choice. Some schemes offer the families a basic dwelling unit to which they can add improvements later.

Women's needs, though, are frequently ignored. Home design and plot sizes and layout rarely consider the fact that many women will want to grow fruit and vegetables for their families, and use their houses as workshops or as shops to sell goods – such enterprise is often forbidden in low-income housing projects. Housing managers as well as aid donors and international financiers must start to recognise women's vital contribution in building new communities and maximise the opportunities for them to be full partners at every stage of the work.[11]

The participatory approach

Both settlement upgrading and site-and-service schemes are based on a high degree of popular participation, often channelled through slum dwellers' own community organisations. Participation offers several positive features: it reduces friction between official agencies and squatters; it mobilises the skills and resources of the community, keeping costs to the minimum. In addition, participation stimulates community interest in the maintenance of services, and the introduction of other kinds of improvements, such as neighbourhood security, where mutual cooperation is essential.

Even outside these official settlement improvement schemes, the quality of life can be changed when community organisations bring basic amenities such as drinking water, sanitation, roads, rubbish disposal, health care and education. Often their most important role is in helping citizens to articulate and fight for their rights.

Mexico City: Casa y Ciudad

In the aftermath of the 1985 Mexican earthquakes, local residents' committees grew up in the parts of Mexico City that were badly hit. People had been living in rented properties and they feared that landlords would evict them in order to sell the land for development. Some land was being earmarked for green space. But poorer people wanted to stay near to the centre with its jobs and services. So, to strengthen their position, they began to refurbish their homes and neighbourhoods and campaign for better services, including rubbish removal.

Casa Y Ciudad (meaning House and City) is an NGO working with poor people in Mexico City to meet their housing needs. Since the 1985 earthquakes, Casa Y Ciudad has been part-funded by Oxfam, developing and strengthening participation in the Urban Popular Movement – a coalition of community organisations. Casa Y Ciudad, which is staffed by architects, planners, social workers and other urban professionals, works alongside existing organisations – neighbourhood associations, trade unions and educational institutions – and it concentrates on four priorities. First, its staff advise groups working with low-income families on the technical aspects of construction, and prepare alternative plans for low-cost housing in the city. Secondly, Casa y Ciudad works with local groups on wider urban problems, offering them advice on government policies and regulations, and analysing social and economic trends. Thirdly, Casa provides education and training on technical issues (such as carpentry and plumbing), on land and water rights and social organisation. Finally, Casa's communications activities provide neighbourhood groups with the resources for writing and printing newsletters and other audiovisual materials, and training in communication.

Casa Y Ciudad emphasises people's participation in decision making at every level of society. It helps neighbourhood groups to acquire the tools of empowerment, and works with other members of the Urban Popular Movement to develop an alternative vision for the city. This is emerging from a number of local demonstration projects which are based upon people's perceptions of the problems, and community approaches to creating neighbourhoods that are better places to live in.[12]

WORKING WITH URBAN WASTE

The collection and disposal of rubbish are major problems for Third World cities – but here too, community organisations are at work. While local recycling schemes are often struggling to survive in Northern cities, and make up only a marginal component of domestic waste treatment, recycling is commonplace in Third World cities. Rubbish collecting, sorting and selling provides an income for some of the poorest of urban dwellers – especially women and children. Community organisations in a number of cities are trying to help these people improve their living and working conditions, and increase their earnings by more effective recycling of the materials they collect.

Waste workers of Calcutta

To the east of Calcutta, in an area called Dhapa where the city's wastes are dumped, thousands of people gain a living from the rotting rubbish. They pick over the piles of garbage, collecting rubber, tin, cork, glass, foil and other items which they sell to middlemen for recycling. Some use the heaps of rotting waste to grow vegetables which they sell in the city.

The Calcutta Social Project, started by a group of women in 1969 to work in some of the slums of the city, moved into Dhapa in 1981. In an abandoned shed, literacy and recreation classes were introduced for the young garbage pickers, and these were followed by training courses in carpentry, masonry and sewing so that, in future, the waste workers have other skills for earning a living. Now there is a primary health care clinic offering an immunisation programme, and a school for the children.

In 1984 and again in 1986, serious flooding threatened to bring epidemics and widespread pollution to the area as sewage channels and tannery effluent overflowed on to the waste tip. Older students, teachers and health workers teamed up to prevent disaster by disinfecting drinking water, distributing food, encouraging the waste workers to be inoculated and teaching them about oral rehydration therapy to treat diarrhoea. Oxfam has helped the Calcutta Social Project to sink a deep tube well for the health clinic at Dhapa and to build the school.[13]

The waste workers of Calcutta show what is possible with limited resources. Groups like this not only help large cities to run more smoothly, but they bring tangible benefits for their members. It is possible, even for very poor communities, to take on a variety of social and environmental activities which help to meet their basic needs, raise their incomes and improve their social status. While outside support is often important for these groups to start making improvements, they have the capacity to innovate and adapt, finding new ways of solving the immense problems they face. Some groups, like the Zabbaleen in Cairo, develop a whole range of responses as they build on their original waste reclamation work.

The Zabbaleen in Cairo

Originally from upper Egypt, the Zabbaleen (literally: rubbish collectors) are Christians whose predecessors were landless agricultural labourers. They occupy seven sprawling settlements on the outskirts of Cairo and they have been subjected to repeated evictions. The Zabbaleen community lives by the collection of Cairo's wastes which are hauled by donkey cart to be sorted in their settlements. The Zabbaleen earn their living by recycling materials from the waste. Organic materials are fed to pigs which they raise, and tin, plastics and glass are returned to the industrial system via local traders.

The right to collect refuse was formerly the monopoly of the 'wahiyya' – traditional administrators of the system. They received fees from householders and sold the Zabbaleen their licence to collect household refuse. Because of the Zabbaleen, the municipality has not had to establish a waste disposal system. Householders have been

PETER COLERIDGE/OXFAM

The Zabbaleen community earn their living by collecting, sorting and recycling Cairo's domestic and industrial refuse.

satisfied with the low-cost service and the Zabbaleen have sustained their livelihood.

But the influx of poor migrants to Cairo strained the system. Poor households could not pay fees to the wahiyya and the Zabbaleen found the quality and quantity of refuse hardly worth recycling. An alternative plan emerged in 1981, after months of discussion between the municipality and a representative of the Zabbaleen. The Zabbaleen began to collect from the low-income areas and from commercial establishments. They, rather than the wahiyya, collected the fees for the service and transported the wastes – by donkey and by tractor – for recycling. The wastes are now processed at a recycling plant with a capacity of 35 tonnes a day. Oxfam and the Ford Foundation have contributed to the core costs of the scheme.[14]

This was a big step forward for the Zabbaleen as it involved taking over the management of the programme, setting up accounting procedures and a bank account and devising a system for contracting out, and supervising, the collection of wastes from the city.

The success with waste collection has encouraged the Zabbaleen to try other ventures. They started small businesses to add value to the waste products by recycling them. In 1985, with Oxfam support, a small fund was created by the Zabbaleen Association to provide credit for local entrepreneurs to set up workshops for carpentry, repairing vehicles and processing used plastics.[15] But the small business scheme soon revealed its weaknesses. Repayment rates were very low and the beneficiaries were almost all men. The very poor were excluded from the scheme because they could not guarantee the large loans.

In 1988, the small business scheme with its credit programme was expanded to include women. The loan size is now too small to be of interest to any but the very poor, and loans are given to women only after they have formed themselves into a group, whose members act as guarantors for repayment: if one individual defaults, the entire group is disqualified from receiving a subsequent loan. So far the repayment level is high – 98 per cent of loans are recovered. The scheme presently covers 24 groups and more than 70 women. They use the credit to invest in goats and pigs, and to set up handloom weaving and other small businesses. In addition to the practical benefits, women are becoming more self-confident, going out of their homes in groups to make their repayments.

The Zabbaleen enthusiasm and determination is also at work in the field of health and sanitation. The local Association for the Care of Garbage Collectors is trying to change health attitudes and behaviour through providing antenatal care, vaccinations, nutrition advice and the low cost treatment of diarrhoea.

But many problems remain for the Zabbaleen. Poor drainage is one of them, for many of the city's drains are clogged with discarded plastics. Paradoxically, the provision of better drinking water without simultaneous improvements in drainage capacity has added to the problems – for three years the Zabbaleen community has been trying to persuade the city authorities to act. Another problem is the limited space available to the Zabbaleen for all their activities. With no permission to extend their residential borders, their compounds are overcrowded and insanitary – with humans, animals and garbage all competing for space.

WAYS FORWARD

Whether it is in Mexico City, Calcutta or Cairo, community organisations are emerging as major actors in the struggles of poor people to secure shelter, security, basic services and the protection of health and livelihoods in the city. Alone, this approach cannot begin to solve the massive social, economic and environmental crises that Third World cities face. But small-scale, people-based solutions point the way: they are resourceful, affordable and sustainable.

> Raising Southern cities to present Northern levels of consumption and greenhouse gas emissions... is probably impossible and would be a disaster if successful. Northern urban development will require less wasteful resource consumption, less fossil fuel use and less pollution; Southern urban development will require more provision of goods and services, but with less pollution and more efficient resource use.[16]

In most Southern cities, there is neither the investment nor the political will to improve conditions for the poorest people. What funds there are continue to be wasted on Western-style models of urban development that are too expensive and totally inappropriate for Third World cities. Increasingly, it is argued that urban 'environments of poverty' can be improved only by programmes, devised in partnership with local people, which help them to develop their own housing and services, using local materials, local labour and the organisational strength of local communities.[17] What they need urgently from governments is the fundamental support which makes this possible – investment in basic services, secure access to land for building and tougher environmental regulations, which are fully implemented, to limit pollution.

Despite the devastation all around, daily life goes on. A shepherd takes his herd through the ruins of Nacfa, Eritrea. People went on living here, in underground shelters, for years during the war.

8

CONFLICT AND THE ENVIRONMENT

We were attacked at 8 in the evening, when it was dark. There was no time for us to collect our things, we just had to run...Everything was destroyed... they burnt our houses and our crops; all our animals were lost. We ran to save our lives.

Chief Chipawa, an Angolan refugee in Zambia, describing a UNITA attack in November 1985.

Oxfam was established as a response to war and famine 50 years ago during World War Two and has remained closely involved in relief and development work in many war-afflicted countries. The absence of major wars between the leading states of the developed world since the Second World War has coincided with growing numbers of wars and armed conflicts in the South, both within and between states. All but two of the 127 armed conflicts recorded between 1945-89 have been in the South.[1] Although most have been so-called civil wars, many of them have had international involvement.

In the sense of dispute, conflict is universal in human societies. Where channels of dialogue are blocked and basic needs go unmet, growing resentment can erupt into violence: the two sides define their interests in irreconcilable terms and violence is a possible outcome. When one or other side acquires arms, the violence escalates into armed conflict. This may be at a local level, as in Brazil or Bangladesh, where armed conflict has occurred over land rights; but the term is more usually applied where one side to the conflict is government or army.

The Northern image of conventional warfare which includes formal declarations of war, battles and battlefields, and distinctions between soldiers in uniform and civilian populations, does not help in understanding armed conflict in the South. The reality of conflict for so many of Oxfam's Southern partners is an unpredictable continuum of lesser or greater violence, from occasional harassment to mass murder and devastation.

Civilian suffering

The nature of war has been changing; nowadays, far more of the casualties of armed conflict are civilians. Whilst during the Second World War 52 per cent of deaths were of non-combatants, now, according to the International Committee of the Red Cross, more than 90 per cent of those killed are civilians.[2] The total number of war-related deaths since 1945 has been estimated by the UN to be in excess of 20 million.[3] Civilians and their livelihoods have not only been the main victims but often the main targets. Wars have resulted in 17 million refugees around the world and a further 24 million people have been displaced within the borders of their own countries – most of them as a result of conflict.[4]

In 1989, as much as half (£20 million) of Oxfam's total overseas expenditure was related to conflict.[5] A large part of those funds was spent on emergency work in response to the needs of refugees and those internally displaced by wars.[6] In Africa, where the problem has been most severe, 70 per cent of grants are spent on conflict-related work, assisting the civilian casualties. Oxfam is involved in emergency relief in many conflict-ridden African countries, including Ethiopia, Sudan, Angola, Mozambique, Somalia and Liberia. In many countries, conflict has created a semi-permanent emergency and undermined prospects for longer-term development work.

The lives and development efforts of poor people are affected by conflict both directly and indirectly. The most direct effect of war on people's livelihoods is in the terrible destruction of lives, resources and infrastructure by armed conflict, particularly bombing and the laying of mines. Even where military activity is at a fairly low level, people may find it difficult or impossible to maintain their normal way of life. Land mines have inflicted terrible casualties and caused severe economic disruption in many of the countries where Oxfam works, such as Cambodia, Angola, and, more recently, Iraq.

THE REFUGEE CRISIS

Conflict during the 1980s has created a dramatic and unprecedented rise in the numbers of refugees from wars in places as far apart as Afghanistan, Cambodia, Southern Africa, Central America and the Horn of Africa. The UNHCR estimates that in 1991 US$164 million was required to meet the needs of the world's 17 million refugees. When people cross the border into another country, they are classified as refugees and are guaranteed international protection and the support of UNHCR. But the millions of people forced to move from war-zones within their own country receive no such attention. There is no agency mandated to protect or care for people displaced by internal conflicts.[7]

The majority of the world's refugees are women and children, whose husbands, sons, fathers or brothers have been killed or are fighting. Women face special problems as refugees because of their gender. They are very likely to be harassed and their needs are frequently not recognised. Many will not have been accustomed to decision-making roles but they are faced with building new lives for themselves and their families. They are very likely to be ill and distressed as a result of the traumas they have suffered.

In the Horn of Africa, many thousands of people have been forced to flee their homes because of the combined effects of poverty, environmental degradation and war. The Horn accounts for 60 per cent of Africa's refugees – some 2 million people who have been uprooted from their countries. Another 10 million people have been internally displaced within their own countries. During the 1977-78 Ogaden War, an estimated 650,000 refugees fled from their homes in war-torn Ethiopia into Somalia, putting unprecedented pressures on an already fragile environment and economy. Ten years later, the flow of people was reversed when, according to UNHCR sources, 440,000 Somalis fled into Ethiopia to escape fighting in the north of their country in mid-1988. There were also massive movements of people into and out of Sudan. By the mid-1980s nearly half a million people were estimated to have migrated into Sudan from Ethiopia and Eritrea as a result of the combined effects of war and famine.[8] In 1987, the civil war being waged in the south of Sudan caused 350,000 people to move into western Ethiopia.

Malawi is home to many thousands of refugees from neighbouring Mozambique, and its economy is under strain as a result. This is a woodlot at Dedze, for building materials and fuel for nearby refugee camps. Refugees can place great demands on environmental resources in the countries where they find sanctuary.

In addition to the misery of the people involved, migration can lead to neglect of the land and loss of agricultural production and can cause immense problems in the places where the refugees make their new homes. Massive movement of people has a ripple effect as competition for resources between newcomers and local people leads to further tensions and increased environmental degradation – and potentially more conflict.

Malawi, for example, already one of the poorest and most densely populated countries in Africa, is having to accommodate large numbers of refugees fleeing from the civil war in neighbouring Mozambique, where there has been almost continuous war since 1960. From a trickle of refugees in 1970, the numbers have increased dramatically. In 1986, 70,000 people crossed to Malawi in one month when the Mozambique National Resistance (MNR) launched an attack to try to split the country in two. There are now 980,000 refugees living in Malawi, more than one-tenth of the population, to whom Malawians must give up land and with whom they must share their country's meagre resources. There is increasing pressure on Malawi's health services and water supplies. Environmental damage is on the increase as more and more trees are cut down for firewood and building.

ARMS DIVERSION

In addition to the poverty and suffering caused by the direct impact of armed conflict, the diversion of scarce resources into military expenditure has crippling indirect effects on development prospects. It is estimated that during Colonel Mengistu Haile Mariam's fourteen-year long regime in Ethiopia, 65 per cent of its national budget was spent on

JOHN CAMPBELL/OXFAM

Military parade, Addis Ababa, Ethiopia, to celebrate the 13th anniversary of the Mengistu regime, in 1987.

'internal security',[9] diverting desperately needed resources away from development towards the military. Government expenditure on health and education combined is dwarfed by military spending in a number of countries, as illustrated in figure 8.1. Services such as agricultural extension are often abandoned, partly because of the danger involved in carrying them out, and also the need to pay for military hardware and activities.

FIGURE 8.1

Total amount spent on arms, health and education in Ethiopia, Sudan and Somalia in 1987.

	Arms millions	Health millions	Education millions
Ethiopia	$472 * (9 per cent of GNP)	$67 (1.3 per cent of GNP)	$225 (4.2 per centof GNP)
Sudan	$800 (6 per cent of GNP)	$27 (0.2 per cent of GNP)	$563 (4.2 per cent of GNP)
Somalia	$23 (2.4 per cent of GNP)	$2 (0.2 per cent of GNP)	$6 (0.6 per cent of GNP)

Source: *World Military and Social Expenditures, 1991*, Sivard[10]

* Note: Given the end of the civil war and demobilisation of the old army, there is a likelihood that this figure will go down.

The effect of the diversion of resources to military spending has been well documented. Total global spending for military purposes amounted to US$980 billion in 1990, or US$185 for every person on earth. The international trade in conventional arms is a profitable and thriving business. During the past 20 years arms with an estimated total value of US$588 billion were traded. The USSR and America alone account for 65 per cent of this total, with France, Britain, West Germany and China also acting as major suppliers. Developing countries are the biggest market for these arms. In any country, military expenditure is a drain on resources that could be used more productively, but it is particularly serious in developing countries. Many Third World governments spend twice as much on the military as on health or education and a few – Angola, Iran and Pakistan, for example, spend twice as much as on both combined.[11] In 1988 African countries imported $4.9 billion worth of arms amounting to roughly 10 per cent of the world's arms imports.[12] Clearly, even a fraction of these vast resources used constructively for appropriate kinds of development work would have made a difference to the lives of poor people.

POVERTY AND CONFLICT

Poverty and conflict are often closely linked. In most developing countries there are huge disparities in access to power and control over resources. Existing social, political and economic structures reinforce the dominance of privileged elites and the powerlessness of poor and marginalised sectors of society. This unfair distribution of wealth, power and land is a recipe for conflict. Those with power battle with disadvantaged groups to hold on to their advantages. For example, settled farmers are often in conflict with pastoralists, urban with rural populations, one ethnic group with another, black with white, peasants with landowners.

El Salvador

During the 1980s, much of Oxfam's work in Central America was a response to poverty and suffering exacerbated by armed conflict. As in the case of El Salvador, the roots of this conflict lay in the unequal distribution of power and resources.[13]

El Salvador is the smallest Central American republic, a mountainous country about the size of Wales. The population density is high – seven times higher than neighbouring Honduras – and almost all of the people derive their livelihood from the land. In the 1930s, coffee was the basis of the country's economy, producing over 95 per cent of export earnings, financing some infrastructural development and providing extensive seasonal employment. The eastern provinces of Morazán, La Unión, San Miguel and Usulafter cover nearly one-third of the country and used to be vital to El Salvador's coffee production. These agricultural activities were virtually the only sources of employment in the region.

The expansion of cash crops in the eastern provinces resulted in the decline of subsistence crops of maize and beans which destroyed the means of survival of peasants farmers. Environmental problems associated with monocropping for export were common, such as overuse of pesticides leading to health problems and contamination of soil and water supplies. Most of the wealth created fell into only a few hands. The country was said to be run by a national oligarchy of the 14 families most closely involved with the export of agricultural products. Those same families played a key role in government and the military establishment. Military governments had been in existence almost continuously since 1932 following an uprising of landless peasants which had been savagely suppressed.

When the economy began to decline in the 1970s, the inequities upon which it was based became very striking. Employment opportunities plummeted and by 1975, 40 per cent of the rural population nationwide was landless and jobless. Much destruction of pine and tropical deciduous forests had taken place in the lowlands when the large plantations were established. With the collapse of employment opportunities, peasant farmers were forced to move into marginal lands to try to make a living. Many people moved higher up the mountain slopes, where they produced two harvests of maize or sorghum a year on land that was unsuited to cereal production. The serious erosion which followed years of intensive cropping is probably irreversible.

Increasingly, throughout the 1970s, poor people throughout the country became involved in organisations to press for fairer access to the country's resources. Efforts to bring about political and economic change through electoral means were met with brutal repression. As many landowners demonstrated their unwillingness to consider structural change and prepared to use violent means to defend their interests, more and more people became convinced of the need to resort to arms. Unequal access to power and land meant a diminishing resource base for those dependent on land for their survival. This inequality in access to power and land was the underlying cause of the full-scale civil war in El Salvador that was raging by 1979.

Guerrillas in El Salvador.

Environmental destruction as a tool of war

In addition to the untold suffering caused by war, the environmental consequences of armed conflict can be severe. Environmental degradation was a feature of the countryside before the civil war in El

Salvador but, according to one aid worker in the area: 'the wholesale destruction of the environment became a "military objective"'. The strategy adopted by the armed forces involved indiscriminate bombing of the rural areas in which the guerrilla organisations were assumed to have their social and logistical base. According to the human rights organisation Americas Watch, in the early 1980s the north and east of the country became known as 'free fire' zones in which bombing was 'a systematic and, apparently ... deliberate, practice'. A Salvadorean peasant from Morazán described it at the time like this:

> The whole area is subject to bombing, strafing, rocketing and machine-gunning from the air, by the military. At worst, this results in deaths and injuries within the civilian population. At best, it prevents people from working in their fields. The military system- atically burn large tracts of brush and trees each year to reduce undergrowth for the [guerrilla fighters] to hide from air attacks. This burning has resulted in destroying 75 per cent of the water table in the area – and is gradually going to convert it into desert.

Attempts by the inhabitants to preserve or repair their environment have all too often been thwarted. Hills which were reforested after being denuded in armed conflict in 1981, are now almost totally bare again due to aerial bombing.[14] Rocketing and strafing caused a fire which destroyed all the pine trees in a community wood planted only ten months earlier.

Massive migration resulted from the civil war: about one million people were killed or forced to leave their homes, almost one-fifth of the population of El Salvador. Some fled to urban areas within the country, whilst others made the hazardous journey to the United States via Mexico. Many thousands fled over the border into Honduras and about 8,000 of them formed refugee camps at Colomoncagua. They came from north Morazán, and were mainly women, children and elderly men. The establishment of the camps was a difficult task because of the physical conditions and the unfriendliness of the host government and military authorities. The camps were enclosed and social interchange between the refugees and the local Honduran population was prohibited. For people who were accustomed to living off the land and being self-reliant in respect of most staples, this new life of dependency was an alien one.

The Gulf War

Destruction of enemy infrastructure and key resources has long been a strategy in war. The devastating environmental consequences of modern warfare were clearly illustrated by the 1991 Gulf war. Kuwait and Southern Iraq and Iran were severely affected by smoke from burning oil following the firing of oil wells by the retreating Iraqi army. Some scientists claim that, at a high estimate, three million barrels of oil a day were burned from more than 600 wells for nearly ten months. 'Black rain' containing dust and hydrocarbon particles and 'oil rain' have fallen on Kuwait, Iraq and Iran. Up to one-third of Iran is said to have suffered from black rain at one time or another since the end of the war. This could have serious effects on Iran's main agricultural area, between Bandar Khomeyn in the north and Bandar Busherer on the coast.

The social and environmental effects of the Gulf War on Iraq's agriculture and water supplies have been devastating. The breakdown of electric power supplies following Allied bombing has created a cycle of contamination. More than 90 per cent of the sewage treatment plants in the country are out of action which means massive amounts of untreated domestic and industrial sewage are pumped into the rivers. A Harvard Study Team which visited Iraq in 1991 reported that:

> In all of the seven southern governorates surveyed, the onset of unsanitary conditions and the increase in water-borne diseases followed the loss of electric power in the first days of the war.[15]

Agricultural production has been sharply reduced as a result of the breakdown of the electrically-powered network of irrigation pumps. The Harvard Team estimates that the irrigation network is currently operating at 40-50 per cent of pre-war capacity. In addition, there is an acute shortage of fertiliser and seeds because the main fertiliser plant at Al Qaim was destroyed during the war. Before the war, Iraq produced 30 per cent of its food needs. Today it produces 10-15 per cent.[16]

In May 1991, Oxfam began an emergency relief programme in Iraq, working through local authorities in the south by providing spare parts and pumping equipment for water and sewage treatment and cooperating with UNICEF to re-establish primary health care. In the north-east of Iraq, Oxfam is working in cooperation with UNHCR to provide shelter, water supplies and sanitation to Kurds in the Sulaimaniya region.[17]

The wider impact of the Gulf War
The repercussions of conflict in causing suffering, threatening livelihoods and disrupting economic development can extend far from the war-zone. A report commissioned by Oxfam and five other development agencies identified 40 developing countries which had experienced costs greater than 1 per cent of GNP as a result of the Gulf War.[18] The total cost to these 40 countries is estimated at US$12 billion. Worst affected are Jordan (32 per cent of GNP), Yemen (10 per cent of GNP), and Sri Lanka (4 per cent of GNP). The list includes most of the

poorest countries in all regions and four African countries – Ethiopia, Sudan, Mozambique and Liberia – where millions of people were at the time facing starvation as a result of drought and war.

Increases in oil prices, loss of remittances from workers in the Gulf, loss of export markets, and withdrawal of aid are some of the ways that countries have been affected economically. The increase in oil prices during the Gulf War adversely affected all oil-importing countries, resulting in further stress for fragile economies struggling to meet their foreign exchange needs. In Zambia, for instance, costs of fuel for transportation increased dramatically as a result of the Gulf War.[19] Many thousands of workers, mainly from India, Bangladesh, Sri Lanka, and Middle East states such as Yemen and Egypt, were forced to leave their jobs in Kuwait and Iraq, thereby cutting off a valuable source of income to their families, and accentuating poverty at home.

ENVIRONMENT AND CONFLICT

The Gulf War illustrates both the far-reaching human suffering and the environmental devastation that result from war. Environmental degradation can also be a factor generating conflict as pressure on a shrinking natural resource base leads to competition for control of resources. A vicious circle of environmental degradation and conflict can develop, where inequitable distribution of natural resources leads to environmental degradation, which exacerbates conflict over shrinking resources. Further environmental damage takes place as a result of the conflict, with disruption of agriculture or destruction of forest cover. The resource base is further diminished and insecurity increases so that any peace achieved is only tenuous, with a strong potential for future conflict.

Together with poverty and drought, conflict is one of the key factors in a complex syndrome that has pushed many countries, in Africa especially, towards food insecurity and political disintegration. All the indications are that conflict will remain a continuing problem on the continent. The consequence of this cycle is that lives are shattered and long-term development made difficult or impossible.

The Horn of Africa

The interrelated causes and effects of poverty, conflict and environmental degradation are well illustrated in the Horn of Africa, an area in which Oxfam has had substantial involvement over a long period. The countries of the Horn – Ethiopia, Somalia, Djibouti and Sudan – are amongst the world's poorest. It is an area where African and Arab cultures, Christianity and Islam, pastoralism and sedentary farming meet. Underdevelopment, environmental degradation and drought, coupled with the effects of war, have contributed to devastating famines. Over the past 20 years these have claimed the lives of millions of people and displaced many millions more.

Throughout the Horn of Africa, traditional methods of coping, such as mutual food lending and seed banks, are eroded as the margin of survival of rural civilians is squeezed. An Oxfam report concluded that the variety of ways in which people survive has proved to be more important than the provision of food relief, in withstanding famine.[20] When war disrupts 'coping strategies', destitution and starvation for the poorest people can easily follow. All the famines in the Horn of Africa which have witnessed extremely high casualties, have been conflict-related, whereas starvation is rare or unknown in famines where conflict is not a feature.[21]

Hunger and malnutrition are recurrent problems in this region. In 1991 the UN estimated that 6 million people in Ethiopia, and 7.7 million in Sudan were at risk from starvation.[22] Since 1955, wars in the region have caused 5 million civilian deaths and as many people again have been severely disabled. A report of the United Nations Environment Programme in 1989 comments:

> While the causes of political conflict in this region are complex and multifaceted, deteriorating environmental conditions clearly contribute to instability. Environmental degradation has heightened political tensions, aggravated existing conflict and in some cases been a catalyst for hostilities.[23]

Longer-term management of the region's scarce and fragile natural resources in the interests of all its people cannot be successful unless there is an end to conflict. Rangelands and water are essential resources right across the region and demand cooperation across national boundaries for proper management. The Ethiopian highlands are the source of nearly all the water used to irrigate commercial crops in Sudan and Somalia. Ethiopia has made little use of irrigation so far but there is now a possibility of dams being built on the Ethiopian headwaters of the Blue Nile and the Shebelle, which could create more tension with countries downstream. Rangelands for pastoralists often span national boundaries. Catering for their needs will require regional cooperation if their livelihoods are to be sustained and they are not to join the ranks of refugees already uprooted by conflict and worsening environmental conditions.

Ethiopia
The World Bank classifies Ethiopia as being the world's second poorest nation with a GNP of only $120 per head in 1989.[24] Eighty per cent of its population are dependent on agriculture for their survival. Between 1970-80 real average annual GDP growth is estimated to have been only

0.6 per cent, and the trend during the 1980s was downwards. In 1990, Ethiopia's debt service ratio was 36 per cent.[25] Ethiopia earns most of its foreign exchange from export of one primary commodity – coffee. It was affected by falling prices between 1979 and 1982, in 1987, and again in 1989 with the collapse of the International Coffee Organisation's (ICO) quota system.

Famine in the Ethiopian highlands helped to trigger the 1974 revolution which overthrew Emperor Haile Selassie. That famine, like the more recent famines in the region, had its roots in socio-economic conditions and government policies as well as environmental degradation. Traditionally the highlands of Ethiopia were the main farming areas of the country. Owing to the combination of drought, deforestation, poor agricultural practices and population pressure, the fertility of the land had deteriorated markedly by the early 1970s. Ethiopia has been largely deforested; in 1900, 40 per cent of the country was covered with forest but today this is down to only 4 per cent. An estimated 77 million hectares of land has suffered serious erosion, and 1 billion tonnes of topsoil are reckoned to be lost each year. Protests against corruption, inflation, unemployment, food shortages and indifference to the famine in Wollo Province escalated into the 1974 revolution.

Falling agricultural production resulting from drought, soil erosion, and other problems, had gradually driven farmers out of the highlands into marginal areas not suitable for intensive agriculture. A slow movement of people out of Wollo and Tigray provinces developed towards the west and south. After the famine of 1984-5, the post-revolutionary Mengistu government decided that in order to speed-up migration, people should be forcibly moved and resettled. The plan was deeply unpopular, as was the 'villagisation' programme which forced people to leave their homesteads and to live in concentrated settlements. Their crops were bought by the government at very low prices, providing little incentive to raise yields. A former Oxfam country representative reported that the resettlement programme was detrimental in that it displaced indigenous farmers, accelerated environmental degradation and impoverished the settlers both culturally and materially.[26] The unpopularity of the resettlement programme fuelled the conflict between the people and the government which eventually contributed to the overthrow of the Mengistu Government.

Up until 1991, fighting had gone on for 30 years between the government of Ethiopia and the Eritrean People's Liberation Front (EPLF), who were fighting for an independent Eritrean state, and since 1975 between the government and the Tigray People's Liberation Front (TPLF). Fighting in some of the most drought-prone areas of the country has aggravated poverty by undermining rehabilitation programmes and

Tigrayan soldiers, with weapons captured from the Ethiopian government troops against whom they were fighting.

efforts to prevent famine. Relief work has been essential, including the 'cross-border' transport of food into Eritrea and Tigray with large international donors channelling food through non-governmental organisations, including Oxfam.

Oxfam's work in Ethiopia has consisted of a combination of relief and development work at community level aimed at helping communities meet their basic needs, strengthen their coping mechanisms and withstand periods of stress by rehabilitating the degraded environment. For example, in Eritrea, Oxfam contributed to a three-year programme which involved 75,000 families.[27] Each family received seeds and tools and 15,000 families were given either oxen or camels for ploughing. Another 5,000 pastoral families were helped to restock their herds. Community activities were part of the programme too, with village water supplies and irrigation schemes in some areas. An initial reafforestation project involved the planting of 95 acres and the repair of nearly 3,000 acres of terracing. Oxfam hopes to support the local Eritrean relief and development agency, ERA, in its efforts to establish 500 small agricultural workshops. They aim to produce and repair tools, which will make village communities more self-sufficient.[28]

Sudan

In South Sudan, Oxfam is concentrating its efforts on the less insecure west bank of the Nile and is currently funding many development projects which assist war-displaced people to return to the countryside and begin to farm again.

Oxfam field staff report that since the war, people are showing a renewed interest in traditional agricultural technologies such as the use of oxen for ploughing and traction, and local seed varieties. Integrated agricultural systems were very much part of the southern Sudanese economy. The Sudan Relief and Rehabilitation Association (SRRA), have set up local seed banks and employed local farmers to grow out the seed and multiply stocks.[29] The aim is to produce 160 tons of local varieties of maize, sorghum and groundnuts which will be distributed mainly to women's groups and cooperatives. Seed can thus be bought locally for a fraction of the cost of buying outside the area. The SRRA is also promoting systems which incorporate piggeries, chicken hatcheries, fishponds and intercropping. Sim-sim and sorghum, for example, are being planted together. Lack of foreign exchange has encouraged the use of non-chemical means of pest control; an effective insecticide can be made by boiling up tobacco leaves. Provision of basic tools, often using scrap metal from derelict trucks, is important, and traditional trading routes are once again being used for exchange of cattle for grain. The almost total absence of transport infrastructure means that people are travelling by foot and bicycle, often over huge distances, to barter their goods. People are increasingly concerned about excessive cutting of timber, mostly for construction purposes. Agroforestry projects have been started, including tree-nurseries.

But the continuing armed conflict seriously hampers this type of work by making it impossible to plan more than six months ahead. Environmental rehabilitation upon which people's livelihoods are based is essentially a medium- to long-term activity which is made very difficult in conditions of such instability.

Surviving and rebuilding

Oxfam experience with refugees who had fled from the war in El Salvador and were living in camps in Honduras, illustrates how important community-led organisation can be in helping people rebuild their lives.

UNHCR provision of shelter, food and health services to over 8,000 people concentrated in one of the camps at Colomoncagua, a remote settlement a day's drive from any sizeable town, was a daunting task. The refugees were determined not to become passive recipients of aid programmes designed and delivered by outside agencies. It was assumed that their return home – their eventual goal – could be later rather than sooner and a long-term approach was adopted. They quickly formed teams and elected coordinators to identify ways to ensure that their needs for food, shelter, health care, education and social organisation, were met. Community development was central to survival.

Training and production workshops were set up as an important first step, with part-funding from Oxfam. In this way, the refugees could build on existing strengths and also develop new skills. The workshops were initially in practical skills such as carpentry, tin-smithing, pottery, tailoring, shoe-making and weaving. On the insistence of the refugees, workshops expanded to include literacy and community health care, with teachers increasingly being drawn from amongst their own numbers. With the support of aid agencies, the refugees became increasingly ambitious in their aspirations. Training was given in administrative skills, and a semi-industrial approach to workshop management was developed, employing new machinery and thereby developing skills in maintenance, repair and recycling of equipment. This culminated in the inauguration of a technical school in 1986. With women forming the majority of adults in the camp, the traditional sexual division of labour was overridden, and vehicle maintenance, for example, was often carried out by women.

With material and educational assistance, the refugees of Colomoncagua had successfully built what amounted to a sizeable, almost self-contained town. Public health infrastructure included chlorinated water systems, latrines, showers and laundries; an irrigation system and terracing meant that in spite of restricted space, the camp was self-sufficient in vegetables. Collective kitchens were used as a way of saving fuel; and fishponds and small animal husbandry were organised collectively, to maximise productivity.

Colomoncagua was one side of the story; meanwhile, in northern Morazán from which the refugees had fled, those left behind also managed to achieve a degree of development in spite of the armed conflict around them. Together with some of the people who began filtering back into the area from about 1985 onwards, they formed community development councils to try to secure basic rights and needs. These in turn joined together to form a region-wide association, Patrimony for the Development of Communities of Morazán and San Miguel (PADECOMSM). Refused credit from official sources because they lived in a war zone, PADECOMSM began to administer a revolving loan fund, with money provided by development agencies.[30] Through this, small amounts of credit were provided for the production of basic grains. Between 1984 and 1987, there were serious droughts which brought many other communities to the brink of disaster. Peasant communities that had benefited from the PADECOMSM revolving loan fund, were better able to withstand the pressures.

Return to El Salvador

The refugees looked upon themselves as part of PADECOMSM, so when they were able to return from Colomoncagua to Morazán there was close and positive cooperation between them and the PADECOMSM membership. As part of a much larger re-population process, the returning refugees were settled in a newly created town which they named 'Segundo Montes', in memory of one of six Jesuit priests assassinated in 1989. Cooperation was crucial to the success of the plan, which involved integrating over 8,000 people, with a recently acquired high level of technical skills, with communities who were in much the same material conditions as they themselves had been when they had left some nine years earlier. The returning refugees were essentially dependent for food on what the PADECOMSM members could produce. Given the problems of subsistence farmers in meeting even their own needs, the scope for friction was enormous. The potential for ecological disaster was even greater as the land which had been abandoned for so long was to be intensively, 're-colonised'. Recognising the importance of human development to achieving more sustainable development, the refugees were eager to share their newly acquired skills. Largely as a result of the high degree of social organisation and PADECOMSM's credit project, food production was greatly increased. Several farmers said they had doubled their output, and sufficient extra food was produced to feed the returning refugees as well.

In spite of having operated under enormous constraints, the returned refugees and PADECOMSM members have together managed to avert disaster in their area by creating a positive cycle of self-help and co-operation to counter the effects of environmental degradation and conflict. The biggest single constraint on the regeneration of the environment was the war.

The Government was initially hostile to the repatriation and the armed forces insisted that permits had to be obtained for supplies. Access to essentials such as building materials, tools and fertiliser was severely restricted and repression continued. Yet, despite attempts to undermine the efforts of the community to build new livelihoods for themselves, Segundo Montes has survived and prospered.[31] The signing of a peace agreement in January 1992 at last brought the prospect of an end to the civil war in El Salvador.

CONFLICT IN A CHANGING WORLD

The late 1980s and early 1990s have seen global political and economic changes happening at breath-taking pace. In Latin America, military dictatorships have been replaced by elected governments and in Africa moves towards multi-party democracy are gathering pace. This is not to suggest that the lives of millions of poor people have materially improved, or that armed conflict has lessened.

The end of the cold war and moves towards the resolution of proxy East/West armed conflicts in the South should offer real opportunities to take advantage of the peace dividend to promote sustainable development. However, as the Worldwatch report, *State of the World 1992* states, 'At roughly US$980 billion in 1990... global military spending is way out of line with the diminishing magnitude of military threats. Efforts to ward off far more pervasive environmental and social hazards, meanwhile are grossly underfunded.'[32]

At the same time the likelihood of new armed conflicts is very real. The political and economic collapse of the former Soviet Union (the Commonwealth of Independent States) and other former communist states and the disintegration of the nation state in many parts of Africa have resulted in a resurgence of ethnically-based movements and brought previously suppressed religious and ethnic tensions back to the surface. Fragile new democracies, particularly in Africa and Eastern Europe, will be unable to meet popular economic expectations at a time of acute economic crisis. To reduce tensions and conflict in the South, the North needs to show political will to create the conditions for equitable and sustainable development.

> Just as a new set of relationships is taking shape between East and West, one that dismantles mutual threats and creates a climate of economic cooperation, so is there a need for a new partnership between wealthier countries... and the developing world... that embraces the common goals of restoring the planet's health and promoting sustainable progress.[33]

Conflicts will not be resolved without a wider notion of security which includes not only the absence of wars, but recognition that action to reduce poverty and injustice and tackle environmental problems are essential to global security.

A more dynamic role for the United Nations is also key to resolving conflict. A revitalised UN system would have a crucial role in conflict mediation, curbing the arms trade, protecting human rights and responding to humanitarian need. The UN also has a crucial role to play in the realisation of North–South agreements on global environmental issues and greater equity in international economic relations.

The enabling context for sustainable development must operate also at the national level. Popular pressure for political and social change in the South is leading to calls for democratic participation, equity, good governance and respect for human rights.

9

THE POPULATION QUESTION

When we talk of emancipation, we are not saying that we should be emancipated from childbirth and motherhood. What we are saying is that we should be given the right to choose when to start motherhood and how many children we want to have.

Miriam Tabingwa, a founder-member of Action for Development (ACFODE) in Uganda.

In recent years, high population growth rates have been a feature of many countries in the South. At the same time, environmental degradation is also occurring at an unprecedented rate in many of these countries. It is tempting to see the rapid increase in numbers of people in the world as a major cause of environmental degradation. However, the relationship between environmental degradation and population increase is highly complex and not fully understood. It is certainly not possible to make a simple, direct link between the two; there are too many other factors at work. The link is increasingly the subject of research and debate.

From an Oxfam perspective, the debate must include consideration of poverty and inequitable access to resources both within countries and between North and South. We need to look behind the global statistics and consider the different situations in different countries. If we are to understand the causes of rapid population growth, we must also consider the social, cultural and economic pressures on individuals and the choices open to them, which together influence the number of children they have. For it is the life choices of individuals and family groups which together go to make up the raw data of the statistical information.

Patterns of population growth
The global population reached 5.4 billion in 1991. On the latest UN estimates, this will rise to 6.2 billion by the turn of the century, and to

11.5 billion before there is stabilisation.[2] Overall, population growth rates are slowing down – from 2.1 per cent in the late 1960s to 1.8 per cent in 1992 – but the global statistics conceal wide variations between North and South and between different regions of the South.[3] Over the next ten years, growth rates of 0.5 per cent are expected in the industrialised North, with 2 per cent growth in the South. Rates in Latin America and Asia are slowing down but in sub-Saharan Africa, which has most of the poorest countries, rates are still increasing, although in some countries the spread of AIDS may have an effect.[4] It is difficult to predict to what extent AIDS might reduce population growth rates, but because the death-rate from AIDS is highest among children and young adults, it could have a serious effect on future development in certain countries.

More important than growth rates are the actual numbers of people added each year and the amount of resources they consume. Every year, there are 93 million more people, perhaps 98 million by the end of the decade. Whatever reduction takes place in growth rates, the world's population will be nearly half as large again by 2025, because the parents of the future generation have already been born.

Resource depletion

The population statistics are a cause for concern in terms of the capacity of Southern economies to support fast-growing populations against a background of highly inequitable distribution of resources and access to technology. But to equate sheer numbers with resource depletion and environmental damage is to miss a highly significant point. Even though the total population of the industrialised countries is much lower than that of the developing countries, it is clear that the former generate significantly more damage per person to the global environment than do people in the developing countries.

Commercial energy consumption is a useful measure of environmental impact per person. Four-fifths of the world's commercial energy is used by a quarter of its population living in 42 countries; one fifth of the world's energy is used by three-quarters of the population living in 128 countries. An average person in a 'high consumption' country uses 18 times more energy than a person in a 'low consumption' country. Moreover, although the high consumption countries' populations are stable or declining, consumption levels continue to rise.[5] Examples from Bangladesh and the United States of America further illustrate the disparities. The population of Bangladesh is set to expand in 1992 by 2.9 million people (growth rate 2.5 per cent) and that of the US by 2 million (growth rate 0.8 per cent). But each Bangladeshi consumes energy equivalent to 3 barrels of oil per year and each US citizen 55 barrels. The total impact of the Bangladeshi increase will be 8.7

million barrels, that of the US will be 110 million. In terms of the consumption of a non-renewable natural resource and the pollution which that consumption generates, the US bears a huge responsibility for global environmental degradation even though its population growth rate is only 0.8 per cent.[6]

The impact of the population of the rich countries with high levels of energy consumption is directly related to global warming and the depletion of the ozone layer – environmental problems which will affect North and South alike. The environmental impact of people in the South is largely related to depletion of natural resources such as forests and soil. These problems are widespread but mainly localised in their effects and are most serious for the day-to-day lives of the poorest people. But it is not just poor people, forced to over-use scarce resources, who are responsible for environmental degradation in the South. For example, in the case of the destruction of the Brazilian rainforest, it is the activities of rich land speculators, as well as small-scale farmers, which have caused deforestation.

A view from the South

People in the South can find the Northern preoccupation with the 'population problem' highly offensive. They see this anxiety as based on a concern for the preservation of power and a lifestyle of extravagant consumption, rather than a genuine worry about the future carrying capacity of the planet. Only when the North shows some sign of being prepared to reduce its consumption of scarce global resources and to tackle inequities in the world economic system will people in the South believe that concern over population increase is anything other than selfish.

While many people in the South would not deny that rapid increase in population presents a major problem for some countries – though not all – they believe that one of the main causal factors for rapid population growth is poverty – and until poverty and inequality are addressed, nationally and internationally, population growth is unlikely to slow down.

POVERTY AND POPULATION GROWTH

The countries with the poorest people are in general those with the highest rates of population growth. These are the people who are landless or are trying to survive in marginal areas of low agricultural potential or in the squatter settlements of the urban fringes. Poverty, high population growth rates and the low status of women are all interconnected and are symptomatic of fundamental inequalities in people's access to power and resources. Yet it is too simplistic to say that increasing population pressure leads inevitably to environmental degradation.

Increasing population is only one of a number of complex, interacting social, economic, political and ecological factors which contribute to environmental degradation. It is neither the most direct nor the main cause, let alone the only cause, of environmental degradation.[7] In some countries, it is not a major concern. Yet in other countries, such as Rwanda and Pakistan, the effects of rapidly increasing populations are clearly a problem, for different reasons.

The case of Rwanda

About the size of Wales, with a population of 7.5 million growing at 3.5 per cent each year, Rwanda is already more densely populated than any other African country.[8] At this rate of increase there will be 10 million Rwandans by the end of the century and double that by 2025. Ninety per cent of Rwanda's population depends on agriculture. A third of the population are extremely poor with hardly any land.[9]

Serious efforts to reduce soil erosion have been made but in general, fallow periods are shorter, and soil fertility is declining. Farm holding sizes have been reduced to an average of less than half a hectare per family and are often very fragmented. More than half the cultivated soils are on slopes of 10 per cent gradient or more. Many of the steepest slopes used to be tree covered and the soils that are exposed when trees are felled are acid and fragile. Within a few years of being cleared, the soil and nutrients that were held in place by the forestry cover are washed away by increased surface runoff. Recent figures show the nutritional value of food produced per person to be falling steadily since 1984 and the population steadily rising.[10] For poor families who lack access to sufficient land to make ends meet, migration offers a possible solution.

> Christine and Emmanuel are in their mid-sixties and live in south-west Rwanda. They have six children. One single girl, the widow and three children of one of the sons, another son and his wife and three children, and one disabled son, all still live at home – seven adults and six children in all. Their plot is very small, about one-tenth of a hectare, but they also farm another small plot belonging to their son, Joseph, and they look after a friend's pig and piglets, which provide manure. They grow beans, sweet potatoes and soya, with some coffee and bananas (to make beer) as cash crops. In 1989, their crops failed because of drought and they were forced to rely on food aid and eating the bitter bananas which would have been used to make beer for cash. Christine believes that the famine had been coming for some time, and she had noticed climatic changes and a decline in soil fertility. In 1990, with better rains and

the produce from Joseph's land, things might have improved; but the price of coffee fell and the prices of necessities increased, owing to the war and devaluation.

Joseph, their second son, decided to leave the area and look for land elsewhere. He walked 140 kms. to Bugesera, in another part of the country, in search of land. Most of the land was already taken, many people were looking and there was resistance to strangers moving in. An arrangement he made with a local farmer to buy a small piece of land came to nothing and he had to start looking again. He found a very small plot which he could use for one season only with no guarantee for the future. They survived the period until the harvest with the help of the landowner. Then Joseph went east to Tanzania to look for land. But Tanzania had just decided to repatriate all Rwandans so Joseph hurried back to try again to find better land before all the others arrived back. He managed to renew his arrangement with the first farmer but it was not recognised by the authorities. When people arrived back from Tanzania, there was nothing for them to come back to. Many went to the local parish in search of food aid and others turned round and went straight back to Tanzania.

Migration is important both on an informal basis and in a more organised way with government support. But environmental and economic trade-offs are involved where internal migration is organised at the national level. People from land shortage areas have moved to the areas around the Volcanoes National Park and other previously forested areas, to valley bottoms previously used for grazing, and to more marginal areas such as Bugesera, the area to which Joseph migrated. By 1990, no more land was available in these areas. Some suggest that the Nyabiringo Valley which runs for 150 kms. through the country should be used but it serves as a reservoir for the headwaters of the Nile. Others suggest using the Nyungwe Forest and the Akagera National Park but both are regarded as important ecological conservation areas and would not support intensive agriculture.

Many thousands of people have migrated into the surrounding countries of Uganda, Burundi, Zaire and Tanzania in search of land, work, and safety from political harassment. But surrounding countries may be reluctant to allow this to continue. In a survey carried out in 1984 on the effects of migration,[11] it was found that poverty, measured by food consumption per head, was most severe not amongst the 20 per cent with least land but amongst the next 20 per cent with more land. This was because some members of the families with least land had been forced to migrate in order that those remaining could survive. Food security then improved for those remaining. Those with a bit more land struggled to survive on it and suffered progressively as years went by.

In common with many developing countries, there are very strong economic, social and cultural pressures towards high fertility in Rwanda and people tend to have several children. In an effort to tackle what was seen from the outside as a population problem, the National Office of Population Activities (ONAPO) was created in 1981 with funding from USAID. Its objective was to balance population growth and available resources. Unfortunately ONAPO activities were not integrated with other aspects of primary health care and were not a government priority. This made ONAPO ineffective. After seven years, only 4 per cent of women were using contraceptives and many more had become prejudiced against them because of side effects which went unexplained and were not dealt with. Much greater medical supervision was needed than was available. ONAPO activities were re-launched in 1989 and there has been a marked increase in contraceptive use, up to 12 per cent in 1992. The reasons for this increase are presumed to lie in the cumulative effect of several factors, including community education activities, the 1989 famine, the modification of the position of the Catholic Church, and the integration of family planning and health services.

At present rates of population growth, Rwanda will have to accommodate 3 million more people by the end of the century. The key issue is not so much whether or not Rwanda could eventually support a larger population, but whether it can do so fast enough to keep up with the rate of population increase.[12] In a country completely dependent on agriculture, which is pushing at the limits of available agricultural land, the question is what development strategy could be devised to absorb a further 3 million people in such a short space of time. Further agricultural intensification and land redistribution could offer some possibilities since 16 per cent of the population owns 40 per cent of the land. But experience of land reform elsewhere (as shown in Chapter 5) does not give cause for optimism, and migration offers limited possibilities.

Oxfam field staff working in Rwanda have become increasingly aware that, despite resources having been relatively well managed, the problems facing the country are extremely serious. Pressure of a rapidly rising population is probably already an important factor in food shortages, conflict and environmental degradation – and ways ahead towards solutions are far from clear.

The case of Pakistan

Pakistan is another country where, at a national level, there are significant environmental and development problems. They have been described in detail in the National Conservation Strategy (NCS), a comprehensive report presented to the government in May 1990. National Conservation Strategies were prepared in many countries as part of the follow-up to the World Conservation Strategy published in 1980.[13]

The birth rate in Pakistan has changed very little in the past 40 years but the death rate has fallen substantially, resulting in a population growth rate of 3 per cent, one of the highest in the world. The population has increased from 31 million in 1947 to 123 million in 1990 and is projected to rise to 162 million by the end of the century.[14]

These large increases in population have been accommodated by three major agricultural advances which occurred in the 1960s: increased water from the Indus river for irrigation; many more tubewells; and the use of high-yielding grain varieties. There seems to be little hope of gaining much more now from these 1960s innovations. According to the National Conservation Strategy document, for the past 30 years the ecosystem has been greatly damaged and natural resources are being depleted at an alarming rate. Forest cover is down to 5 per cent of the land area; various forms of land degradation have affected 60 per cent of the land – soil erosion threatens 11 million hectares; water-logging and salinisation 5.5 million hectares; destruction of river and mangrove systems are threatening many plants, animals and fish with extinction; and the level of pollution, mostly from human effluent, is described as 'horrific'.[15]

In addition, there is pervasive land hunger which increases pressure on the forests and aggravates water supply problems for agriculture and public health. Agricultural technology has enabled Pakistan's food production to keep pace with population growth for the past 40 years. But it has probably not been sustainable in the recent past. It remains to be seen whether food production can meet the needs of the increasing population in the future and particularly whether distribution systems will ensure that food requirements of all the people are met. The National Conservation Strategy document is outspoken in laying a large part of the blame for the present predicament on neglect of women's development which is closely related to poverty, population growth rates and environmental management.

WHY DO PEOPLE WANT CHILDREN?

Desired family size is conditioned by a wide range of factors – cultural and religious views, the status and level of education of women, the general social and economic situation, and attitudes to replacement of children in situations where infant mortality rates are high, and access to health and birth planning services limited.[16]

Large families are seen in some societies as a sign of high status. Men may see it as 'macho' to have a large family, and producing many children, preferably males, is seen by women in many societies both as their principal social role and as a means of providing security in their old age. Gender relations, determined by social and cultural attitudes, are slow to change; it is because of the low social and economic status of women in so many societies that the bearing of male children is highly valued. Where women are able to claim an equal role in decision making, and take control over their own lives, there are other possibilities for status-conferring activities open to them, besides child-bearing. Early marriage, a feature of many societies, can be another reason for high birth rates.

In the rural areas of developing countries, where people have access to few resources beyond the family, children provide labour and income for family survival. A large family provides the only insurance for old-age; security depends on the number of surviving healthy children a family produces. Male children are often important in securing continued ownership of land or property so women will wish to ensure that they have one, preferably more, sons. In countries where health care provision is limited and child mortality rates high among poor families,

IAN BRAY/OXFAM

Young herders, Mozambique. Children are a valuable source of labour in a rural family, and take responsibility for caring for animals at an early age.

many children may be born but only a few may survive. Women may need to have several children to ensure enough survive into adulthood. Rwanda, for example, has one of the highest infant mortality rates in the world and one of the highest fertility rates.[17] In economic terms at the household level, large families are the only source of security, in the present and for the future, for millions of the very poor, and especially for women.

Clearly there are many complex and inter-related factors contributing to large families and so to rapid population growth – but poverty appears to be a major underlying cause.[18]

For the urban poor, it can be rather a different story where, instead of being a source of wealth or insurance, a large family may be a drain on resources. Cities are nevertheless growing very rapidly throughout the developing world because of a combination of migration and natural population increase, as described in Chapter 7. People perceive and express their needs differently in rural and urban areas depending on their access to land, income, employment, health and education services. Leela is an Indian woman trying to cope in a harsh urban environment:

> Leela is known to an organisation supported by Oxfam. She had eight children. One boy died when he was one year old. She was pregnant again and had no milk to feed him so he weakened and died. Her eldest daughter committed suicide because she was unhappily married. Leela explains that she had eight children because her husband wanted them to make him wealthy – but now times have changed. They live in the city where everything costs money – school fees, medicines, clothes, food and fuel for cooking. Her next daughter is pregnant. Leela told her: 'Have only two children – any more is crazy!'. [19]

In spite of cultural, social and economic pressures to do otherwise, many poor families do take the decision to limit the number of children they have. But it is often very difficult for them to get access to the contraceptive information and services they need, and to overcome family or cultural pressures.

WAYS FORWARD

Tackling the interlinked problems of poverty and rapid population growth calls for an integrated response including most importantly poverty alleviation, improving the health, education and status of women, and providing access to birth planning information and services.

Actions to address poverty must involve tackling the inequitable access to resources both within and between countries.

Focusing on women

The role of women is central to finding solutions to problems of poverty, environmental degradation and rapid population growth. The poorest people are usually women. Women often have no decision-making power over their fertility; and women play a crucial role in the management of natural resources as the means of providing for their families. For example, in Sri Lanka, India, Colombia and Chile, all countries where Oxfam works, it has been shown that fertility rates are very closely linked to the health status, education and income-generating capacity of women.[20] When women's prospects are improved and they gain the strength to take decisions for themselves, they are more likely to limit their families.

In Sri Lanka, female literacy rates are in excess of 80 per cent and there is a strong primary health care programme which encourages rural women's involvement. The general fertility rate declined by 18 per cent between 1965-70 and by the same rate again between 1975-80. Desired family size is steadily declining also. The Indian state of Kerala has a strong public health sector and a female literacy rate more than twice as high as India's average. Infant mortality is less than one-third the national average, giving parents confidence that their children will survive to adulthood. A comparison with the Indian state of Uttar Pradesh is illuminating: with 85 per cent lower female literacy and infant mortality four times higher, the fertility rate was more than double that of Kerala.[21]

Education is one key factor enabling women to take control of their lives and their fertility. In addition, lack of education can translate into poor health and nutrition for women and their children, which leads in turn to high infant mortality and so to more births. Some observers believe that education is the most important factor in improving women's lives.[22]

The need for birth planning

Access to appropriate birth planning information and services is also essential so that when people take decisions to limit child-bearing, they are able to act on their wishes.

There is a very clearly established need for birth planning which at present is not being met. The World Fertility Survey[23] carried out in 41 developing countries between 1972 and 1984 revealed that about 300 million couples wanted to limit their families but lacked access to appropriate and acceptable family planning services. More recent figures taking into account increased use of contraception indicate that the number of women using contraception could increase by 100 million if their contraceptive needs were met.[24] If appropriate services were available to all the people who wanted them, it is estimated that the number of births would be reduced by 27 per cent in Africa, 33 per cent in Asia and 35 per cent in Latin America. The prevalence of present contraceptive use is 20 per cent, 30 per cent and 40 per cent in those regions respectively, compared with around 70 per cent in Europe.[25]

This striking unmet need for family planning is borne out by the desperate measures taken by women – the immense number of illegal and dangerous abortions, the numbers of abandoned children and even infanticide.[26] Abortions are estimated at 50 to 70 million per year, mostly in developing countries.

The following stories from Rwanda and Vietnam illustrate the problems faced by many of the world's poorest women.

> Born into a rural family in Rwanda, Odette was the third of eight children. She did not go to school because her parents could only afford to educate some of the children and sent the boys to school. She stayed at home helping with farming, cooking and looking after the younger children. She was married about ten years ago and moved away from her home area. Since then, Odette has had six children of whom four survived. At present she is able to feed all the family on the produce from the family plot of land and is able to educate the older one. She would prefer not to have any more children for a while. She feels weak from repeated pregnancies, breastfeeding the youngest child and doing all the work on the farm but she considers herself lucky that her husband helps in the fields. Odette visits the health centre 5 kms. away when she is pregnant and receives advice there on some contraceptive methods. She would like to have a contraceptive injection at a different centre 20 kms. away but her husband would never agree to her taking the time it would need to get there and back. He does not like to use contraception because he believes that children are a blessing from God. Odette agrees, but she would like to have a rest before having the next child.

A recent Oxfam report on Kyanh district of Vietnam found that the local Women's Union branch was very well-informed about methods of contraception but unfortunately only one method was available to its members. This was a form of intra-uterine device which caused such severe side-effects that most women found it intolerable and had to have it removed. Some women had undergone as many as four abortions and most had had at least one. Vietnam is no different from other countries in that contraception is regarded as very much a woman's problem and male contraceptive methods are hardly used at all. One in three pregnancies end in abortion – there are 1 million each year. Women want quite small families, two or three children, which is not surprising in a country where women marry late, the great majority are literate and most are engaged in work outside the household. A better birth planning service is obviously badly needed in which personnel are trained to offer advice and follow-up, and which can offer a wider choice of methods for women and men, suited to their personal needs.

Birth planning can have a significant effect on improving the health of women and their children. The negative effects on women's health of too many pregnancies, too early, and too closely spaced are well documented. It is estimated that 25 to 40 per cent of the half million maternal deaths worldwide per year (mostly in developing countries) could be avoided by proper family planning provision. The health of those who survive, and their children, would also be improved if they were able to plan their families. Good birth planning programmes should enable people, especially women, to decide how many children to have, and when to have them.

'Population control'

In the past, there has often been an over-emphasis on narrowly focused approaches which have led to target-oriented birth control programmes. The aim has been population control, rather than concern for the well-being of the individual and their family. They have been coercive in implementation and counterproductive in terms of reducing rates of population increase.

Partly as a reaction to such coercive programmes, development planners have tended to emphasise reduction of poverty as the best, or even the only, way to slow down population growth rates. For a while, access to contraception was considered to be of secondary importance. But lack of emphasis on provision of contraceptive advice can lead to 'coercion' of a different kind where women are forced to go through unwanted pregnancies because they lack access to the means to control their fertility. The level of unmet demand, and the number of abortions, attest to the need for contraceptive information and services to be more generally provided as part of development programmes.

Oxfam field workers and project holders in some countries have been well aware of the negative effects on people's health and well-being of coercive birth control programmes. These provided an array of inducements and targets, often financial, to health personnel and clients, which often led to abuses and even to violence. Features of such coercive methods of birth control delivery have been the lack of information, the limited range of methods, often unsuitable for individual circumstances, with a heavy reliance on sterilisation. These programmes were frequently put in place without wider health care support.

In Bangladesh, for example, payment of financial incentives for sterilisation led to abuses amounting in some cases to infringements of human rights. A more appropriate and effective approach would include sensitive provision of information, choice of methods and follow-up. Bangladesh is one of the world's most densely populated countries. To deal with the high population growth rates, successive Bangladeshi governments, under pressure from multilateral and bilateral agencies including the World Bank, USAID and some UN agencies, formulated various 'five-year' plans to deal with the high population growth rate, which was perceived by some international agencies to be the country's major problem.

The story of a Bangladeshi couple illustrates the problems of abuse which can arise in target-orientated birth control programmes.

> Taibur and Shakina Rahman have six children. They live in a small village in Noakhali, Bangladesh. Shakina is 35 years old. Her oldest daughter is 22 and already married. Shakina's right leg is paralysed so she cannot do any work outside her home. Taibur, her husband, is a landless agricultural labourer. Their second daughter has come back to live at home as her husband divorced her. One of their sons, Babu, has a job on a tea stall, and is able to send his parents some money.

> The Rahman family is fairly typical of rural Bangladeshi families. Their daily food consists of rice or wheat which they eat with peppers or lentils; they can no longer afford oil and onions. They depend on cast-off clothes and are worried about their debt to a relative of Taka 300 (£6).They do not know how they will ever repay it.

> Shakina was told by a village health worker that if she was sterilised, she would receive in return Taka 175, a sari and a ration card entitling her to 40 pounds of wheat every two weeks. The wheat came from the UN World Food Programme, intended to feed vulnerable families. It is, however, often used by local officials to bribe people into having sterilisations so that they can meet their sterilisation 'targets' and so receive their wages on time. Shakina agreed to have the operation to help feed her family. Taibur was also told that if he would agree to a vasectomy, he would receive Taka 200, some clothing, and a card entitling him to 40 pounds of wheat monthly.

> Taibur and Shakina are now both sterilised but neither has received a single ounce of wheat from the local office, despite the ration cards and promises that entitle them to a regular supply.[27]

Birth planning

The experience of Taibur and Shakina Rahman illustrates the unacceptable aspects of some birth control programmes. It is generally acknowledged now that the approach to contraceptive provision should be one of birth planning rather than birth control with the latter's overtones of coercion and disregard of individual needs. Birth planning is about ensuring that contraceptive provision and advice is integrated with other health and education initiatives, especially those that focus on the status and rights of women.

Provision of good quality birth planning services and advice can play a highly significant role in enabling women to take control of their fertility. In the context of general poverty alleviation measures and initiatives to improve the health, education and status of women, birth planning provision can play an important part in reducing population growth rates.

Oxfam attempts to take a sensitive approach to birth planning services, supporting organisations which try to assess people's needs, provide information and advice. Birth planning should be an integral part of primary health care programmes involving advice, choice of methods appropriate to people's needs, and follow-up.

Oxfam also supports projects which are involved in sex education, female literacy and provision of information to women about broader aspects of their health. In Western Kenya, for example, Kima hospital runs a health care programme supported by Oxfam which provides

JENNY MATTHEWS/OXFAM

Sex education is an integral part of this women's health scheme in Recife, Brazil.

birth planning advice and services as one part of a broader programme which is designed to improve people's health and quality of life. Traditional birth attendants are trained in nutrition and provision of contraceptives. General development work includes, for example, improvement and protection of water supplies, and agricultural extension services. In 1990, about 5,500 women attended talks about birth planning at the clinic. Close to 1,000 of the women who participated have decided to use some method of birth control.

Working with teenage girls has been an important part of the work of the Centre for Information and Advisory Services in Health (CISAS) in Nicaragua.[28] Set up in 1983 to offer community health information services, by the late 1980s, CISAS had decided to concentrate its efforts on working mainly in the area of women's health, including giving priority to sex education with teenage girls still in school and to working with health professionals at the women's hospital in Managua to tackle issues of fertility control, pregnancy and childbirth. Workshops run by the Centre provide an opportunity for women and teenagers to start to make their own choices through gaining understanding of how their own body functions and an awareness of reproductive rights, including contraception.

Oxfam's experience in Pakistan demonstrates an evolving approach to the integrated provision of birth planning services in a country where, as described above, rapid population growth is recognised as a constraint on sustainable development. Oxfam and the Family Planning Association of Pakistan (FPAP) have had a long relationship which has changed over the years in response to improved understanding of the problems facing the women FPAP was involved with. Over a period of almost 40 years, the Association's strategy for providing family planning services has evolved from one of simply making contraceptive supplies available to one of integrating the delivery of contraception with very broad education and training programmes aimed at improving women's lives. In 1965, Oxfam started contributing to an educational campaign to provide information about birth planning. Resistance from elderly relatives and the restrictions of the purdah system still proved powerful obstacles preventing women from taking up birth planning services. A more integrated approach was developed, working with traditional health practitioners to provide mother and child health care services including birth planning. This approach proved highly successful and was eventually extended to include traditional birth attendants.

Despite small successes at an organisational level, it was realised that social, cultural and economic factors prevented many women from participating in the Association's programmes. So in 1978, FPAP embarked on a more broad-based programme to develop women's self-

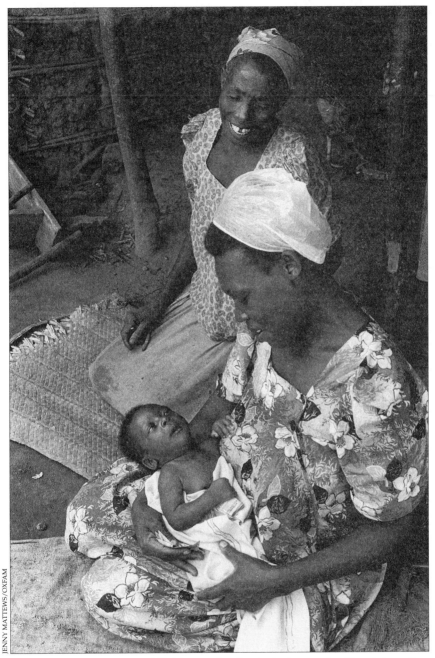

Traditional birth attendants (TBAs) can often be the best way of getting information across to new mothers. This is Amina Nakabugo, a Ugandan, who has been delivering babies for 40 years, with Nulu Kawaya and her son, Moses. Amina recently did a TBA training at the Semuto hospital. Maternal and child deaths are prevented by teaching basic antenatal care and hygiene practice to TBAs.

awareness, confidence and solidarity to a point where they would be able to take control of their fertility. This was done through practical programmes of skills development, health education, adult literacy, income generation, and workshops. In 1991, Oxfam funded 30 grassroots workers in over 25 urban and rural locations, who helped women to organise a wide range of activities – educational, health training and services, including birth planning. Oxfam has also funded FPAP for day-care services, skills development and awareness-raising in urban slums, and is now supporting a similar programme in five rural areas.

Oxfam believes that it is the right of people, particularly women, to be able to choose the number of children they want, when they want them and when to stop having them. The priority is to listen to the needs of the people concerned and to fund birth planning information and services, usually in the context of primary health care systems. Special attention should be given to informed choice and back-up health services. Women should be consulted at an early stage and be involved in programme design. Male awareness and participation is particularly important. Birth planning services should be part of a broader programme of reproductive health care which includes sex education for women and men.

If population growth rates are to be reduced, the priorities must be to tackle poverty, improve the status and education of women, and respond to their right to control their fertility by providing access to birth planning information and services. The improvement in the quality of life of individual men and women and their children that results from the provision of good birth planning programmes should be an overriding reason for investing in them.

10

RICH WORLD, POOR WORLD: TRADE, DEBT AND AID

We are all now in the same lifeboat. The continued health of the North depends on the survival and sustainable development of the South.

Ambassador Jamshead Marker, Permanent Representative of Pakistan to the UN.[1]

In the struggle to reach a fairer, more secure and sustainable world, poor countries face a fundamental problem. Rich nations in the North remain preoccupied with the symptoms of poverty and environmental degradation whilst for the nations of the South, it is the causes of deepening poverty and a worsening environment that must be addressed. At the heart of these problems lie the structural inequalities in economic relations between the North and the South – unjust terms of trade, crippling debts and inadequate aid flows.

The rich countries of the North recovered from the recession of the early 1980s to record eight years of uninterrupted economic growth. Even with the downturn in 1991, average living standards in the 24 member countries of the OECD are still rising slightly. By contrast, the world's poorest countries have been trapped, for over a decade, in a profound crisis. For most of them, the 1980s were a decade of lost development, marked by economic decline, and abysmally low living standards which are still falling. In Latin America, average incomes today are lower than they were in the early 1980s. In sub-Saharan Africa, they have fallen to the levels of the mid-1960s. Only Asia (taken as an economic grouping) has grown more rapidly than the North, but with wide regional variations; the growth in some parts of Asia is counterbalanced by the poverty of countries like Bangladesh and the Philippines.

Economic mismanagement in many of the poorer countries was a factor in their economic downturn in the 1980s. But the sheer scale and geographical spread of the crisis point to the importance of wider structural forces rooted in the international trading and financial systems. Paramount among these has been a decline in the prices which countries in the South receive for the commodity exports on which many of them depend.

Commodity dependence

Most of the countries in which Oxfam works are heavily dependent on selling a small number of primary commodities, such as tea, coffee, cocoa or copper. In sub-Saharan Africa, ten countries rely on single commodities for more than half their export income. Zambia, for example, earns 97 per cent of its foreign exchange from copper; Uganda earns 95 per cent from coffee.[2]

> Tanzania is dependent on primary commodities for 79 per cent of its total exports and cotton accounts for 15 per cent of its export earnings. But in recent years, the price of cotton on the world market has been low – its level determined not by farmers or producer governments, but by traders on the international market. By producing more cotton (though earning less) Tanzania has contributed to the slump in world prices. Buying a kanga – the traditional garment worn by women and men in Tanzania – costs farmers only a little less than their entire earnings from the annual cotton crop. Yet the cotton they can grow on one hectare is enough to make 720 kangas.[3]

Between 1980 and 1988, the terms of trade for developing countries, that is, the purchasing power of exports against the price of imports, dropped by 30 per cent.[4] This deterioration in the terms of trade meant a loss to sub-Saharan Africa alone of US$50 billion in the second half of the 1980s – equivalent to nearly a year's export earnings.[5] Protectionism, which denies Third World countries access to Northern markets, has in effect added to this revenue loss, depriving developing countries of potential sales of more than US$100 billion annually.[6]

The debt burden

> Being a severely indebted country means being in a state of perpetual financial haemorrhage.[7]

While the deteriorating trade environment has eroded the purchasing power of exports from the South, debt repayments are claiming a growing proportion of trade earnings for many poor countries.

In 1991, developing countries transferred US$20 billion more to the rich nations of the North (in the form of interest and capital payments)

Fig 10.1
Total debt as a per cent of GNP, and annual debt service as a per cent of exports

	Total external debt to GNP '89	*Total debt service to exports '89 (debt service ratio)*
Severely Indebted Low-Income Countries	116.5%	27.2%
Somalia	210.5%	47.6%
Mozambique	416.7%	24.4%
Severely Indebted Middle-Income Countries	51.3%	31.9%
Philippines	64.3%	25.3%

Source: *World Debt Tables 1991-92*, (1991)[8]

than they received in new loans and investment.[9] They have been caught in this trap every year since the debt crisis broke in 1982, yet most are further away from paying off their debts than ever. By the end of 1990, the total external debt of developing countries stood at US$1,430 billion, compared with US$900 billion in 1982. This sum is close to half the total national income of developing countries, or about US$327 for every woman, man and child.[10] By 1991, indebted Latin American countries owed more than US$423 billion in long-term loans, and some are spending 5 per cent of their entire GDP servicing them.

Although sub-Saharan Africa's total debt of US$72 billion is smaller than that of Mexico or Brazil alone, the burden it imposes is even more severe. Despite its poverty and underdevelopment, the region transferred US$81 billion in debt service payments between 1983 and 1990, with just under half of this going to Northern governments and multilateral agencies such as the World Bank and the IMF.[11]

There is a deadly interaction between trade and debt pressures operating on the world's poorest economies. Debts have to be paid for in hard currency – which has to be earned through trade. As debt service obligations rise and the real prices of exports fall, an increasing proportion of trade earnings are being diverted away from domestic expenditure and towards creditors in the North. Both Latin America and sub-Saharan Africa now spend more than a quarter of their foreign exchange earnings on debt servicing. For an increasing number of developing countries, international trade – once an engine of growth – has become part of the mechanism for maintaining a haemorrhage of capital resources from South to North.

The debt crisis of the 1980s exposed the structural weaknesses of Southern countries within the international economic system. It also forced Southern governments, faced with a sharp cut in export revenues and a rising debt burden, to introduce painful policy reforms, often under the auspices of World Bank and IMF structural adjustment programmes. These programmes sought to increase export competitiveness through currency devaluation, and to reduce budget deficits by cutting public expenditure, deregulating prices, liberalising trade and encouraging private sector investment.

Faced with a need to reduce domestic expenditure and consumption to levels commensurate with the smaller amount of financial resources available, policy reforms were inevitable. Also it is clear that reforms were needed to promote exports and to facilitate more efficient management of the balance of payments. However, the adjustment programmes of the 1980s were unbalanced and inequitable. Geared towards maximising short-term foreign exchange gains to meet debt repayments, they failed to create the conditions for a sustainable, investment-led recovery.

Moreover, adjustment programmes were not supported by sufficient external finance and were based on unduly optimistic assumptions about the effects of market liberalisation. Most seriously, however, they displayed a complete disregard of equity considerations in their prescriptions, with especially harmful consequences for the most vulnerable social groups.

The most visible victims of structural adjustment have been the poorest, most marginalised people with whom Oxfam works – particularly the urban poor, and especially poor women. The withdrawal of government subsidies on basic goods such as food, kerosene, and on public transport hits hardest at those on the lowest incomes, particularly when devaluation (a common component of adjustment programmes) boosts inflation. The poorest also lose out when cuts in government spending lead to the closure of primary health care clinics and other welfare services. In the Philippines, where at least half the population of 62 million is officially categorised as poor, 44 per cent of the government budget was devoted to debt servicing in 1989.[12]

> Women are bearing the brunt of adjustment. Women's burden of unpaid labour is always implicitly expected to fill the gaps caused by cut-backs in health and education....and reductions in other basic services. Similarly, women as household managers are held responsible for absorbing the impact of steeply rising food prices. Restructuring means that someone has to change, and those changes are falling very heavily on women.[13]

ENVIRONMENTAL COSTS: MORTGAGING THE FUTURE

Oxfam is increasingly aware of deep and pervasive environmental problems associated with the trade and debt crisis in the South. The most direct link between external economic pressures and the escalation of environmental degradation discussed in this book can be stated in a single word: poverty. As people are pushed further into poverty, in part by government measures to deal with debt, and as prices rise faster than incomes, the daily struggle for survival forces poor people to exploit ecologically fragile areas. For example, as their incomes fall, they cut trees to make charcoal or to sell as firewood. Some travel long distances to collect wood to sell in urban markets. They may clear more forest and woodland to grow food or raise animals. In desperation, they may adopt methods which cannot be sustained, even temporarily, such as exploitive fishing. These activities can generate a modest increase in meagre incomes, but often at the cost of soil erosion, land degradation and the loss of long-term environmental security. Oxfam has seen all these pressures at work in the Philippines, where debt and poverty have created a powerful cycle of environmental destruction.

Fishing communities in the Philippines

Many of the communities with whom Oxfam works in the Philippines are dependent on fish for their nutrition and for an income. Eight million fishing families are amongst the poorest people in the Philippines.

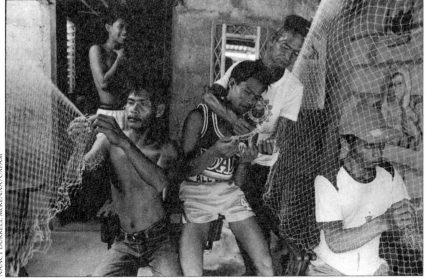

Philippine fishermen from Laguna Bay mending nets. Fishing communities are faced with declining catches as pollution and over-fishing have devastated fish stocks.

The unique environment of mangrove swamps and coral reefs once provided rich breeding grounds for fish. But the pressures are intensifying on these fragile fisheries: pollution and industrial trawling result in lower and lower catches for the fishing communities. The once-extensive mangrove swamps are disappearing fast: some 1,700 hectares have been cleared to make way for large commercial prawn farms, financed by Japanese loans and serving the Japanese market. Mangroves now cover just one-tenth of the area they occupied in the 1920s, and the destruction of these mangrove breeding grounds means a progressive and serious lowering of fish catches each year for local fishermen.

Inland, deforestation leads to soil erosion. Soil is carried by rivers out to sea and clogs the deltas, destroying more breeding grounds – the coral reefs. On the island of Negros, the government estimates that 88 per cent of the reefs have been damaged or completely destroyed in this and other ways. As the fishing communities become more impoverished, some turn to desperate – and illegal – measures to increase their catch. They use cyanide and blast fishing (with dynamite), both of which damage the remaining coral and endanger lives. Many fishermen report that daily catches have dropped from 40 kilos 30 years ago to just 2 kilos now. Oxfam is supporting FESFIN – a local grouping of small fishermen on Negros – who are working to reverse this trend by opposing illegal fishing methods and by protecting marine habitats.[14]

There are other environmental consequences of indebtedness and economic decline – national and local. At local level, family and personal indebtedness mean that farmers can no longer afford to invest in long-term conservation measures and land and water management suffer as a result. At a national level, environmental protection measures are abandoned as governments divert resources away from domestic expenditure to service debts. There is evidence from Latin America that imports of pollution control equipment and investment in environmental management programmes have been stopped or curtailed. Austerity measures have left environmental agencies underfunded and understaffed. As the World Resources Institute has argued in relation to Latin America

> So long as the economic crisis...continues, investment in environmental improvements – such as cleaning up the heavily polluted urban areas – will be difficult.[15]

Debt and deforestation

The need for foreign exchange for debt servicing, and attendant efforts to expand exports, have added to the pressures on natural resources, especially tropical forests. According to recent estimates, more than 20 million hectares of tropical forest are being destroyed and degraded each

Timber being measured, Mozambique. Commercial logging operations can supply scarce foreign exchange, but most logging is unsustainable, and a vital natural resource is lost for ever.

year (an area similar in size to that of England and Scotland) and the rate of destruction is accelerating.[16] However, the pressure to generate foreign exchange is only one of many factors which lead to deforestation. The destruction of the Amazon rainforest is not directly debt-related, but caused by internal factors such as road building, land speculation and clearance by cattle ranchers and small farmers.

In some countries, however, notably Côte d'Ivoire, Malaysia and Papua New Guinea, the link between debt and deforestation is direct and clear. In Côte d'Ivoire, the government is engaged in a desperate bid to increase foreign exchange earnings. Timber extraction is carried out primarily for export and so controls on logging operations have been withdrawn and companies are encouraged to cut into the dwindling tracts of remaining natural forest. Cocoa and other export producers then move into this newly cleared land.

In Central America, the expansion of cattle ranching to meet the import demands of the USA and Canada is one of the main causes of deforestation. During the last 25 years the area has lost two-thirds of its tropical forests, much of which has been cleared to raise beef for export.[17] In Costa Rica, logging and slash-and-burn cultivation are continuing to claim more than 120,000 hectares of rainforest annually. In Brazil, the migration to forest areas by impoverished urban dwellers and landless labourers, often displaced by large farms producing crops (such as soya for animal feed) for export to the European Community, has also contributed to deforestation.

One commentator writes: 'The debt burden is damaging the environment through extraction, encroachment and neglect.'[18] The pressure to earn foreign exchange is speeding up the extraction of natural resources. Increased poverty among small farmers fuels the process of encroachment on forests and other fragile areas. And governments are propelled by debt to cut back on public expenditure which leads to the neglect of good environmental management.

EXPORT-LED ENVIRONMENTAL DEGRADATION

Structural adjustment programmes have often intensified environmental pressures. Central to these programmes is an assumption that developing countries can export their way into recovery. However, some of the policy reforms introduced to promote export-led growth have been inevitable and long overdue: devaluation of over-valued currencies is one example. Devaluation encourages export crop production because it is likely to increase the prices for traded goods, although all too often the resulting income gains accrue to rich and powerful traders rather than peasant producers.

Viewed from an environmental perspective, devaluation can have both positive and negative consequences. By increasing the local currency costs of imported agro-chemicals, which can cause severe environmental problems (such as groundwater pollution), devaluation provides an incentive for farmers to return to organic production methods, as it did in Zambia (see Chapter 5). Conversely, in Chad, cotton producers responded to shortages of inputs by expanding the acreage planted in an effort to maintain output.This resulted in lower cotton yields and long-term environmental damage to ecologically fragile soils.

Particularly serious problems arise when devaluation is introduced as part of a package of policies designed to maximise commercial export crop production to the exclusion of all other considerations. This is partly because a common feature of all the major export crops – such as coffee, cocoa, cotton and groundnuts – is that they are extremely demanding in their nutrient requirements. Yet large-scale monocultural production is not the only way in which such crops can be grown. When they are carefully intercropped with nitrogen-fixing crops (like cow peas) which act as natural fertilisers, or with bananas or millet, crop yields can be high and the prospects for sustainability are good. The denser vegetative cover provided by multiple cropping reduces soil temperature and erosion, and increases water in filtration. Weeds are less likely to get established, so fewer herbicides are required. Many

Third world farmers are highly knowledgeable about intercropping, and well aware of the dangers of intensifying production to maximise short-term income.

However, as governments have come under pressure to increase output to repay debts, they have encouraged intensive, monocultural forms of production. In West Africa, this has taken place without due regard for the nature of local soils and weather patterns and the results have been ecologically – and economically – disastrous. In Senegal, soils have become so depleted by mechanised groundnut cultivation, the country now has difficulty supplying the groundnut refineries (created mainly with borrowed money).

The rapid expansion of cotton production in countries like Burkina Faso, Chad and Mali has been even more damaging, causing extensive soil erosion and deforestation. In the Koutiala area of Mali, problems of environmental degradation have been accelerated by the development of cotton production which has led to the clearance of wooded areas and encroachment on to land previously used for food crops. The result of this pressure on resources is a shortage of land for small-scale farmers and a breakdown of the traditional system of agriculture which allowed fields to rest by remaining fallow. Because of land clearance, there are few trees left for fuel and the villagers have to use cow dung and cotton stalks, which would otherwise be used to replenish soil fertility. These factors have combined to exhaust the soil and reduce its fertility in an area already vulnerable to drought and soil erosion.[19]

Apart from these 'primary' effects, the expansion of cash cropping has caused a wide range of 'secondary' problems by further marginalising poor subsistence farmers and herders. Evicted from their plots or denied access to pastures to make way for commercial agriculture, they are often forced to work nutrient-deficient soils, easily eroded hillsides (which are rapidly stripped of tree cover) and areas of virgin forest. The result is a vicious cycle of increasing poverty and a deteriorating environment.

More for less

The ecological costs of the headlong rush to generate more foreign exchange have been exacerbated by deteriorating terms of trade. Take the case of cocoa, one of West Africa's main sources of foreign exchange. Between 1985 and 1989, the region increased cocoa production by 26 per cent, as governments diverted resources to the export sector. But over the same period, the equivalent of more than US$3 billion was lost in foreign exchange as world prices for cocoa fell to their lowest-ever levels in real terms.[20] Exporters of coffee and cotton have also seen falling prices wipe out the gains they anticipated from increased production. At the same time as the value of their commodity exports has been falling, the cost of imports for Southern countries (mainly oil and manufactured goods) has risen dramatically. Every year, the pressure is on to produce more and more, yet this earns less and less. Dozens of debtors have simultaneously tried to meet their debt service obligations by exporting more of the narrow range of commodities on which they rely. Since world demand for most of these commodities is relatively static the inevitable result has been market gluts and a downward price spiral. In this way, countries become locked in a 'trade trap'.[21]

Ironically, the 'success' of structural adjustment programmes in expanding export production has compounded the problems facing commodity-dependent countries. It has left them trying to climb a downward escalator – producing more at mounting environmental cost just to stand still.

Northern protectionism

Trade measures adopted by industrialised countries contribute to the cycle of environmental deterioration by ensuring that much of the value added to primary commodities never reaches the South. While most primary, or unprocessed, commodities exported by producer countries attract only modest trade barriers in Northern markets, higher value processed products are subject to heavy tariff duties. This 'tariff escalation' is designed to protect manufacturing industries in the North from potentially more efficient competitors in the South. But it has the effect of depriving Southern countries of the increased foreign exchange which domestic processing would bring. Practices such as transfer pricing (the manipulation of prices to avoid local taxation and maximise the remittance of profits back to the North) have a similar effect. In both cases, the outcome is a further loss of revenue for Southern countries and increased pressure on the natural resource base.

The tropical timber trade provides a clear illustration of these problems. Japan, for example, allows raw logs to enter the country duty free, while imposing 9 per cent tariffs on high value plywood. Furniture makers in Europe enjoy even higher levels of protection. The result is that manufacturers in developing countries are discouraged from making the investment which would add local value to exports.

Unlike tariff escalation, transfer pricing is illegal (and therefore vastly under-reported); but it too has the effect of shifting profits away from exporting countries. By understating the price of exported logs, firms can evade taxes in the producer country but raise their profits when the timber is sold at its real market value in the importing country.[22] Within transnational corporations (TNCs), it is relatively simple for a subsidiary to over-invoice its parent company, thus artificially depressing local profits. According to an official inquiry in Papua New Guinea, Japanese TNCs were evading export duties by stating the price of logs to be, on average, 10 per cent to 20 per cent below those paid by foreign buyers.[23] In Indonesia, logs are often undervalued by as much as 40 per cent.

The outcome of these trade practices is that Third World timber exporters are trapped at the lower value – and most volatile – end of commodity markets. A recent analysis of six countries exporting raw logs showed that they retained less than 10 per cent of the product value that was finally obtained on Northern markets. Had they been able to process the logs, that share could have risen to 35 per cent.

ENVIRONMENT AND THE GATT

The interactions between trade and the environment are increasingly widely recognised. Energy intensive, trade-based growth in the North is polluting the global commons by ozone-depleting chemicals, carbon dioxide emissions and waste dumping. In the South, debt-fuelled export expansion continues to destroy the natural resource base. Against this sombre background, it is no longer possible to ignore the simple fact that trade is an environmental issue.

Responsibility for setting the framework within which governments address the implications of environmental policy for the global trading system rests with the General Agreement on Tariffs and Trade (GATT). Created in 1947, the GATT sets out rules for the free and open conduct of world trade and its agreements cover nearly 85 per cent of international trade. Not surprisingly, environmental problems did not figure prominently in the minds of its architects. But as environmental awareness has grown, the GATT's failure in this area has emerged as its Achilles' heel. Seven years after Brundtland, the GATT makes no mention of environmental sustainability as a legitimate objective of government policy, and it does not allow for the use of subsidies or trade restrictions to encourage more sustainable forms of production. Inevitably, this approach exposes the conflict between environmental policies and GATT obligations. Indonesia, for example, has been accused by the European Community and Japan of violating the GATT by imposing export restrictions on unprocessed timber – a measure introduced to increase local value-added processing. Any government subsidies to industry aimed at reducing carbon dioxide emissions would also fall foul of the GATT, if the letter of the treaty is to be strictly applied.

The tuna ruling

The limitations placed by the GATT on progressive policy making for environmental management were well illustrated by the 1991 'tuna ruling'. At issue was a successful case brought by Mexico claiming that US restrictions on the import of yellow-fin tuna were contrary to GATT rules. The ban had been imposed under the 1988 US Marine Mammal Protection Act which was passed – after intensive lobbying by conservation groups – because of the large numbers of dolphins killed by Mexico's tuna fleet. This fleet operates in an area of the eastern Pacific Ocean where dolphins swim above tuna and are caught in the tuna nets. The GATT ruling in Mexico's favour stunned marine conservationists. But its implications are much wider, as they concern environmental sustainability and political sovereignty. In effect, the ruling prevents governments from using trade restrictions either to protect environmental resources beyond their national borders or to register an objection to the methods of export production.

Environmentalists, North and South, fear this ruling could now jeopardise international efforts to protect 'extra-territorial' resources, including atmospheric ozone. The Montreal Protocol on ozone depletion, which envisages trade sanctions against countries which do not reduce ozone-destroying chlorofluorocarbon emissions, could be deemed to be in contravention of the GATT. So could agreements such as the International Convention on Trade in Endangered Species (CITES), and the proposed UN moratorium on drift-net fishing.

Clearly, environmental deregulation in the manner implied by the GATT tuna ruling is undesirable. But Third World countries are aware of another danger – 'green protectionism'. They fear that as governments in the North move to clean up their industries, they will seek to protect them from industries in the South operating at lower environmental standards. There are already moves, notably in the US, to introduce legislation aimed at offsetting the price advantages enjoyed by 'dirty' industries (those that do not meet US standards) by imposing import duties. At one level, this approach makes good sense, especially given the failure of market prices to reflect environmental costs. At another, it could open the door to a wave of arbitrary and discriminatory trade restrictions. Inevitably, many of these would be targeted against Southern producers who, because of inadequate investment, are unable to meet Northern environmental standards.

Understandably, developing country governments resent the prospect of having the industrialised countries dictate production standards which, they would argue, are inappropriate given the resource constraints under which they operate. Environmentally, it is in the interests of the North to enable Southern countries to leap-frog wasteful and polluting production methods by learning – and importing – environmentally sound technologies. By the same token, it is not in the long-term best interests of North or South for poor countries to become the repositories of toxic and other wastes discarded in the rich world but dumped in Southern countries with inadequate pollution control standards.[24]

The GATT may assume an increasingly important environmental role; the GATT Working Group on Environmental Measures and International Trade has been reconvened and is expected to make recommendations on how environmental policies could be incorporated into the GATT, or into any new multilateral trade organisation that could replace it.

COUNTING THE COSTS

The farmers, pastoralists and marginalised urban people with whom Oxfam works have long been aware of the real costs of environmental degradation. A major factor which perpetuates unjust trading practices is the failure of policymakers and economists in the North to take account of these costs. But this is beginning to change as the discipline of environmental economics, which seeks to assign market values to environmental resources, becomes increasingly accepted. Current research in this area has focused on forests.

Tropical forest destruction accounts for more than 20 per cent of the greenhouse gas emissions which cause global warming. Large quantities of carbon dioxide and other gases are released when they are burned to clear land. In this context, forests also play an important role as absorbers of carbon dioxide, and the earth's capacity to absorb this greenhouse gas is reduced as forest vegetation is destroyed. In addition, the accompanying loss of biodiversity and the genetic material for plant breeding directly affects Northern agriculture.

Conventional economic accounting fails to register environmental costs such as these, or the social costs of impoverishment, because national income figures record changes in wealth only when they pass through the market. When a forest is cut down and sold, a country appears to grow richer – even though a valuable resource has been lost, food and fuel supplies have been reduced for local people and soil erosion and flooding may have increased. The world as a whole has lost some capacity to regulate climate. In the distorting prism of market economics, the value of a single plank of wood from a felled tree can appear greater than the true value of the forest left intact.

Measuring the real cost of destroying tropical forests is, of course, impossible. The relationship between these complex ecosystems and the global climate is little understood, and the future value of undiscovered plants for medical, agricultural and other commercial purposes can only be guessed at. Similarly, the value of forests to those who live in them is incalculable. Yet even the known economic values of natural resources are seldom taken into account in the rush to generate foreign exchange.

One study of the annual market value of edible fruits, cocoa and rubber from a hectare of Peru's Amazonian forest showed that, averaged out over the years, the revenue was approximately six times the amount that could be realised from harvesting the timber from that hectare in a single year.[25]

In 1987, the Brundtland Report drew attention to the need for a new economics which measured the future costs of resource depletion:

> In all countries, economic development must take full account, in its measurements of growth, of improvement or deterioration in the stock of natural resources.[26]

Since Brundtland, attempts have been made to devise national resource accounting systems which can measure the effects of natural resource exploitation on the generation of future wealth. Although still in its infancy, this 'green accounting' has come up with some interesting results. One study of Indonesia, covering the period between 1971 and 1984, concluded that the annual average 7.1 per cent growth rate would have been reduced to 4 per cent had natural resource depreciation been costed in.[27] And this is before the 'hidden' costs of soil erosion, loss of fertility and increased sedimentation are taken into account. Mali, for example, is currently losing the equivalent of 4 per cent of its GDP each year because of soil loss caused, in part, by over-intensive cultivation for export markets.[28]

WAYS FORWARD ON TRADE AND DEBT

The crux of the challenge facing Northern policy makers is to reduce the external pressures which hinder a return to economic growth in the South. Above all, this means they must assume responsibility for ending the transfer of resources from poor countries to rich, whether in the 'disguised' losses associated with declining terms of trade, protectionism and transfer pricing by transnational companies, or in debt servicing.

In an increasingly interdependent world, it would be foolhardy to suggest any diminution in the volume of world trade. What the South needs is to trade with the North on more favourable terms. There are a number of ways forward. At their current depressed levels, primary commodity prices do not provide a fair return to producers and they do not allow for ecologically sustainable production. Governments in the North and South cannot avoid assuming responsibility for regulating supplies in order to raise producer prices. There is also a need to end protectionist and other trade barriers, to widen Third World access to Northern markets and to allow value to be added to primary commodities in producer countries. Selective protectionist measures aimed at safeguarding both local food security and the environment should be permitted within the framework of the GATT. Governments in the North could implement policies designed to stop the dumping of their subsidised agricultural exports on world markets in unfair competition with Third World produce. Finally, any new trading organisation set up to replace the GATT could be charged with improving appropriate technology transfers to the South, controlling the activities of transnational corporations and protecting the environment.

Governments in the North have now recognised that economic recovery and sustainable development in the South will not happen unless debt burdens are substantially reduced. But progress is slow. Some 60 per cent of Southern debt is owed to private creditors, mainly Northern banks. This commercial debt is concentrated in some 20 middle-income countries, although low-income countries also face a heavy burden. In 1989, the Brady Plan proposed official financial support – of some US$30 billion – for countries seeking voluntary debt and debt service reductions with private banks. So far, the results have been disappointing: of the five agreements concluded, only those involving Mexico and Costa Rica have brought significant reductions. Meanwhile, debt arrears have accumulated in other debtor countries, especially in Latin America. Resources under the Brady Plan are recognised to be inadequate and private banks have failed to play a positive role in negotiating debt reductions. This has strengthened calls for a new multilateral agency to buy up and reschedule outstanding bank debt, and for more government pressure on banks to reduce debts.

This nuclear power station in the Philippines will never produce electricity, because it has been built on a natural fault line and would be too dangerous to operate. Yet the enormous cost of construction is still being paid for in debt servicing – at the rate of almost £200,000 a day.

On official debt, the British government has taken a lead. It has persuaded the 'Paris Club' of official creditors to adopt more radical measures for debt reduction, known as the Trinidad Terms. In his original proposals, the then Chancellor, John Major, called for two-thirds of debt stock to be cancelled, with the rest to be rescheduled over 25 years. Other governments have diluted these proposals, so that the final package allows for only one half of debt service obligations to be written off. Even so, the latest agreement, adopted by the Paris Club in December 1991, will bring substantial relief to severely indebted low-income countries. Oxfam believes that governments should be pressed to implement in full the original Trinidad Terms, and to extend the provisions, in special cases, to severely indebted middle-income countries.

Likewise, whilst economic reform is necessary in many Southern countries, structural adjustment programmes need to be redesigned to enhance the prospects for sustainable development. Policies designed for economic growth can also reduce poverty if investment in social welfare, job creation and sound environmental management increases. Measures to protect vulnerable people and their environment need to be integral to the design of adjustment programmes, not added on as supplementaries.[29]

AID: VALUE FOR MONEY?

At a time of unprecedented need, when the interlocking trade and debt crisis is straining Southern economies as never before, investment and aid flows from Northern countries are stagnating or falling in real terms. Since 1969, when the UN called for developed countries to give 0.7 per cent of their GNP in development aid, very few donors have come anywhere near this target. On average, they contribute 0.33 per cent, and almost a half of this aid goes to high- and middle-income countries. The UK is fourteenth in the league table of OECD donors, with an aid budget down to 0.27 per cent of GNP in 1990 from 0.47 per cent in 1965.[30]

Foreign aid underwrites a major part of development expenditure in many Third World countries. But, against the background of economic crisis, and mismanagement and lack of political will on the part of Third World governments, international aid is making little impact on poverty. At best good aid is being wasted; at worst bad aid is blocking sustainable development.

In 1990, the UN Summit for Children set certain modest goals for Third World development by the end of the century.[32] To achieve these goals, an extra US$20 billion would have to be committed. If all OECD members had reached the 0.7 per cent minimum of aid spending in 1989, this would have generated an extra US$52 billion. Such an increase is not

Fig 10.2
Official Development Assistance as a per cent of GNP for OECD countries

Norway	1.17
Netherlands	0.94
Denmark	0.93
Sweden	0.90
France	0.79
Finland	0.64
Belgium	0.45
Canada	0.44
Germany	0.42
Australia	0.34
Italy	0.32
Japan	0.31
Switzerland	0.31
UK	0.27
Austria	0.25
New Zealand	0.22
USA	0.21
Ireland	0.16

Source: *British Overseas Aid*, (1990).[31]

beyond the economic power of donor countries: the World Bank has estimated that a cut of just 10 per cent in the military spending of NATO members could allow a doubling of aid budgets.[33]

The quality of aid

While there is an urgent need for increased aid, the quality of aid is as important as the quantity. What is crucial is who gets the assistance and what it is used for.

Some blame for the failure of the 1980s' 'lost decade' of development must be apportioned to official aid agencies. Billions of dollars were poured into development assistance (much of it in the form of loans rather than grants) but this failed to solve the problem of mounting poverty. Indeed, all too often, it helped local elites to increase their power and personal fortunes. Together with the loans that were readily available from Northern banks throughout the 1970s, development assistance often funded expensive 'white elephants' – projects which have done little for economic growth but which have contributed greatly to the Third World's mounting debt burden and environmental problems.

The once popular theory of the 'trickle down of wealth' had largely been discredited (it being apparent that the poor rarely benefit from economic growth unless there are government policies to ensure that they do). It had become evident that the 'trickle down of poverty' is a surprisingly efficient mechanism. When the screw is turned, those with power can readily ensure that it is not they, but someone weaker, who feels the squeeze. Hence rich governments were able to push the burden of recession on to poor countries; the elite in poor countries were able to pass on the burden to their poorer neighbours, and through short-sighted mining of the environment, the burden is being passed on to those whose voice is the weakest of all, because they are not yet even born.[34]

Brazil is one of the World Bank's largest borrowers and, at the close of the 1990 financial year, it accounted for almost 10 per cent of accumulated Bank lending. Much of the funding for the rapid development and colonisation of the Amazon was provided by the World Bank, which during the 1970s and 1980s implemented a number of large projects ranging from power generation to integrated rural development. On the World Bank's own admission, many of these projects contributed significantly to Brazil's subsequent environmental problems. Added to this, Brazil, which is the tenth largest economy in the world, has become one of the world's most unequal societies:

Brazil continues to register one of the most skewed income distributions in the world, as the wealthiest 10 per cent of the population claimed 46 per cent of the national income in 1985, while the lowest 20 per cent received just 2.4 per cent.[35]

The benefits of aid were clearly not evenly distributed: during the 1980s the number of Brazilians living in absolute poverty rose from 29.4 million to 44.8 million. Large-scale export production was promoted at the expense of the production of food for internal markets. By 1985, according to FAO, 85 million Brazilians were consuming fewer than 2,240 calories a day (considered to be the minimum daily requirement) and were classified as undernourished.

Aid and poverty

The proportion of donor spending aimed at poverty alleviation is still small in comparison with that given for large capital projects such as dams and power plants. In India, during the 1980s, only 17 per cent of British bilateral aid was spent on reducing poverty, while 76 per cent went to infrastructural projects in mining, civil engineering and power generation. There is little evidence that this kind of expenditure assists the poor, indeed it can be positively damaging to them.

A high proportion of the bilateral aid from EC member states is tied – that is, aid is conditional on procurement in the donor country. The recipient has little or no choice in the purchase of materials, even though more appropriate goods may be available locally or from another exporter. Tying of aid also places undue emphasis on projects with a high import component, compared with those which may need more investment in management and personnel (such as the Primary Environmental Care projects, described in Chapter 2). In 1990, 62.2 per cent of Britain's public expenditure on aid was tied, one of the highest proportions of all OECD countries.[36] At EC level, the amount of tied aid stands at some US$10 billion – or 58 per cent of the total bilateral aid budgets of member states.

But the untying of aid would not automatically help developing countries. While aid donors may be less tempted to design aid programmes and projects to benefit their own industries, increased competition for aid contracts may still not benefit Third World companies, unless they are given priority in bidding for them.

Large projects: the problems of resettlement
Most infrastructural projects are geared towards building up a country's industrial base and promoting the large-scale production of crops, often for export. All too often, they have had disastrous impacts on the rural poor. During 1979-1985, 39 dam projects were approved for financing by the World Bank in 27 countries and these entailed the relocation of 750,000 people who lived in the reservoir areas. Every year, between 1.2 million and 2.1 million people are displaced worldwide as a consequence of new dam construction. Aggregate statistics for China, for example, document that the water conservancy projects of the last 30 years have caused the evacuation of over 10 million people. Other infrastructural programmes also involve land expropriation, depriving many families of their habitat and livelihoods and forcing them to relocate. Some estimates put the numbers of people affected by such programmes in India during the last four decades as perhaps 20 million. And it is likely that involuntary displacement will increase further as part of future urban and agricultural development.[37]

In the late 70s and early 80s Oxfam field offices in India and Brazil became increasingly concerned about the forced displacement of tribal people and peasant families. Partner organisations (with Oxfam support) began to press for adequate compensation for people affected by large dams and this developed into an active campaign by Oxfam and others to press the World Bank to establish effective resettlement and rehabilitation policies.

Sociologists working for the Bank also took issue with the way in which forced displacement had been treated simply as an administrative problem. They pointed out that consulting firms who designed the projects usually left out population relocation from their feasibility studies and cost estimates, disregarding the traumatic social and personal effects of resettlement.

> When people are forcibly moved, production systems are dismantled. Long-established residential communities and settlements are disorganised, while kinship groups and family systems are often scattered. Life-sustaining informal social networks that provide mutual help are rendered non-functional. Trade linkages between producers and their customer bases are interrupted, and local labour markets are disrupted. Formal and informal associations or self-organized services are wiped out by the sudden departure of their membership, often in different directions. Traditional authority and management systems tend to lose their leaders. Abandonment of symbolic markers, such as ancestral shrines and graves... sacred mountains, water courses and trails, severs physical and psychological linkages with the past and saps at the roots of people's cultural identity...The cumulative effect of all these processes is that the social fabric is torn apart.[38]

The common factor underlying all the different consequences of displacement is the onset of impoverishment. Extending far beyond its immediate and visible effects, forced displacement can lead to a spiral of deepening poverty which amplifies the initial damage.

During the oil crisis of the 1970s, Brazil made energy production a priority. In 1974, the World Bank approved a loan for the Paulo Afonso IV Hydropower Project on the São Francisco River, which included the construction of the Sobradinho regulating dam. Although the project increased the generation and distribution of electric power throughout North East Brazil, it forcibly resettled some 70,000 people, 30,000 of whom received little or no compen-sation. According to the Bank's own subsequent evaluation, the project has had serious environmental consequences; it has destroyed livelihoods and increased poverty and human suffering.

In 1980, in the light of both external criticisms and internal pressure for change, the World Bank became the first multilateral development bank to issue a resettlement policy. After a number of subsequent revisions, this policy now provides a set of guidelines by which the Bank deals with resettlement. Involuntary displacement is to be avoided because of its disruptive and impoverishing effects. Where displacement is unavoidable, resettlement plans are to be formulated with due care given to people's needs and to environmental protection. Displaced people are to be compensated for their losses at replacement cost, given opportunities to share in project benefits, and assisted with the move. Indigenous peoples, ethnic minorities, pastoralists, and other groups that may have informal customary rights to the land or other resources taken from them by the project must be provided with adequate land, infrastructure and other compensation. The fact that such groups lack formal legal title to land is not a reason for denying compensation and rehabilitation.

These resettlement guidelines (which in December 1991 were adopted by all the major aid donors at the OECD's Development Assistance Committee) are an important advance, but problems remain with their effective implementation. Borrower governments have the final responsibility and have often proved reluctant to comply with the new policy.

In 1987 the World Bank approved a loan for its first free-standing resettlement project – the Itaparica Resettlement and Irrigation Project. In 1988 when the Itaparica reservoir (downstream of the Sobradinho dam) was flooded, over 65,00 people were relocated from the fertile lower São Francisco Valley in the states of Pernambuco and Bahia to a semi-arid zone. The Polosindical, a rural trade union consortium which led the long campaign for compensation, negotiated a resettlement agreement with the São Francisco Hydroelectric Company (CHESF) which built the dam. However, this agreement was only reached after an occupation of the Itaparica dam site that brought work to a standstill for six days. At this point the World Bank stepped in and agreed to finance the Itaparica Resettlement project.

Itaparica marked a breakthrough in the treatment of displaced people. But although the families have now been rehoused, their claims to land have not been met, irrigation has yet to reach all but one of the new agricultural areas and CHESF's monthly payments to each family have fallen below the agreed figure. Repeated failures of the Brazilian government to comply with the terms of the World Bank loan could mean the cancellation of Bank funding for the entire project and even greater hardship for the displaced families.[39]

Oxfam's research on the effects of big projects confirms that if development assistance is to meet the needs of the poorest people and promote sustainable development, then aid programmes and projects must adopt four essential components – a poverty focus, popular participation, gender awareness, and full environmental appraisal.

Large projects: the development of environmental guidelines
During the early 1980s, World Bank operations in Brazil came under increasing scrutiny from the burgeoning environmental movement. The

European Community was criticised by two British NGOS (Survival International and Friends of the Earth) for its contribution to the World Bank-funded Projecto Grande Carajás, without any prior environmental impact assessment. This project has led to the devastation of Indian lands and destruction of much of the rainforest of the Eastern Amazon.

US pressure groups like the Environmental Defense Fund sought Congressional support for the suspension of loans for projects like Polonoroeste, an integrated rural development project in Rondônia, Brazil, which had brought social and ecological disaster.

> The Polonoroeste project began as an attempt to create a self-sustaining agricultural frontier which would also protect the environment and indigenous groups. It ended up as the most notorious, the most expensive and the largest failure of development planning in the history of Amazonia.[40]

One result of this criticism of World Bank funding for Polonoroeste was that the then President of the Bank, Barber Conable, initiated a series of internal reforms in 1987. By 1990 the Bank's environmental staff had increased tenfold and environmental concerns were beginning to be integrated into country development strategies through the preparation of environmental action plans. According to a recent Bank report, environmental strategies will have been prepared, by mid 1993, for the 130 or more countries which are members of the International Development Association (an affiliate of the Bank which provides assistance to poorer developing countries).[41]

At the end of 1989, the Bank's Operational Directive on Environment Assessment was approved. The directive is supposed to ensure that an environmental assessment is carried out for all projects that may have a significant and negative impact on the environment. The Bank's four regional Environment Divisions coordinate and oversee the process of environmental assessment, which remains the responsibility of the borrower government. Pipeline projects are classified according to their likely environmental impact, with Category A projects requiring a full and detailed environmental assessment. Category B projects are subjected to a more limited analysis, and Category C projects are deemed not to require any assessment.

One important innovation is that Bank staff are now expected to seek the views of people who may be adversely affected by a proposed project. The Bank now acknowledges that project success often depends on effective local participation throughout the project cycle.[42]

Over the past ten years, most bilateral agencies such as the ODA have strengthened both their environmental procedures and the institutional arrangements for implementing them.[43] Though the development of these and the Environmental Assessment procedures at the World Bank and other multilateral development banks is an important step forward, much still depends on the political will of the borrower governments. Local communities and NGOs are usually denied access to project proposals and to confidential environmental assessment reports. The attitude of Bank staff responsible for projects is crucial: most still see their primary objective as fulfilling lending quotas rather than ensuring environmental sustainability. An internal memorandum from Lawrence Summers, the Bank's Chief Economist argued (allegedly tongue in cheek) that 'the economic logic behind dumping a load of toxic waste in the lowest-wage country is impeccable'. His observation that 'under-populated countries in Africa are vastly under-polluted' will have done little to reassure public opinion that the Bank, at its most senior levels, is indeed set on a course of promoting sustainable development.[44]

New challenges for aid

The key issue which has influenced official aid policy so far in the 1990s is the importance of 'good governance'. There is growing recognition that economic reform has failed to deliver equitable development. This recognition, together with the political developments in Eastern Europe and South Africa, have ensured that democratisation and its relationship to development have become major themes of the official aid debate. But much depends on what is understood by democratisation and how it is translated into action. At present, aid donors make much of the need for good governance, yet only parts of their aid budgets are directed to ensuring this. Official support for democratisation is at times in danger of being sacrificed for rival economic or political goals.

Promoting poor people's rights to participate in the political decisions which affect them has long been a hallmark of Oxfam's work. For many years, the experience of working in situations of armed conflict and of providing support for groups which challenge the causes of poverty, has confirmed that greater empowerment of poor people is a necessary precondition for their development. What counts for Oxfam is that the process of democratisation should include three essential elements: democratic access to political power and equality of economic opportunity; the introduction of democratic institutions which respect human rights and help to resolve conflict; and the implementation of mechanisms for full popular participation.

The new international consensus on the importance of democrat-isation creates an unprecedented opportunity for official resources to be directed towards people-centred development. The positive new emphasis in donors' statements on the importance of popular participation, poverty reduction and sound environmental management now needs to be translated into practice. One priority is for donors to increase the volume of aid spending, over five years, to reach the UN target of 0.7 per cent of GNP. Meeting the UN target means a virtual doubling of the British aid budget: the challenge is to achieve this as soon as possible while at the same time improving aid quality. One way towards this goal is to direct a larger proportion of aid to the poorest groups and make Primary Environmental Care programmes and projects a priority for aid spending – perhaps by channelling more aid through appropriate NGOs whose projects meet the new social and environmental criteria. Effective development assistance could not only promote PEC projects and programmes, but also help to create an enabling context at national level in which PEC can flourish.

EXTRA RESOURCES

In addition to more and better quality aid, and action on trade and debt, other new financial mechanisms are needed to accelerate progress towards sustainable development, not least to enable Southern countries to adopt appropriate technologies. There are various ways in which the flows from the rich world to the poor world can increase – greater spending through UN institutions, the transfer of revenues from an energy tax in the North, and through more environmentally sound private investment.

Global Environment Facility (GEF)

The GEF is a multilateral fund set up in 1990 to help developing countries address global problems – ozone depletion, climate change, loss of biodiversity and the pollution of international seas. The GEF is jointly managed by the World Bank, UNDP and UNEP and the funds committed to it must be in addition to existing aid flows. Its objective is to enable donors and recipients (as well as other agencies) to develop a better understanding of the global environment and promote the action necessary to protect it. To the annual GEF budget of US$1.5 billion, Britain pays £40.3 million (and a further £9.4 million under the Montreal Protocol fund to help Southern countries phase out chlorofluorocarbons).

Projects under the GEF must be based in a developing country with a per capita income of less than US$4000, and show substantial benefits for the global community (how indirect this can be is not yet clear). Projects are to be innovative, sustainable and take account of the interest of local people, and there is a Small Grants Programme to encourage small-scale ventures by NGOs and community groups.[45]

The priorities of the GEF are drawn from a Northern environmental agenda. During 1991, NGOs and others registered concern over a number of matters, including the GEF structure and management, and the increasing dominance of the World Bank. They fear that GEF funding may divert attention away from the need for reforms in Bank lending practices as a whole. The GEF does not yet have an obvious mechanism for finding out and taking account of local views. So far, it lacks any commitment to the ideal of public accountability. While participating donor governments have subsequently agreed to review the scope and structure of the GEF, doubts remain about its effectiveness.

THE WIDENING GAP

Repeated emergencies in the Third World reinforce the commonly-held notion that the rich North is transferring vast sums of money to the poor South. Nothing could be further from the truth. The reality is that, over the last decade, there has been a net transfer of funds from South to North. According to the OECD, between 1982 and 1990, total resource flows to Third World countries amounted to US$927 billion. Over the same period, these countries paid out US$1345 billion in debt service alone.[46] The figures for resources transferred showed a steady increase, and in 1989, the net transfer from South to North had reached US$51 billion.[47] Although the transfer from South to North was reduced in 1990, the World Bank predicts that the net flow of financial resources from the poor world to the rich world will continue until the mid 1990s, and possibly beyond.

For poor countries in the South, the interlinked trade and debt crisis presents a major obstacle to sustainable development. These structural inequities between North and South, and within the South, underly deepening poverty and rapidly deteriorating environments. The problems can be tackled, but only if governments in the North and the South show the political will to address them. The final chapter of this book offers an agenda for action.

11

NO TIME TO WASTE:
AN AGENDA FOR ACTION

Will the growing awareness of 'one earth' and 'one environment' guide us to the concept of 'one humanity'? Will there be a more equitable sharing of environmental costs and a greater international interest in the accelerated progress of the less-developed world?

Indira Gandhi, Stockholm 1972

Twenty years on, there are still no answers to the questions asked by Indira Gandhi at the first United Nations Conference on the Human Environment in 1972.

All the chapters of this book have stressed how dependent the poorest people are upon the natural environment, and how that environment is degrading fast, perhaps faster than at any other time. Many poor people use natural resources wisely, conserving them for the future. Yet a growing number have no option but to damage their environment further in the daily struggle to stay alive, forced into a downward spiral of increasing poverty as they over-exploit natural resources which they have traditionally managed in sustainable ways.

Their actions are driven by poverty but compounded by environmental changes which have their roots elsewhere. Economic development that serves the interests of a minority whilst threatening the livelihoods of poor communities, unjust terms of trade, crippling debts and armed conflict all contribute to environmental destruction. Alongside the inequities in North-South relations are the corruption and greed of powerful minorities in the South. All these factors keep poor people trapped in their poverty.

In spite of everything, against all the odds, poor communities are responding to environmental damage by evolving more resilient ways of living. For 50 years, Oxfam has been working at grassroots level with some of the poorest people, supporting them as they cope when their environments are under threat. But Oxfam believes that poor people cannot be expected to conserve resources for the future when they are struggling for survival now. It is equally unfair for the high-consuming, high-polluting countries of the North to expect people and governments in the South to protect their resource base, unless the North shows the political will to address global poverty, and reduce its own contribution to environmental destruction.

Throughout this book, the links between environmental degradation and poverty have been stressed. There is an urgent need to tackle both. Reducing poverty could relieve the pressure on poor people to exploit natural resources when they have no other option. Environmental regeneration provides one way out of the vicious spiral of a deteriorating resource base and increasing poverty.

This final chapter concentrates on Oxfam's priorities for translating its vision of a fairer, more sustainable world into the practical action to achieve it.

UNCED

The United Nations Conference on Environment and Development (UNCED) in Rio de Janeiro, offers a unique opportunity to make tangible progress towards more equitable and sustainable development – in both the North and the South. But, at the time of writing, the agenda is dominated by Northern concerns about the symptoms of the crisis and there is no sign of the political will necessary to tackle the underlying causes. From Oxfam's perspective, it is crucially important that the action agenda of UNCED ('Agenda 21') promotes changes aimed at reducing poverty as well as threats to the global environment.

People in the South want more rapid progress towards democratically accountable governments that are committed to equitable development. But change in the South must be met by an adequate response in the North. There is an urgent need for greater equity in North-South relations, including action on fairer terms of trade, debt reduction, improved aid and additional financial resources for the South, and the transfer of appropriate technologies and information.

Targets agreed at the Earth Summit have to be backed by the necessary institutional support for progress to be reviewed. Agenda 21 and its follow-up strategies for action need to be implemented at all levels from village associations to the UN Security Council. The rest of this chapter sets out some of the issues which require action at local, national and international levels.

SUSTAINABLE DEVELOPMENT AT THE LOCAL LEVEL
Primary Environmental Care

For development to be sustainable, it has to be about change: change shaped by people to meet their perceived needs. This change must be firmly rooted at the local level, but must be carried through to regional, national and international levels. From an Oxfam perspective, the most effective approach to sustainable development, especially at the local level, is the three-pronged approach which has come to be known as Primary Environmental Care. This involves popular empowerment, securing basic rights and needs and caring for the environment, and as Chapter 2 argued, PEC is a strategy that will succeed only if all three elements are tackled together.

- Oxfam believes that faster progress towards sustainable development can be made if governments, aid agencies, non-governmental organisations and the private sector all promote the practice of Primary Environmental Care.

At present, PEC is a response to locally expressed needs for environmental and social changes, preventative as well as curative, which go well beyond any technical solutions. Many wider environmental problems are aggregations of local problems: if replicated widely enough, the PEC approach could contribute to the solution of global problems such as deforestation and the loss of biodiversity.

Whilst Primary Environmental Care is principally a strategy for achieving change at local level, it will not succeed without a supportive national and international framework and the political will to tackle the obstacles to sustainable development operating at these different levels.

Women

The vital role of women as environmental carers and managers has been emphasised throughout this book. Oxfam believes that sustainable development can only take place when women have the power, status and independence to shape the decisions which profoundly affect their lives, including those which relate to the environment. Chapter 2 argued for positive action by many institutions to recognise and enhance women's role in caring for the environment and its resources. Practical action at all levels will be needed to:

- reduce the continuing damage to women brought about by misguided development policies and individual development projects (aid agencies, for example, will need to introduce early project screening procedures to assess potential problems and opportunities for women);

- improve the capacity of women and their organisations to be effective environmental resource managers and to benefit directly from this role (this will require, for example, greater empowerment and participation of women in development decisions, with increased training and the deployment of more women as project managers and extension workers, and action to reduce their work burdens);

- enable women to use and share their knowledge and traditional skills (through, for example, exchanges of project personnel within and between countries in the South and between the South and the North).

SUSTAINABLE DEVELOPMENT AT THE NATIONAL LEVEL

Democratisation

Oxfam's experience suggests that popular participation in decision making, and democratic accountability are key factors in moving towards sustainable development. Three aspects of democratisation are especially important.

First, there is the issue of 'fair shares' – democratic access to political power, and equality of economic opportunity. The absence of 'fair shares' results in stark contrasts between rich and poor, marginalisation of the powerless, and environmental degradation. The systematic marginalisation of people – expressed in ethnic, class, ideological, religious or geographical terms, is at the root of armed conflict. Sustainable, peaceful development cannot be achieved against a background of structural inequality. Secondly, there is a need for democratic institutions which respect human and minority rights and are capable of resolving conflicts peacefully. And thirdly, democracy means people having a fair say in the formulation of policies and programmes which affect their lives. A democratic society means open, responsive and accountable government.

Equity

Governments have also to tackle the massive inequalities in people's access to resources of all kinds, including water and land. People must be enabled to secure their basic rights and needs – for food, shelter, education, employment, health care and access to the means to control fertility. Investment in human resource development is a fundamental requirement for economic growth, and should be a priority in economic reforms.

Reduced military spending

Excessive military expenditure is diverting limited resources away from more productive investment in people-centred development, particularly in meeting health, education and employment needs. The problems are acute in some of the world's poorest countries, where enormous suffering is caused both directly by armed conflict and indirectly through the diversion of scarce resources. A significant reduction in military expenditure could release resources to be used for sustainable development.

Population

Oxfam's work suggests that the impact of high population growth rates is one of several complex and interacting factors which impede sustainable development in some developing countries. There is considerable evidence to show that, especially in the context of the health of women and children, control of fertility is an unmet need. It is also a democratic right – especially for women – and a demographic necessity. Chapter 9 argued that when rapid population growth is a problem, it is best addressed through an integrated approach which tackles poverty, improves the education and status of women, and widens access to appropriate birth planning services in the context of effective primary health care.

Environmental care

To implement effective programmes of environmental care, many Southern governments will require significant additional funding as well as the transfer of appropriate technologies and information on fairer terms.

Some of the poorest people in the South are most threatened by the impact of global environmental degradation, and governments in the North are beginning to recognise their responsibility for contributing to the problems. But it is time for these responsibilities to be reflected not only in policies at national level, but also in the international agreements now under negotiation.

It is generally recognised that two principles are vital to policy development: the 'polluter pays principle' so that industrialised countries accept full responsibility for their role in causing such environmental problems as global warming and ozone depletion; and the 'precautionary principle' – that, in the absence of conclusive scientific evidence, policies which have environmental implications are formulated and implemented with care and restraint.

Climate change

Global warming is likely to lead to climatic and ecological changes which could severely threaten food production, water supplies and increase the frequency of extreme weather patterns. Greenhouse gas emission from human activity is a major contributing factor to global warming and it is the industrialised countries, with their high energy consumption, that are primarily responsible. Countries in the South believe that they will have to increase their greenhouse gas emissions in the short term, in the interests of their own development, so this places an even greater responsibility on the North to reduce emissions, if global warming is to be slowed down. Energy-saving technologies need to be adopted, certainly in the North, but also in the South, particularly by the larger and more industrialised countries such as Brazil, India and China.

The commitment of the countries of the European Community to stabilise carbon dioxide emissions at the 1990 level by the year 2000 is welcome as a limited objective for tackling global warming. But this commitment needs to be acted on as soon as possible. Some see the implementation of an energy tax as one way towards tackling the problem. A percentage of the revenues generated by such a tax could be a source of additional funds for sustainable development in the South.

Fundamental changes will be necessary in energy and other resource consumption patterns in the North. These could include:

- greatly increased emphasis on reducing energy consumption;

- investment in energy conservation and efficiency programmes to meet social as well as environmental needs;

- more research into, and implementation of, renewable energy strategies;

- pricing of energy supplies to reflect the true social and environmental costs.

SUSTAINABLE DEVELOPMENT AT THE INTERNATIONAL LEVEL

There is growing recognition of global interdependence over problems such as global warming, deforestation, the narcotics trade and migration. Countries in the North as well as the South are now concerned about the impact of some of these problems on them – and this provides an incentive to negotiate on solutions.

At the same time, the countries of the South argue that it is their sovereign right to use their resources to advance economic development. In an increasingly interdependent world, this gives the South a bargaining counter in its negotiations with the North. But the prospects for sustainable development, and the success of the UNCED commitments and continuing negotiations, are poor unless inequities in the international economic system, which underlie poverty and foster the unsustainable use of resources, are reduced.

- It is vital that the environmental and social implications of trade, debt, structural adjustment programmes and aid policies are addressed, with proposals for early action on these issues.

Trade

As the previous chapter outlined, the interlinked problems of heavy dependence on commodities and declining terms of trade are shared by many of the countries in which Oxfam works. There are a number of possible ways forward, to benefit poor producers and commodity-dependent countries:

- Governments in the North and South could seek to regulate Commodity Markets so that prices are maintained at levels that reflect the ecological costs of production and give a fair return to producers.

- Northern governments could improve developing countries' access to markets in the North, in particular by reducing tariff escalation and withdrawing discriminatory non-tariff barriers to trade.

- Mechanisms could be established to counteract transfer pricing and other restrictive business practices.

- Governments in the North could implement policies designed to stop the dumping of subsidised agricultural exports on world markets in unfair competition with the Third World produce.

- Any new trading organisation to replace the GATT could be charged with improving appropriate technology transfers to the South and protecting the environment.

Debt

Oxfam has direct experience of the negative social and environmental impacts of the debt burden in many of the countries in which it works. The transfer of funds from South to North for debt servicing is draining resources urgently needed for development and to reduce poverty. The World Bank predicts that the net flow of wealth from the poor to the rich nations will continue at least until the mid-1990s and possibly beyond. Action on debt reduction is urgently needed at international level, and Oxfam suggests this could include the following measures:

- Building on the Trinidad Terms initiative, more creditor governments could implement significant debt reduction for the poorest, most indebted countries and increase the proportion of debt eligible for write-off from 50 per cent to two-thirds.

- At the same time, flexibility is required in applying eligibility criteria so that these recognise alternative structural adjustment programmes which prioritise social and environmental action alongside economic growth.

- Similar terms for official debt reduction are needed by other indebted Third World nations which are currently ineligible because they are not low-income countries.

- A substantial proportion of private commercial debt could be written off, with mechanisms established for refinancing on concessional terms.

- Action could be taken to ease the burden of servicing the debts owed to multilateral institutions, such as the World Bank and IMF.

Structural adjustment

Debtor nations have been encouraged to adopt structural adjustment programmes. Oxfam has direct experience of the serious impact on poor people of the cuts in government expenditure introduced under these programmes. Whilst far-reaching economic reforms are necessary in many countries to achieve growth and sustainable development, the needs of the poor should be paramount in any structural adjustment programmes.

- Structural adjustment programmes in poor countries can be designed to promote poverty alleviation alongside economic growth and to safeguard crucial investment in human resource development, health care and environmental protection and improvement.

- Structural adjustment policies could be reviewed to shift their focus towards domestic needs and reduce the over-supply of primary commodities on world markets.

Aid

At a time of unprecedented need, aid flows have been falling, with UK development assistance now down to 0.3 per cent of GNP (in 1992). More and better quality aid is required. The positive new emphasis in donors' statements on the need for poverty reduction, environmental management and popular participation is welcome, and can be translated into practice by:

- setting a five-year timetable for increasing the volume of aid to meet the UN target of 0.7 per cent of GNP;

- making local level Primary Environmental Care projects a priority for aid spending.

Aid donors could foster the linkage of democracy with development by making aid conditional on the following criteria:

- people having democratic access to political power with equality of economic opportunity;

- the maintenance of democratic institutions, the rule of law, respect for human rights and a free press;

- people having a decisive voice in issues which affect their lives and development.

Financial mechanisms

In addition to greater equity in the international economic system, other new financial mechanisms are needed for faster progress towards sustainable development. Ways in which the volume of North-South financial flows can be increased include:

- greater spending through UN institutions;

- the transfer of revenues from a tax on Northern energy consumption;

- more environmentally sound private investment.

The Role of the United Nations

The UN has a vital part to play in the move towards sustainable development, peace and greater North-South equity. But this will require member nations to take immediate steps to invest the UN with a more effective role in mediating armed conflict, protecting human rights, curbing the arms trade (notably through the UN Arms Register) and improving the environment. The distinction between 'environment' and 'development' programmes has little meaning in practice and could usefully be replaced by programmes based on 'sustainable development'. Within the context of a strengthened UN, action to promote sustainable development and to tackle the underlying causes of poverty and environmental degradation can be accelerated by increasing the effectiveness and budget allocations of UN agencies.

Conventions and agreements

Efforts to develop legally binding Conventions on Climate Change and Biodiversity and a Statement of Forest Principles have been under way for several years. But they are unlikely to be concluded in time for the Earth Summit. The gap between North and South in all these negotiations is extremely wide and the needs of the world's poorest people are not adequately recognised. A major difficulty lies in the reluctance of the North to provide more funds for the South. The Conventions are likely to fail unless the North agrees to give additional funds to the South.

- In Oxfam's view the needs of poor people have to be fully addressed in international agreements currently under negotiation.

Convention on Climate Change
Poor people in many countries where Oxfam works are at risk from climate changes which are predicted to result from global warming.

- If major climatic disasters and continuing environmental degradation are to be avoided, and opportunities for development in the South to be enhanced, then the North will need to recognise its major responsibility for global warming, reduce energy consumption, increase energy conservation and efficiency, and the use of renewable energy sources.

- Appropriate mechanisms for funding and technology transfer will need to be agreed for Southern countries themselves to pursue policies of energy conservation and efficiency.

Convention on Biodiversity
Countries in the South are rich in biological diversity but its continuing loss is undermining options for the future. The best way to ensure the long-term conservation of biological diversity in the South is through the promotion of sustainable development and a balanced agreement on access to genetic resources and appropriate technologies.

- The Biodiversity Convention could promote fairer access to genetic resources, to the research based on them and to appropriate technologies. It could ensure that national laws and policies, and international agreements such as the GATT, particularly on intellectual property rights, do not restrict access.

For the Biodiversity Convention to be successful in practice, it is important that small farmers, many of whom are women, and indigenous communities, participate fully in decision making. They have to be able to assume a major role in managing – and benefiting from – the biological resources on which they rely. These measures could be integrated into Primary Environmental Care projects and include:

- protecting and enhancing local knowledge and innovations;
- strengthening locally based conservation, research and development;

- greater participation of local communities in formulating and implementing national plant genetic resources programmes and those of the International Research Centres.

Agreement on the protection of forests
Chapters 1 and 6 described how the world's forests are disappearing at an ever-increasing rate. Forest losses threaten the livelihoods of many millions of traditional forest people and have far-reaching implications for biological diversity, global warming, and climate patterns.

Despite international concern over deforestation, the gap between North and South is very great on this issue. The North is calling for an agreement to protect tropical forests, whilst the countries of the South are insisting on their sovereign right to develop their forests and trade in forest products in the ways they choose. Given the rate of forest destruction, securing some agreement is vital. The root causes of deforestation, which often lie in the international economic system and in the spread of poverty, are central to the discussion and to any agreements to deal with the issue.

Deforestation is likely to bring an increase in poverty rather than its resolution. Governments wishing to avoid forest loss have a variety of options; but they need to look at the social inequalities which underlie deforestation, such as the lack of land rights for poor people. From its experience in working with forest dwellers, Oxfam believes that progress could be made by concluding agreements which:

- take into account the needs of large numbers of people (including indigenous communities) whose livelihoods depend on forests. These 'guardians of the forest' deserve to be recognised and suitably compensated for their role in forest management;

- promote popular participation in a decentralised manner taking special account of women's changing activities in the community;

- ensure that if plantations or forest reserves are created, they do not displace landless peasant families offering them little alternative but to encroach on other fragile lands;

- address the question of land rights;

- include a moratorium on rainforest destruction, and a major aid programme to invest in the infrastructure required to set forest products and the livelihoods of indigenous forest dwellers on a firm economic footing;

- address the issue of appropriate technology transfer: developing countries have been calling for this in return for taking steps to limit deforestation;

- incorporate the concept of Primary Environmental Care into any measures concerning deforestation and forest policy.

The Global Environment Facility (GEF)

The Global Environment Facility's objective is to enable donors and recipients, as well as international agencies and others, to develop a better understanding of the global environment and to promote action to protect it. Oxfam suggests that:

- the GEF be regarded as complementary, but not an alternative, to moves towards debt reduction, fairer terms of trade or other means of providing extra financial resources for the South;

- the GEF is not used as a means of mitigating the harmful effects of World Bank projects where the issue is their fundamental redesign;

- the management of the GEF be shared equally between donors and recipients; NGO views on the management structure of the GEF should be taken into account in its design;

- GEF projects and the Small Grants Programme are carefully monitored to ensure they take account of the needs of local people and their environment by, for example, providing for a review by local community representatives and social scientists;

- local people and NGOs have timely access to information and are able to participate in decision making;

- the disbursement of funds for a project be delayed until agreement is reached on the management structure and financial mechanisms.

No time to waste!

In an interdependent world, the solutions to environment and development problems require global cooperation. The 1992 United Nations Conference on Environment and Development – the Earth Summit – is only one stage in the process of countries, organisations and individuals committing themselves to the action required for sustainable development, which underpins the reduction of poverty.

Many agreements scheduled for conclusion at UNCED, and other agreements that are necessary, will have to be negotiated in other fora, such as the GATT and the Paris Club. UNCED may provide the impetus for these negotiations to take place; they now have to be concluded and implemented. Appropriate mechanisms for reviewing progress will be needed, designed to monitor and evaluate the agreements and ensure that follow-up efforts are not dissipated.

Continuing action on structural change at national and international levels is crucially important if progress is to be made towards sustainable development. Oxfam's purpose in publishing this book is to create understanding and a sense of urgency about the problems of poverty and the environment. It is imperative that the rich world listens more carefully to the voices of people in the South and learns from their experience. Faced with the global environmental crisis, North and South alike must recognise that working interdependently and with a common purpose offers the best hope, not just for relieving poverty and suffering – but for securing a sustainable future for all the world's people.

Children in Orissa sing a song about their forest. The environmental organisation, Friends of Trees and Living Beings (p.9-10), regards work with young people as vital for ensuring sustainable development for the future.

NOTES

INTRODUCTION
1 UNDP (1991) *Human Development Report 1991*, Oxford: Oxford University Press.
 Oxfam: *The Oxfam Report: It's Time for a Fairer World*, Oxford: Oxfam.
2 World Commission on Environment and Development (1987) *Our Common Future*,
 Oxford: Oxford University Press.

CHAPTER 1
1 Quoted in Lean G (1992) 'How they cut down the tree woman of Kenya', *The Observer*, 8 March.
2 The World Bank defines absolute poverty as an income within the range of US$275–370 per year; or, less than US$1 a day. World Bank (1990) *Development Report 1990*, Washington DC USA: World Bank.
 Poor people as a proportion of the world population (23%) has remained the same since 1975, but as the total population has grown, so has the number of those in absolute poverty.
3 UNDP (1991) *Human Development Report 1991*, Oxford: Oxford University Press.
4 ibid.
5 UNICEF (1991) *State of the World's Children 1991*, Oxford: Oxford University Press.
6 UNDP (1991) op. cit.
7 ibid.
8 Dankelman I and Davidson J (1988) *Women and Environment in the Third World*, London: Earthscan.
9 Shiva V (1988) *Staying Alive: Women, Ecology and Development*, London: Zed Books.
10 Banda F 'The buffalo gone, times are hard', *Oxfam News*, Autumn 1991.
11 Durning A (1989) *Poverty and the Environment: Reversing the Downward Spiral*, Worldwatch Paper 92, Washington DC: Worldwatch Institute.
12 Human J (1992) 'Friends of the Trees and Living Beings', unpublished internal Oxfam paper. Oxfam project ORS 091.
13 Leach M and Mearns R (1992) *Poverty and Environment in Developing Countries – An Overview Study*; report prepared for the Economic and Social Research Council and the Overseas Development Administration; to be published by the Institute of Development Studies, University of Sussex, Brighton.
14 The links between poverty and environment are complex. It is not always the case that poverty leads to environmental degradation – sometimes it can limit people's impact on natural resources. In the rich world, increasing wealth evidently does lead to environmental damage. For a further analysis of the linkages see:
 Leach and Mearns (1992) op. cit.
 Lipton M (1991) 'A note on poverty and sustainability' in *IDS Bulletin* 22:4, Institute of Development Studies, University of Sussex, Brighton.
15 Oxfam project TAN 343.
16 Oxfam (1991) *The Oxfam Report: It's Time for a Fairer World*, Oxford: Oxfam; and Timberlake L (1988) *Africa in Crisis*, London: Earthscan.
 Countries of Africa severely affected by famine and conflict are Sudan, Ethiopia, Somalia and Liberia.
17 *Oxfam, Poverty and the Environment*; Oxfam Information Leaflet, 1991.
 see also: UNDP (1991) op. cit.
18 The Relief Society of Tigray (REST), Oxfam project KHT 053.
19 Dwip Unnayan Sangstha (DUS), Oxfam project BGD 215.
20 Foley G (1991) *Global Warming: Who is Taking the Heat?*, London: Panos.

21 The section on Bangladesh is derived from a case study commissioned for this book and written in 1991 by Ro Cole, formerly Oxfam Deputy Country Representative in Bangladesh.

22 Statistics are drawn from:
Brown L et al (1990) *State of the World 1990*, Washington DC: Worldwatch Institute;
World Commission on Environment and Development (1987) *Our Common Future*, Oxford: Oxford University Press;
Food and Agriculture Organisation (FAO) Rome, Italy and United Nations Environment Programme (UNEP) Nairobi, Kenya.
See also Chapter 6, endnote 7.

23 UNEP (1991) *Environmental Effects of Ozone Depletion, 1991 Update*, Nairobi: UNEP.

24 Commonwealth Group of Experts (1989) *Climate Change: Meeting the Challenge*, London: Commonwealth Secretariat.

25 Intergovernmental Panel on Climate Change (IPCC) (1990) *Scientific Assessment of Climate Change; Report of Working Group 1*, World Meteorological Organisation and UNEP, Geneva and Nairobi.
see also: Foley G (1991) op. cit.

26 Calculated from statistics given by the IPCC (1990) and the Commonwealth Group of Experts (1989) op. cit.

27 IPCC (1990) op. cit.

28 UNDP (1991) op. cit.

CHAPTER 2

1 Judd F (1991) in Oxfam's *Annual Review*; Oxford: Oxfam.

2 All the material on Brazil and Amazonia is drawn from a case study commissioned by Oxfam for this book and written in 1991 by Raja Jarrah, formerly Oxfam Deputy Country Representative.

3 Clark J (1991) *Democratising Development*, London: Earthscan.

4 World Commission on Environment and Development (1987) *Our Common Future*, Oxford: Oxford University Press. (Also known as the Brundtland Report, after the Chair of the Commission, Gro Harlem Brundtland, Norwegian Prime Minister.)

5 This quotation comes from a speech delivered in Cambridge in 1990, published in Angell D, Comer J and Wilkinson M (eds.) (1990) *Endangered Earth*, London: Macmillan.

6 Jackson B (1990) *Poverty and the Planet: A Question of Survival*, London: Penguin Books.
See also: IUCN, UNEP, WWF (1991) *Caring for the Earth: A Strategy for Sustainable Living*, Gland, Switzerland: IUCN.

7 Commonwealth Secretariat (1991) *Sustainable Development*; report by a Commonwealth Group of Experts on Environmental Concerns and the Commonwealth, London: Commonwealth Secretariat.

8 Preparatory Committee for UNCED (1992) *Combating Poverty*; report of the Secretary General of the Conference, New York: UNCED Secretariat.

9 Chambers R (1988) 'Sustainable rural livelihoods: a key strategy for people, environment and development', in: Conroy C and Litvinoff M (eds) *The Greening of Aid*, London: IIED/Earthscan.

10 Dankelman I and Davidson J (1988) *Women and Environment in the Third World*, London: Earthscan.
see also: Commonwealth Secretariat (1991) *Sustainable Development*; report by a Group of Experts on Environmental Concerns and the Commonwealth, London: Commonwealth Secretariat.

11 Shiva V (1988) *Staying Alive: Women, Ecology and Development*, London: Zed Books.
See also: Antrobus P (1991) 'Women in development', in: Wallace T and March C (eds) *Changing Perceptions: Writings on Gender and Development*, Oxford: Oxfam.

12 Holmberg J, Bass S, Timberlake L (1991) *Defending the Future: a Guide to Sustainable Development*, London: IIED/Earthscan.

13 PEC is an idea in progress, developed so far by work in Oxfam, International Institute for Environment and Development (IIED), Instituto Superiore di Sanita in Rome, and other agencies. See, for example:

Holmberg J (1992) *Primary Environmental Care – Building Participatory Approaches to Local Conservation of the Environment*, unpublished paper, London: IIED.

Pretty J and Sandbrook R (1991) *Operationalising Sustainable Development at the Community Level: Primary Environmental Care*, unpublished paper presented to the members of the Working Party on Development Assistance and the Environment of the Development Assistance Committee of the OECD.

Ministero degli Affari Esteri (1990) *Supporting Primary Environmental Care*; report of the PEC Workshop, Siena, to OECD/DAC Working Party on Development Assistance and the Environment; Direzione Generale per la Cooperatione allo Sviluppo, Ministero degli Affari Esteri, Italy.

14 Dwip Unnayan Sangstha (DUS) Oxfam project BGD 215.

15 Khetan N, McGean B, Dangi M (1990) *Wasteland Development through Community Action*, Udaipur, India: Seva Mandir; and

Seva Mandir (1990) *Annual Report 1989–90*, Udaipur, India: Seva Mandir.

16 Affolé, Oxfam project MTA 016.

17 MacDonald N (1991) *Brazil: a Mask Called Progress*, Oxford: Oxfam.

18 MacDonald N *The Andes Report*, forthcoming book, Oxford: Oxfam.

19 Further details from Groundwork Foundation, 85–87 Cornwall Street, Birmingham B3 3BY.

20 See for example:

Davidson J (1988) *How Green is Your City?* Bedford Square Press, London.

CHAPTER 3

1 Lean G, Hinrichsen D and Markham A (1990) *Atlas of the Environment*, London: Arrow Books/ WWF.

2 Lean et al (1990) op. cit.

3 *Oxfam and Water*, Oxfam Project Fund leaflet, March 1991.

4 UNICEF (1987) *Water Supply and Sanitation in UNICEF 1946–86*, New York: UNICEF.

5 Lean et al (1990) op. cit.

6 UNHCR (1982) *Handbook for Emergencies*, Geneva: UNHCR.

7 Matthew B (1991) 'The planner-manager's guide to Third World water projects' in Wallace T and March C (eds) *Changing Perceptions: Writings on Gender and Development*, Oxford: Oxfam.

8 Brett A (1987) 'Changing the approach? The Wollo water experience', *GADU Newspack* 3, Oxford: Oxfam.

9 GVVS, Oxfam project RJN 28.

10 Oxfam and Kenya; Oxfam Information leaflet, 1991.

11 Turkana Restocking Programme, Oxfam project KEN 195; Samburu Livestock De/restocking Programme, Oxfam project KEN 198.

12 Wolaiyta Water Project, Oxfam project SID 188.

13 Phnom Penh Waterworks, Oxfam project CAM 041.

14 Dyke Construction Programme, Oxfam project RVN 090.

15 The section on Bangladesh is derived from a case study commissioned for this book and written in 1991 by Ro Cole, formerly Oxfam Deputy Country Representative in Bangladesh.

16 Ives J (1991) 'Floods in Bangladesh: who is to blame?', *New Scientist*, 13 April.

Pearce F (1991) 'The rivers that won't be tamed', *New Scientist*, 13 April.

17 Own Village Advancement, Oxfam project BGD 226.

18 Clark, J (1990) Oxfam internal memorandum.
19 ARCH, Oxfam project GUJ 078.
20 *Oxfam and Water*, op. cit.
21 Pearce F (1991) 'Wells of conflict on the West Bank', *NewScientist*, 1 June.
22 *Jerusalem Post*, 18 August, 1991
23 According to Malin Falkenmark, people experience water stress if they have less than 44 litres per day available in aquifers and rivers. 'Absolute water scarcity' exists when people have less than 3 litres per day. Falkenmark M and Adiwoso Suprapto R (1992) 'Population–landscape interactions in development: a water perspective to environmental sustainability', *Ambio: A Journal of the Human Environment*, 21:1. Royal Swedish Academy of Sciences.
24 Palestinians argue that this violates the Fourth Geneva Convention governing the rules of belligerent occupation.
25 Report by an Oxfam worker.
26 Leader of the Palestinian Hydrology Group quoted in *The Guardian*, 31 May 1991.

CHAPTER 4

1   Pramod Unia, Oxfam's Regional Manager for Bangladesh.
2   Whittemore C (1981) *Land for People: Land Tenure and the Very Poor*, Oxford: Oxfam.
3   Graham O (1991) 'Pastoral women and drought: social dislocation in Central Somalia', *GADU Newspack* 6, Oxford: Oxfam.
4   Salinisation is the accumulation of salts in soil, often from over-irrigation, particularly with water having a high concentration of mineral salts. This can degrade the land beyond the point at which it can support plant life.
5   Worldwatch Institute (1990) *State of the World, 1990*, Washington DC: Worldwatch Institute.
6   Sfeir-Younis A (1986) *Soil Conservation in Developing Countries: A Background Report*, Washington DC: World Bank.
7   'Thinking about desertification', *Baobab* 5, 1990, Oxford: Oxfam.
8   Oxfam project BKF 093.
9   Critchley W (1991) *Looking After Our Land*, Oxford: Oxfam.
10 Hardin G (1968) 'The tragedy of the commons', *Science*, 162, no. 3859.
11 Leach M and Mearns R (1992) Poverty and Environment in Developing Countries – An Overview Study; report prepared for the Economic and Social Research Council and the Overseas Development Administration; to be published by the Institute of Development Studies, University of Sussex, Brighton.
12 Jodha N S (1991) *Rural Common Property Resources: A Growing Crisis*, Gatekeeper Series 24, London: IIED; 'Pastoral Land Tenure in Africa', IIED Drylands Programme Proposal, 1990.
13 FAO (1990) *The State of Food and Agriculture*, Rome, Italy: FAO.
14 Pineda-Ofreneo R (1991) *The Philippines: Debt and Poverty*, Oxford: Oxfam.
15 Oxfam Public Affairs Unit (1984) *An Unnatural Disaster: Drought in North–East Brazil*, Oxford: Oxfam.
16 Feeney P (1992) 'Environmental reform in Brazil: advances and reversals', *Development in Practice*, 2:1, Oxford: Oxfam.
17 Cleary D (1991) 'The greening of the Amazon' in: Goodman D and Redclift M (eds) *Environment and Development in Latin America: The Politics of Sustainability*, Manchester: Manchester University Press.
18 Castilho C (1991) 'The deadly toll of a land war', *Panoscope* 24, May.
19 Information about the death of Expedito Ribeiro de Souza is based on an *Action Alert* from Amnesty International, 4 February 1991.
20 Feeney P (1992) op. cit.
21 The section on Amazonia is derived from a case study on Amazonia commissioned for this book and written in 1991 by Raja Jarrah, formerly Oxfam

Deputy Country Representative in Recife, Brazil.

22 Goodman D and Hall A (eds.) (1990) *The Future of Amazonia*, London: Macmillan.

23 The section on South Africa is derived from a case study on South Africa written for this book in 1991 by Matthew Sherrington, Communications Officer, South Africa Desk, Oxfam.

24 Durning A (1990) *Apartheid's Environmental Toll*, Worldwatch Paper 95, Washington DC, USA: Worldwatch Institute.

25 Oxfam project RSA 380.

26 Blaikie P and Brookfield H (1987) *Land Degradation and Society*, London.

27 Monan J (1989) *Bangladesh: The Strength to Succeed*, Oxford: Oxfam.

28 Samata, Oxfam project BGD 203.

29 Monan J (1989) op.cit.

30 World Bank (1991) *World Development Report 1991*, Washington DC, USA: World Bank.

CHAPTER 5

1 World Bank (1990) *World Development Report 1990*, Washington DC: World Bank.

2 *Oxfam and Food*, Oxfam Information leaflet, 1991.

3 World Bank (1986) *Poverty and Hunger*, Washington DC: World Bank. Quoted in Conway G R and Barbier E B (1990) *After the Green Revolution: Sustainable Agriculture for Development*, London: Earthscan.

4 Jackson B (1990) *Poverty and the Planet: A Question of Survival*, London: Penguin Books.

5 Jacobson J L (1991) 'India's misconceived family plan', *World Watch*, 4:6.

6 The notion of 'entitlements' was first proposed by Amartya Sen. It is developed in a paper by Leach M and Mearns R (1992) *Poverty and Environment in Developing Countries – An Overview Study*; report prepared for the Economic and Social Research Council and the Overseas Development Administration; to be published by the Institute of Development Studies, University of Sussex, Brighton.

7 FAO Committee on Commodity Problems, *International Trade and World Food Security*, quoted in Conway and Barbier (1990) op.cit.

8 Foley G (1991) *Global Warming: Who is Taking the Heat?* London: Panos.

9 Oxfam Information Unit, 1991.

10 The Pesticides Trust (1989) *The FAO Code: Missing Ingredients*, London: The Pesticides Trust.

11 Cole R (1989) 'Changes in tree density on five sites in Red Sea Province early 1960s to 1989' in: Cole R (ed) *Measuring Drought and Drought Impacts in Red Sea Province*, Oxfam Research Paper 2, Oxford: Oxfam.

12 Conway and Barbier (1990) op. cit.

13 Holmberg J, Bass S and Timberlake L (1991) *Defending the Future: A Guide to Sustainable Development*, London: Earthscan.

14 Mosse J C (1991) *India: Paths to Development*, Oxford: Oxfam.

15 Mary Cherry, 1992. Personal communication.

16 Mosse J C (1991) op. cit.

17 ibid.

18 The Pesticides Trust (1989) op. cit.

19 Hazell P and Ramasamy C (1991) *The Green Revolution Reconsidered*, Food Policy Statement 14, December, Washington DC: International Food Policy Research Institute.

20 Mosse J C (1991) op. cit.

21 Clark J (1989) *Zambia: Debt and Poverty*, Oxford: Oxfam.

22 Chiyanjano Group, Oxfam project ZAM 626; Tiyeseko Group, Oxfam project ZAM 635.

23 The section on Zambia is derived from a case study commissioned for this book

and written in 1991 by Gabriel Banda.

24 Chama Drought Relief Project, Oxfam project ZAM 645.

25 From case study by Gabriel Banda, see above.

26 Hobbelink H (1991) *Biotechnology and the Future of World Agriculture*, London: Zed Books.

27 'Traditional plants in Kenya: reversing the apathy', *Seedling 8:2*, April 1991.

CHAPTER 6

1   All the material on Brazil and Amazonia is drawn from a case study commissioned by Oxfam for this book and written in 1991 by Raja Jarrah, formerly Oxfam Deputy Country Representative.

2   Estimates suggest this accounts for up to 30 per cent of CO_2 emissions (see WWF (1990) *Tropical Forests, Gland*, Switzerland: WWF.

3   WWF (1990) op. cit.

4   ibid.

5   Miller G T (1990) *Living in the Environment*, Belmont, CA: Wadsworth Publishing Company.

6   Prance G (1990) 'Tropical forests' in: Winpenny J (ed.) *Development Research: The Environmental Challenge*, London: Overseas Development Institute.

7   FAO estimated in 1990 that the annual rate of tropical deforestation in 87 countries in the tropical region was 17 million hectares (*Forest Resources Assessment 1990 Project*, Rome: FAO). WWF believes that in addition, 4 million hectares each year are degraded by logging. Other researchers believe the estimates are conservative. Norman Myers estimates that 15 million hectares of tropical moist forest was destroyed in 1991, to which should be added a further 7.4 million hectares of dry forest, making a total of 22.4 million hectares (Myers N (1991) 'Tropical forests: present status and future outlook', *Climatic Change* 19).

8   Holmberg J, Bass S and Timberlake L (1990) *Defending the Future: A Guide to Sustainable Development*, London: Earthscan.

9   Myers N (1989) *Deforestation Rates in Tropical Forests and their Climatic Implications*, Friends of the Earth Report, London: FOE.

10 ibid.

11 Prance G (1990) op. cit.

12 World Resources Institute (1991) *World Resources 1990-91*, Oxford: Oxford University Press.

13 Hurst P (1990) *Rainforest Politics: Ecological Destruction in South–East Asia*, London: Zed Books.

14 Pineda-Ofreneo R (1990) *Philippines: Debt and Poverty*, Oxford: Oxfam.

15 ibid. The project in which Ka Rudy Sambajon is involved is Oxfam project PHL 090.

16 World Bank (1991) *World Bank Report, 1991*, Washington DC: World Bank.

17 Pineda-Ofreneo R (1991) op.cit.

18 Lean G, Hinrichsen D and Markham A (1990) *Atlas of the Environment*, London: Arrow Books/WWF.

19 Repetto R (1988) *The Forest for the Trees: Government Policies and the Misuse of Forest Resources*, Washington DC: World Resources Institute.

20 Holmberg et al. (1991) op.cit.

21 ibid.

22 Mosse J C (1991) *India: Paths to Development*, Oxford: Oxfam.

23 Oxfam project RVN 109 and 110.

24 Oxfam project BRZ 285.

25 Beauclerk J (1991) *Hunters and Gatherers in Central Africa*, Oxfam Research Paper 7, Oxford: Oxfam.

26 ibid.

27 ibid

28 Cleary D (1991) 'The greening of the Amazon' in: Goodman D and Redclift M (eds.) *Environment and Development in Latin America: The Politics of Sustainability,* Manchester: Manchester University Press.

29 Fearnside P (1988) 'Causes of deforestation in the Brazilian Amazon', *Pará Desenvolvimento* 23.

30 Oxfam project BRZ 546.

31 Oxfam project PRU 266.

32 Saxena N C (1991) 'Is farm forestry dead in North–West India today?' in *Wastelands News* 6:4.

33 Mosse D (1991) internal Oxfam report.

34 Abhijit Bhattarcharjee, writing in the *Deccan Herald*, 19 November 1987. Quoted in Mosse J C (1991) op.cit. Abhijit Bhattarcharjee is Deputy Regional Director for Oxfam in Delhi.

35 Oxfam project ORS 091.

36 Ie Rai ,Oxfam project IDS 122.

37 World Rainforest Movement (1990) *The International Tropical Timber Organisation: Kill or Cure for the Rainforests?*, Penang, Malaysia: WRM.

38 Colchester M (1991) 'TFAP reforms deadlocked', *Bank Check*, Fall.

39 Feeney P (1991) *The World Bank's Tropical Forestry Policy: An Oxfam Response*, Oxfam internal policy paper.

40 Shepherd G (1990) 'Tropical dry forests' in: Winpenny J (ed) *Development Research:* op. cit.

41 ibid.

42 *The Gaia Atlas of Planet Management* (1985), London: Pan Books.

43 Lean et al. (1990) op. cit.

44 Material on Zambia is drawn from a case study commissioned for this book and written by Gabriel Banda in 1991.

45 Lean et al. (1990) op. cit.

46 Oxfam project TAN 324.

47 Oxfam project UPD 078.

CHAPTER 7

1 Miller G T (1992) *Living in the Environment*, Belmont CA: Wadsworth Publishing House.
see also:
Lean G, Hinrichson D and Markham A (1990) *Atlas of the Environment*, London: Arrow Books/WWF.
Holmberg J, Bass S and Timberlake L (1991) *Defending the Future: a Guide to Sustainable Development*, London: Earthscan.

2 The section on Mexico is derived from a case study commissioned for this book written in 1992 by Deborah Eade, Development Support Unit, Oxfam, with additional material from Mireya Sofia Trejo Orozco, a member of Casa Y Ciudad, Mexico.

3 World Commission on Environment and Development (1987), *Our Common Future*, Oxford: Oxford University Press.

4 Oxfam field reports from these countries.

5 Lean et al (1990) op. cit.

6 All the material on Brazil and Amazonia is drawn from a case study commissioned by Oxfam for this book and written in 1991 by Raja Jarrah, formerly Oxfam Deputy Country Representative.

7 Oxfam project WBE 116.

8 Dankelman I and Davidson J (1988) *Women and Environment in the Third World*, London: Earthscan.

9   PREDES, Oxfam project PRU 310.
10 Hardoy J and Satterthwaite D (1989) *Squatter Citizen: Life in the Urban Third World*, London: Earthscan.
11 Moser C (1991) 'Gender planning in the Third World: meeting practical and strategic gender needs', in Wallace T and March C (eds) (1991) *Changing Perceptions, Writings on Gender and Development*, Oxford: Oxfam.
    See also: Hosken F (1987) 'Women, urbanisation and shelter', in *Development Forum*, May 1987.
12 Casa Y Ciudad, Oxfam project MEX 641. Additional material supplied by Mireya Sofia Trejo Orozco, member of Casa Y Ciudad and Deborah Eade, Development Support Unit, Oxfam.
13 Calcutta Social Project, Oxfam project WBE 048.
14 Oxfam project EGY 068.
15 Oxfam project EGY 066.
16 Holmberg et al (1991) op. cit.
17 Hardoy J, Cairncross S and Satterthwaite D (eds) (1990) *The Poor Die Young: Housing and Health in Third World Cities*; Earthscan, London.

CHAPTER 8

1   Oxfam (1991) *The Oxfam Report: It's Time for a Fairer World*, Oxford: Oxfam.
2   International Committee of the Red Cross, (1991) *Casualties of Conflict*, Uppsala University, Sweden.
3   UN (1985) *United Nations Study on Conventional Disarmament*, New York: United Nations.
4   Oxfam (1991), op. cit.
5   ibid.
6   *Oxfam and Refugees*, Oxfam Information Leaflet, 1990.
7   UNHCR (1990), *UNHCR and the New World Order*, Geneva: UNHCR.
8   Ulrich R (1989) *Environment and Security in the Horn of Africa*; Nairobi, Kenya:UNEP.
9   *The Guardian*, 31 May 1991.
10 Sivard R L (1991) *World Military and Social Expenditures 1991*, Washington DC: World Priorities. US and UK figures, for 1987, for comparison:
    US: Military spending $293,211 million, 6.5% GNP; Health $207,300 million, 4.6% GNP; Education $240,820 billion, 5.3% GNP.
    UK: Military spending $31,489 million, 4.6% GNP; Health $35,026 million 5.1% GNP; Education $35,081, 5.1% GNP.
11 Worldwatch Institute (1992) *State of the World 1992*, Washington DC: Worldwatch Institute.
12 Bennett O (ed) (1991) *Greenwar; Environment and Conflict*, London: Panos.
13 All material on El Salvador, unless otherwise stated, is taken from an Oxfam case study commissioned for this book and written by Deborah Eade, Development Support Unit, Oxfam, Oxford, UK.
14 MacDonald N (1990) *Central America: Options for the Poor*, Oxford: Oxfam.
15 Abdelnour L (1991) *The Impact of the Gulf Crisis on the Environment and Agriculture in Iraq: Environmental and Agricultural Survey*; report by Harvard Study Team.
16 ibid.
17 UNICEF is now involved in long-term development work in this region.
18 *The Economic Impact of the Gulf Crisis on Third World Countries* (1990); report prepared for CAFOD, Christian Aid, CIIR, Oxfam, SCF and WDM, London: Overseas Development Institute.
19 Banda F, 'The buffalo gone, times are hard', *Oxfam News*, Autumn 1991.
20 Duffield M (1991) *War and Famine in Africa*, Oxfam Research Paper 5, Oxford: Oxfam.

21 Alex de Waal (1991) 'Famine and human rights', *Development in Practice*, 1:2. Oxford: Oxfam.
22 UN (1990) *Voices from Africa,* Geneva, Switzerland: UN Non-governmental Liaison Service.
23 Ulrich R (1989) op. cit.
24 Economist Intelligence Unit (1991–92) *Country Profile on Ethiopia*, London: EIU.
25 World Bank (1991) *World Debt Tables 1991-2, Vol.2*, Washington DC: World Bank.
26 Duffield M (1991) op. cit.
27 Oxfam project KHE 034.
28 *Preventing Famine in Ethiopia*, Oxfam Information leaflet, 1990.
29 Oxfam project SDX 045.
30 Oxfam projects ELS 078 and ELS 645.
31 Drury P (1990) 'Model city: repatriates start afresh', *New Internationalist* 212, October.
32 Worldwatch Institute (1992) op. cit.
33 Postel S (1992) 'Denial in the decisive decade', Worldwatch Institute (1992) op. cit.

CHAPTER 9

1 Interview in *Women in Action*, 2, 1991.
2 UNFPA (1991) *The State of the World's Population*, New York: UNFPA.
3 Population growth rate is the difference between birth rates and death rates.
4 UNDP (1991) *Human Development Report 1991*, Oxford: Oxford University Press.
5 IUCN, UNEP and WWF (1991) *Caring for the Earth: A Strategy for Sustainable Living*, Gland, Switzerland: IUCN.
6 UNFPA (1991) op. cit.
7 Overseas Development Administration, Natural Resources and Environment Department (1991) 'Population, Environment and Development'. Paper prepared for the preparatory committee of UNCED.
8 By comparison, Wales had a total population in 1989 of 2.87 million.
9 Material on Rwanda has been drawn from a country report written by David Waller, to be published by Oxfam in 1992.
10 ibid.
11 Rwanda Government 1984. National Inquiry into Household Expenditure.
12 Oxfam field office report, January 1991.
13 National Conservation Strategy. Report to the Government of Pakistan. May 1990.
14 UNDP (1991) op. cit.
15 Rowley J (1990) 'Linking population to conservation', *Earthwatch* 40, IPPF.
16 Oxfam Health Unit (1992) *Population and Birth Planning*, internal draft Oxfam policy paper.
17 UNDP (1991) op. cit.
18 Jacobson J L (1991) 'India's misconceived family plan', *World Watch* 4:6, Washington, DC: Worldwatch Institute
19 Mosse J C (1991) *India: Paths to Development*, Oxford: Oxfam.
20 Lappé F M and Schurman R (1990) *The Missing Piece in the Population Puzzle*; report for IFDP, San Francisco: IFDP. The relationship between fertility rates and women's health, education and income generating capacity worldwide is shown in UNICEF *The State of the World's Children, 1992*, Oxford: Oxford University Press.
21 UNFPA, 1991. op.cit.
22 Jacobson J L (1991) op. cit.
23 UNFPA, 1984. op.cit.
24 UNFPA, 1991. op.cit.
25 UNDP, 1991, op.cit.
26 Berer M (1991) 'What would a feminist population policy be like?', *Women's Health Journal*, 18.

27 Monan J (1989) *Bangladesh: The Strength to Succeed*, Oxford: Oxfam.
28 Oxfam project NIC 045

CHAPTER 10
1 From a statement to the Fourth PrepCom for UNCED, New York, 4 March 1992.
2 Coote B (1992) *The Trade Trap; Poverty and the Global Commodity Markets*, Oxford: Oxfam.
3 ibid.
4 World Bank (1991) *World Development Report 1991*, Washington, DC: World Bank.
5 UN (1991) *Africa: New Compact for Cooperation*, New York: UN.
6 World Bank (1991) op. cit.
7 Pineda-Ofreneo R (1991) *The Philippines: Debt and Poverty*, Oxford: Oxfam.
8 World Bank (1991) *World Debt Tables 1991–2, vols 1 and 2*, Washington DC: World Bank.
9 OECD (1991) *Financing and External Debt of Developing Countries: 1990 Survey*, Paris: OECD.
10 Catholic Institute of International Relations (CIIR) (1991) *Debt: The Lingering Crisis*, London: CIIR.
11 Mistry P (1991) *African Debt Revisited: Procrastination or Progress?*, The Hague, Netherlands: Forum on Debt and Development.
12 Pineda-Ofreneo R (1991), op. cit.
13 *Beyond the Debt Crisis: Structural Transformations*, Final Report of an International Women's Seminar, 23–25 April 1990, New York. Sponsored and published by United Nations Non-Governmental Liaison Service, UN, New York.
See also: Commonwealth Secretariat (1990) *Engendering Adjustment*, London: Commonwealth Secretariat.
14 The material about the Philippines is drawn from a case study commissioned for this book and written by Eric Gamalinda in 1991.
See also: Pineda-Ofreneo R (1991) op. cit.
15 World Resources Institute (1990) *World Resources 1990–91*, Washington, DC: World Resources Institute.
16 WWF (1990) *Tropical Forests*, Geneva, Switzerland: WWF.
17 Miller G T (1992) *Living in the Environment*, Belmont CA: Wadsworth Publishing Company.
18 Judd F and Clark J (1991) 'Debt for democracy', *Fabian Review*, 103:4.
19 Critchley W (1991) *Looking After Our Land*, Oxford: Oxfam.
20 United Nations (1991) *Africa: New Compact for Cooperation*; op.cit.
21 Coote B (1992) op. cit.
22 Arden-Clark C (1992) *South–North Terms of Trade: Environmental Protection and Sustainable Development*, WWF Discussion Paper; Godalming UK: WWF.
23 Jackson B (1990) *Poverty and the Planet*, London: Penguin Books.
24 'Pollution and the poor', *The Economist* 15–21 February 1992.
See also: Vidal J (1992) 'The new waste colonialists', *The Guardian*, 14 February.
25 Peters C et al (1989) 'Valuation of an Amazonian rainforest', *Nature*, 339.
26 World Commission on Environment and Development (1987) *Our Common Future*, Oxford: Oxford University Press.
27 World Resources Institute (1990) op. cit.
28 Winpenny J (1991) 'Environmental values and their implications for development', *Development Policy Review* 9:4. Overseas Development Institute.
29 Killick T (1990) *Problems and Limitations of Adjustment Policies*, Working Paper 36, London: Overseas Development Institute.
30 Lynda Chalker, Overseas Development Minister, estimated this figure to rise to 0.3 per cent for 1991 in a Parliamentary written answer, 26 February, 1992. *Hansard*, 204: 70: column 521.

31 Woodroffe J (1990) *British Overseas Aid*, London: Christian Aid.

32 UNICEF (1991) *The State of the World's Children: 1975–90*, Oxford: Oxford University Press.

33 World Bank (1991) op. cit.

34 Clark J (1991) *Democratizing Development*, London: Earthscan.

35 Quotation from World Bank (1991) *World Bank and the Environment in Brazil: A Review of Selected Projects*, internal Bank report, quoted in Feeney P (1992) 'Environmental reform in Brazil: advances and reversals', *Development in Practice*, 2:1. Oxfam.

36 Woodroffe J (1992) op.cit.

37 Cernea M (1991) 'Involuntary resettlement: social research, policy and planning', in: Cernea M (ed) *Putting People First* (second edition), Oxford: Oxford University Press.

38 ibid.

39 'Brazilian Union Leaders Lobby World Bank', Press Release from the Washington Office on Latin America, 13 February 1992, Washington, DC.
see also: Centro de Defesa Dos Direitos Humanos Do Submedio Sao Francisco (1992) *The hydroelectric plant at Itaparica: a struggle with power*; Petrolandia, Pernambuco, Brazil: Centro de Defesa Dos Direitos Humanos Do Submedio Sao Francisco.

40 Cleary D (1991) 'Amazonia and the environmental question' in: *Brazil, Economist Intelligence Unit Report*, London: EIU.

41 World Bank (1991) *The World Bank and the Environment: A Progress Report Fiscal 1991*, Washington, DC: World Bank.

42 ibid.

43 ODA (1990) *Environment and the British Aid Programme*, London: ODA; and ODA (1991) *Manual of Environmental Appraisal*, London: ODA.

44 *The Economist*, 15–21 February 1992, op. cit.

45 Payments under the Small Grants Programme are made directly to NGOs, rather than through a government.

46 OECD (1990) *Financing and External Debt of Developing Countries: 1990 Survey*, Paris: OECD. These sums include (from North to South): all official bilateral and multilateral aid, charitable grants, trade credits, private investment and bank loans (i.e. some is in the form of new debts).

47 UNDP (1991) *Human Development Report 1991*; Oxford: Oxford University Press.

GLOSSARY AND ABBREVIATIONS

Agroforestry: an integrated agricultural production system for crops, trees and shrubs.

Bilateral Aid: aid which flows directly from government to government.

Biodiversity: the earth's abundance of life forms – plants, animals, and micro-organisms together with the genes they contain and the ecosystems to which they belong.

Common Property Resources: natural resources such as land, ponds or forests in which a group of people have co-equal use rights.

Multilateral Aid: aid which flows from government to government through intermediary agencies, such as the UN, EC, World Bank, or IMF.

Population Growth Rate: the annual growth rate of population calculated from the difference between birth and death rates.

Poverty: the World Bank definition is an income within the range of US$275 – 370 per year, or less than $1 per day. (World Development Report, 1990).

Poverty line: the income level below which a minimum nutritionally adequate diet plus essential non-food requirements are not affordable.

Terms of trade: the ratio of a country's index of average export prices to its average price index.

DAC	Development Assistance Committee of OECD
EC	European Community
ESRC	Economic and Social Research Council
FAO	Food and Agriculture Organisation
GATT	General Agreement on Tariffs and Trade, a multilateral trade agreement designed to negotiate rules and standards for the conduct of international trade, signed in 1947.
GDP	Gross Domestic Product, of a nation state, the value of goods and services produced in a year, i.e. including exports but excluding imports from GNP.
GEF	Global Environment Facility
GNP	Gross National Product, of a nation state, the value of all goods and services produced in a year, before allowing for depreciation (capital consumption) of assets.
HICs	High Income Countries, those with a GNP per capita of US$6,000 or more in 1988.
IIED	International Institute for Environment and Development
IMF	International Monetary Fund, one of the institutions established by the United Nations at Bretton Woods in 1944, to provide finance for governments facing short-term deficits on their foreign balance of payments.

ITDG	Intermediate Technology Development Group
ITTO	International Tropical Timber Organisation
LDC	Less Developed Country; or more usually one of the 43 Least Developed Countries, so designated by the United Nations because of their low per capita incomes and little, if any, industrialisation.
LICs	Low Income Countries, those with a GNP per capita of US$545 or less in 1988.
MICs	Middle Income Countries, those with a GNP per capita of more than US$545 but less than $6,000 in 1988.
MTO	Multilateral Trade Organisation
NATO	North Atlantic Treaty Organisation
NGO	Non-Governmental Organisation
ODA	Overseas Development Administration
OECD	Organisation for Economic Cooperation and Development, whose membership includes the industrialised countries of West Europe, North America, Japan and Australasia.
PEC	Primary Environmental Care
SILICs	Severely-Indebted Low Income Countries
SIMICs	Severely-Indebted Middle Income Countries
TNC	Trans-national Company, a large company operating in several countries and sometimes with owners drawn from several countries.
TFAP	Tropical Forestry Action Plan
UN	United Nations, international organisation established after World War Two, to maintain peace and assist economic and political development through regional Commissions in Europe, Africa, Asia and the Far East, and Latin America, and also through specialist agencies, including the World Bank, IMF, and UNCTAD.
UNCED	United Nations Conference on Environment and Development
UNCTAD	United Nations Conference on Trade and Development
UNDP	United Nations Development Programme
UNFPA	United Nations Fund for Population Activities
UNHCR	United Nations High Commission for Refugees
UNICEF	United Nations Childrens' Fund
UNIFEM	United Nations Fund for Women
WB	World Bank, one of the institutions established by the United Nations at Bretton Woods in 1944. It has two arms, the International Bank for Reconstruction and Development (IBRD) and the International Development Association (IDA). The World Bank provides loans for large scale capital projects, the IBRD provides non-concessionary loans, and the IDA cheaper loans to poorer countries.
WHO	World Health Organisation
WRI	World Resources Institute

FURTHER READING

Agarwal A, Narain S (1990) *Towards Green Villages: A Strategy for Environmentally Sound and Participatory Rural Development*, Delhi: Centre For Science and Environment.

Commonwealth Secretariat (1991) *Sustainable Development*, report by a Commonwealth Group of Experts on Environmental Concerns and the Commonwealth, London: Commonwealth Secretariat.

Coote B (1992) *The Trade Trap: Poverty and the Global Commodity Markets*, Oxford: Oxfam.

International Development Research Centre (1992) *For Earth's Sake: A Report from the Commission on Developing Countries and Global Change*, Ottawa, Canada: IDRC.

IUCN, UNEP, WWF (1991) *Caring for the Earth: A Strategy for Sustainable Living*, Gland, Switzerland: IUCN.

Meadows D, Meadows D and Randers J (1992) *Beyond the Limits*, London: Earthscan.

Oxfam (1991) *The Oxfam Report: It's Time for a Fairer World*, Oxford: Oxfam.

Porritt J (1991) *Save the Earth*, London: Dorling Kindersley.

Rodda A (1991) *Women and the Environment*, London: Zed Books.

World Bank (1992) *World Development Report 1992: Development and the Environment*, Washington: World Bank.

Wallace T with March C (eds) (1991) *Changing Perceptions: Writings on Gender and Development*, Oxford: Oxfam.

INDEX